Married with Special-Needs Children

[A Couples' Guide to Keeping Connected]

Laura E. Marshak, Ph.D.
Fran Pollock Prezant, M.Ed., CCC-SLP

WOODBINE HOUSE   2007

This book is dedicated with love to our husbands,
Edward M. Kramer and Robert S. Prezant.
It is also dedicated, with gratitude, to the couples
whose marriages
have been true inspirations.

© 2007 Woodbine House
First edition

Library of Congress Cataloging-in-Publication Data

Marshak, Laura E.
    Married with special-needs children : a couples' guide to keeping connected / by
Laura E. Marshak and Fran Pollock Prezant.—1st ed.
        p. cm.
    Includes bibliographical references and index.
    ISBN-13: 978-1-890627-10-2
    ISBN-10: 1-890627-10-0
    1. Parents of children with disabilities. 2. Marriage. 3. Marital conflict. I. Prezant,
Fran. II. Title.
    HQ759.913.M27 2006
    646.7'8087—dc22

                                                                2006029340

10 9 8 7 6 5 4 3 2 1

Manufactured in the United States of America

TABLE OF CONTENTS

Introduction

Laura E. Marshak, Ph.D.

There is a general notion that having children with disabilities puts such a strain on a marriage that it places it at great risk. Many people expressed this view to us during the preparation of this book, regardless of whether they were actually experiencing a weakened marriage. For example, one mother wrote:

> **"I** have a three-year-old with CP [cerebral palsy] and I think one of the benefits of having children with special needs is that it forces you to communicate with your spouse. There is constantly something going on that you need to confer about. In the same way though, it diverts your communication from topics such as each other, the marriage, other kids. I know the divorce rate is extremely high among couples with special needs children and I know that I am lucky to have my marriage intact after three years of this."

Another woman, upon entering a support group, recalled being greeted by another mother of a child with a disability: "Are you divorced yet? You will be."

Definitive statistics on the divorce rate of couples with children with disabilities are not available but there is general consensus that it is somewhat higher than in families with typical children. We do know that the divorce rate is terribly high for marriages in general; it is reported as approximately 50 percent for first marriages and close to 75 percent for second marriages.

For readers who are beginning the journey that disability brings, it is likely that some of you may feel it is impossible to cope with your situation *and* sustain a marriage. This feeling is not unusual because this phase can initially cause intense upheaval that may affect the marriage. Over time, however, many marriages thrive.

We heard from a great number of husbands and wives who report healthy marriages while raising children with disabilities. Many of the children had multiple and/or severe disabilities as illustrated in the following example:

> "I myself am disabled (late deafened) and have two daughters who are also disabled. The children: our seven-year-old daughter (adopted, profound mental retardation, CP, heart defects, and chronic lung disease); a five-year-old biological son (no disabilities); and our three-year-old biological daughter (imperforate anus, developmentally delayed, speech delayed, auditory neuropathy, motility problems, swallowing problems, G tube fed, chronic constipation, reflux, mitochondrial disease and reflex epilepsy). We have gone through a lot with all of our children and surprisingly enough our marriage has grown stronger."

While many couples report increased closeness and strength, many others experience serious negative effects, at least initially.

> "I am the mother of a beautiful five-year-old boy with Down syndrome. Since my son was born, my husband and I haven't been close and we don't really talk. I can't help but feel anger toward my husband."

Many marriages become extremely rocky in the early stages of adjusting but later change in positive ways:

"Our marriage is stronger than ever. In the beginning, it was very hard because I had such a hard time accepting the diagnosis. I even looked into adoption, which my husband totally opposed. He said he'd do it if I insisted, but such a decision, I am sure, could have destroyed our marriage. In the beginning the fact that we weren't on the 'same page' made me feel more alone. In the long run, I appreciate and gain strength from his solid optimism and unconditional love. As it turns out we now both adore our son."

"I've been married for eight years. When we first brought our baby home all I could think of was divorce (and just the thought terrified me). But we were in a very stressful situation. We have a good strong marriage. It is not perfect and we are not happy all the time but we tend to each other's needs as best we can and share the joy our daughter has brought us."

Often the impact on a marriage is mixed in terms of both positive and negative effects:

"Having a child with autism has put a strain on the marriage. We have our good days as well as our bad days. I feel that the strain is mainly due to the fact that taking care of a child with autism is an added fulltime job. This tends to wear you out both mentally and physically. There are periods when we go through bouts of depression as well as anger. And yet we have become better people and appreciate the simple things in life as well as every new accomplishment our son achieves."

The question about the impact of a child's disability on marriage cannot be answered by a single equation or formula. But some points are clear:

☑ A child's disability does have a large impact, but it is not predetermined whether this will be detrimental, beneficial, or result in a mixture of effects.

☑ Overall, you can think of having a child with a disability as *amplifying* what occurs in a more typical family and marriage. Closeness may be stronger, divisions greater, anger intensified, sadness deeper, parenting decisions weightier, and happy times more exhilarating.

☑ There is no doubt that marriage is more complicated.

☑ Just as we learn to adapt our childrearing skills to meet the unique needs of a child with special needs, we generally need to do the same with our marriages. Both in childrearing and marriage, having children with disabilities requires that we develop even better skills than others may need to have.

Writing This Book

This book is intended to be of value to a wide range of readers, including spouses who want to make their marriages stronger while raising children with disabilities and those who want to be proactive and prevent problems from developing. The book is also geared for couples who are experiencing significant problems in their marriages. Although we have chosen to focus on marital relationships, the book's principles may equally help couples in longstanding non-marital relationships. The book may be used as a resource for individuals contemplating marriage and wondering how being part of a step-family can work when at least one of the children has a disability.

The book takes an in-depth look at the marriages of husbands and wives who have children with disabilities. We will further discuss the different ways that the disability experiences affect individuals and the marriages they create together. In addition, we will explore a wide range of strategies for handling or preventing problems that detract from the strength or vitality of a marriage, as well as some that enhance strong marriages.

The content for this book is drawn from many different sources. In order to make this book as helpful and realistic as possible, we made extensive outreach efforts to gather the thoughts and experiences of many parents of children with disabilities. We were fortunate enough to receive comments from hundreds of individuals who shared their feelings, experiences, challenges, progress, and advice to others. Many filled out written surveys about handling aspects of marriage that are often affected by the disability experience. Others graciously allowed us to interview them at length in person. Some participants have been well-known to us for years; others heard about the book and volunteered their input. We collected input from parents of children with a broad range of disorders, including autism spectrum disorders, psychiatric disorders, AD/HD, Down syndrome, fragile X syndrome, growth disorders, cerebral palsy, and others.

We have included the perspectives of parents of infants, adolescents, and adult children. You will have the opportunity to "meet" many people whose successes and struggles you may identify with, be inspired by, and learn from. Sometimes you may simply feel less alone with what you are dealing with.

We have also drawn upon our own personal and professional experiences. Both of us are parents of children with disabilities and have longstanding marriages ourselves. We have also spent a major portion of our professional lives immersed in disability-related issues. Fran Prezant brings to this book a wealth of experience based on working very closely with hundreds of parents of children with disabilities while she directed a parent training and support program. She clearly understands the day-to-day issues faced by parents.

My professional background includes an ongoing practice as a psychologist. In this capacity I have worked with many parents of children with disabilities as well as other couples addressing their marriages.

In order to make sure that Fran and I could express our personal thoughts, we wrote our designated chapters in the first person and have identified chapters by author in the Table of Contents. This process enabled us to offer our ideas in a personal and straightforward manner to the reader.

With this range of sources for input, we are confident that each reader will find many valuable thoughts in this book. Nonetheless, we know that some readers will initially approach this book with mixed feelings. Based on my experiences as a marital therapist, I know the topic of improving one's marriage tends to elicit strong feelings which often contain a mixture of hope and skepticism. Be open-minded as you progress through this book and bear in mind that much of the advice comes straight from others who have walked in similar shoes. This includes parents who have multiple children with disabilities as well as those with life-threatening disorders. Other advice is drawn from my experiences as a marital therapist and seeing some very troubled marriages improve in ways that surpassed all expectations. Good observations and strategies from marital experts in the field are also included in the book, along with resources for further exploration.

With some exceptions, advice is not "one size fits all." You will find that some advice fits naturally better than other advice. We request that you mull over some points of view that are quite different from your own. Stepping outside of your comfort zone in considering ways to look at your marriage or solve problems is often most fruitful. There is generally more than one way to solve problems, and you may find that a very different path than you have been taking may lead you to a better outcome.

Individual Challenges and Couples' Challenges

The impact on a marriage of having a child with a disability is affected by each parent's own adjustment, the flexibility of their marriage, and their access to external supports. Often a marriage can improve considerably through a combination of handling individual and couples' tasks, along with acquiring additional resources.

Individual tasks are emotional challenges that need to be managed on a personal basis. Whereas your partner may help you with these tasks, he or she cannot do them for you. Common individual tasks include:

- ☑ Managing grief
- ☑ Maintaining perspective
- ☑ Protecting a corner of life for yourself
- ☑ Finding sources of strength
- ☑ Coping with uncertainty and fears of future
- ☑ Managing guilt, fear and shame

☑ Finding healthy support outside of the marriage
☑ Finding meaning in the disability experience

Common couples' tasks include:

☑ Establishing or reestablishing a bond despite the tendency of a child's disability to be "all encompassing"
☑ Accepting differences in emotional reactions to disability
☑ Adjusting to roles that meet family needs in a manner that feels essentially fair and does not breed resentment
☑ Retaining nuances of romance and the ability to see each other as more than "parenting partners"
☑ Developing a creative vision for the future
☑ Being a team

In addition, some of the building blocks of a strengthened marriage can be put in place by handling practical problems and obtaining external supports and resources. The most determined, best-adjusted individuals cannot make a marriage work with a child (or children) with disabilities if there is not a foundation of external support. Only for a limited time can a couple brave sleep deprivation, have no time whatsoever without their children, and actively battle with systems to obtain proper medical care and educational services. One father of a child with Asperger's syndrome noted:

"**W**hen your child is having problems, it can be overwhelming and hard to support each other, especially early on before you have professional support systems in place."

External supports include:

☑ Obtaining respite from others to permit time away from parenting
☑ Receiving competent medical, educational, and rehabilitative services
☑ Forming relationships with others who can provide support, enjoyment, and emotional intimacy

Marital improvement may be achieved by maximizing just a few of these building blocks of change. For example, marital adjustment may be facilitated by one partner learning to better handle his or her grief, joint realigning of marital roles, and procuring new or additional sources of support from outside the marriage.

Readers will find information, insight, and advice related to handling both individual and joint components that lead to a stronger marriage. In addition, we have included chapters on finding practical solutions to problems; seeking external support networks; dealing with serious marital problems; and coping with divorce or remarriage.

Taking Care of Your Marriage and Your Busy Life

The idea of taking care of your marriage while you're incredibly busy with children may initially feel daunting. Often a parent devotes each ounce of energy to meet the sometimes overwhelming needs of his or her children. If you have no choice between getting your child to therapy, calming an emotional outburst, or preparing meals for special diets, there seems to be no decision to make. You may be used to putting your own personal needs, as well as those of your marriage, on hold. In the short run, this works. Over time, this becomes problematic. All people and all marriages need some care.

Doubts about the Pursuit of Marital Change

When working with people on marital improvement, I always think it is best to get objections out of the way. So, let's begin with the most common ones that readers may have. Protests are often reflected in comments or thoughts such as:

- "I don't have the time to work on my marriage."
- "It takes *two* to change a marriage. He (or she) won't change, so why bother?"
- "Nobody with a situation like mine could expect to have a decent marriage."
- "Someday I'll work on my marriage when things get easier."
- "I've tried before and my marriage didn't change."
- "Caring for the children is what is most important."

Time

I understand the limitations of time. I hate to admit that when overwhelmed with juggling more than it feels can humanly be done in a given day, I have been known to say to my husband, "If you are going to kiss me, do it fast!" On most days I try to do much better. When a couple has a child or children with disabilities, it is not realistic to expect that there will be as much time and attention to devote to each other as there may be in other homes. This does not mean that the quality of a marriage has to suffer. Within this framework I think about the old motto, "Work smarter, not harder." *Being mindful* can help us work *smarter* without having to expend great amounts of energy. Being mindful is different than worrying. It means not letting the rest of life keep you from taking care of the marital relationship. Being mindful involves making small, consistent, deliberate changes in our attitudes and behavior within the marriage.

> If you spent a mindful 20 minutes a day on your marriage, the impact would be considerable and this would still be less than 2 percent of your day.

Are you already thinking, *"I really don't even have this much time for my marriage!"* Let me simply say that marriages need some attention and that the time may need to come from other activities. This brings us to the art of prioritizing, something that will be discussed later in detail because it is an essential aspect of adjustment to disability. People can't "do it all" anyway, and when disability enters the picture, there is a greater need to carefully pick and choose (as much as possible) where you put your energies. A mother of three, one with complications from extreme prematurity and one with autism, shared her opinion on this matter:

"There are certain things you need to give up. A neat house is out of the question. If you are going to torture yourself over making sure everything is neat and clean and in place in your house, you're going to wind up divorced because you cannot do it."

Negative Expectations

There are two main sources of skepticism that may undermine your willingness to address problems in your marriage. First, it is likely that you and your partner are not equally committed to addressing issues in the marriage and you may fear that your efforts at marital change will be futile for this reason. It is unusual for both partners to be equally committed, but both are not needed for there to be *initial* changes in the marriage.

[
Under most circumstances, one person alone has substantial power to effect initial change.
]

One way to begin this transition is to take the lead and change how you function within the marriage. (Trying to *directly* change your partner is often less effective.)

There is a principle in therapy that it is sometimes useful to start with behavior change, and then emotional change will follow. This means that you may not have your heart in changing your behavior in the marriage, but if you accept this concept intellectually, your own attitude may change when you start seeing results. Behavior change tends to be reciprocal and this helps break negative marital cycles.

Changing your behavior is useful even with problems that you feel you have not started. Without realizing it, your behavior may be helping the problem stay in place. Often I have had the experience that only one person is willing to come to therapy, yet the primary concern is marital. In those cases we work on changing that one person's behaviors to ones that are conducive to a good marriage.

I am certain that when you were little you learned the lesson: two wrongs don't make a right. It is totally impractical to be upset with your partner's behavior and then cloud the issue by engaging in many problematic behaviors yourself. I am not advocating that you be a saint and accept whatever happens. Rather, conduct yourself the way that you want your spouse to. For example, if your spouse resorts to low verbal blows in fighting, you still need to fight fairly yourself (while requesting the same). If your partner has problems with communication, don't refuse to talk yourself. One spouse's behavior changes often serve as the catalyst for reciprocal changes; if not, it at least helps the partner recognize the need to change his or her behavior because it will stand out like the proverbial "sore thumb." Although people tend to insist they have tried *everything* in their marriage and their partner won't change, often they have not tried a broad range of strategies.

> People tend to frustrate themselves by trying the same few approaches over and over again (even when they don't work), and then assume the pursuit of change is futile.

For example, I have met many wives who use the principles of reward and punishment (or withholding reward) as a way to modify their spouse's behaviors. Punishment rarely changes behavior and often results in passive-aggressive marital behavior. When I asked one woman why she persisted in "punishing" her husband in a particular manner, she surprised me with her response. Essentially, she stated that she had learned such principles of behavior modification as part of raising her son with an autism spectrum disorder and had extended these strategies to her marital relationship. A broad variety of other approaches to marital change—both effective and ineffective—will be discussed throughout this book.

Stress and Childrearing Demands
Undoubtedly, having children with disabilities exposes a marriage to more stress. It is easy to use stress as a reason not to be mindful of your marriage because it feels as if you have no energy left. People sometimes insist they will address their marriage *when things get easier*. The fallacy is that stress generally does not end. Even more importantly, it is in stressful times that a marriage can be particularly important. It is easier to cope in general if your marriage is strong.

> Making small marital changes takes less energy than imagined and results in an overall decrease of daily stress.

Many parents find it hard to identify the times when it is all right to set aside a child's needs in favor of attending to their personal and married life. This is difficult in many marriages but even more so when a child has a disability or illness.

> On a daily basis, children's needs often do need to be addressed first, yet a steady practice of prioritizing your child over your spouse breeds problems. It is also not optimal for your child.

As will be discussed further in the book, guilt is one of several factors that contributes to this and, although it may feel that time with your spouse takes away from the quality of childrearing, overall this is not true.

Adaptability

Throughout this book, you will read examples of people who demonstrate an enviable strength in handling serious problems. Many of these people have a natural flexibility that helps them cope with parenting and marriage. A good example can be found in the perspective of a mother of three children with fragile X syndrome:

"Well, we have a dream. If it gets too hectic, we are going to pack it all up and go to an island and buy a bed and breakfast. I can teach one boy to make beds, one boy to clean up the yard and one boy to do dishes. We can have dinner every night. That would be heaven. How many typical families think: I'm going to raise these kids eighteen years, then they will go off to college and they are going to move to some other state and I'll be lucky to get a phone call. I think you have to look globally. If my kid has one skill, we can put that to work and have a happy and fulfilled life."

This woman has been able to creatively reappraise her situation. This is one way she adapts to a life that she did not expect.

> The "Serenity Prayer" provides a wise and powerful framework for coping:
> "God, grant me the serenity to accept the things I cannot change,
> Courage to change the things I can and the Wisdom to know the difference."

Setting religious beliefs aside, this two-pronged approach is still a beautiful fit for the problems encountered in marriage and in parenting children with disabilities. It spurs us on to be brave in seeking solutions to daunting problems while also having the ability to find ways to accept and function in realties that can't be changed. It demands two kinds of strength: forging ahead despite obstacles and living well with circumstances that are truly beyond our control.

Managing Perspective

Living well with circumstances beyond our control often requires us not to get stuck in self-pity.

> There is a time for self-pity and a time to contain it.

It is essential not to confuse mourning with self-pity. As discussed in Chapter 2, it is not unusual for a parent to be immersed in mourning when learning of a child's disability. Self-pity is part of this emotional process. Some people may be immersed in these emotions for as long as a year or two, which is ultimately adaptive for some. This period of grieving helps some cope and move forward.

There is also a time to rein in feelings of self-pity. Following is an example of one woman who understood the need to draw the line on self-pity in order to shift into active coping:

> "In the beginning, when I just found out about my son, there was a period of self-pity. Why us? Why me? How can this be? And I would go out and run and bawl my eyes out and cry in self-pity. I knew there had to be a turning point. I said to myself, 'I have to do something to get out of this. I can't get stuck here because these problems are not going away. If I get stuck here feeling sorry for us, we're not going to grow.' We have to accept it and say, 'What do we need to do to make it better?'"

Although many parents report feeling "blessed" and "chosen" to be the parent of a child with a disability, many experience something vastly different and can't fathom how this could feel like a blessing. The issue regarding self-pity is the amount of time spent with these feelings. I agree with the advice provided by one parent: "Pity parties are fine now and then but keep them brief."

This is important because self-pity weakens you over time; compassion for yourself doesn't. Several parents who participated in this book warned others not to be stuck feeling like a victim in life. Based on their experience, they cautioned that it leads to acting out on others.

"People could take a look at any of us having the children we have and feel like we've really been violated. Why us?! If you get stuck there, it affects your reaction to everything and everyone (whether it is your loved one or the teacher)."

Pangs of self-pity need to serve as cues to do something better for yourself, not dwell in those feelings.

[Practice self-compassion, not self-pity.]

Self-compassion is a great alternative to self-pity. It is harder to parent children with disabilities, and self-compassion can make it easier. Rather than feel entitled to feel bad, feel entitled to treat yourself with compassion. Ways to practice self-compassion include:

- ☑ Giving yourself a break by accepting your limits, practicing self-forgiveness, and treating yourself kindly.
- ☑ Releasing yourself without guilt from activities you would have undertaken under easier circumstances and which often involve doing things for others. This might include volunteering at school and being the host for holiday meals.
- ☑ Not feeling guilty if you just can't stretch yourself enough to meet everyone else's needs.
- ☑ Being less harsh with yourself when stress causes you to act in a manner that is personally disappointing.

[Change your frame.]

How do people find their way out of self-pity? You must find a way to step back and view a larger picture of your own making. When we are in a state of self-pity, we focus on the part of our life that is distressing—this is the picture we see. It is as if it has a frame around it. One important way to genuinely feel better about your life is to *change your frame of reference.* Using a photography analogy, it is like switching from a zoom lens to a wide angle lens.

This new view can be accomplished in a few ways. One way to switch your focus is to use a structured way to make yourself look at what is good in your life. For example, on one awful afternoon, I made myself enumerate out loud (while driving) all the things that I felt grateful for. It got easier. Some people use a similar strategy to start or end their day.

[In general, it is better not to compare.]

Adjustment to disability involves learning not to compare your child or situation to that of others. The challenge is to find value and enjoyment in what you have, even if it differs greatly from the norm. This is also an important aspect of learning to avoid self-pity. Many parents we interviewed spontaneously offered their thoughts on the importance of not comparing.

"There is no normal. There is no such thing. Don't watch too much TV or look at the soccer moms and feel that you have to live up to what they are. Don't worry if you are different from those other women."

"Don't compare your child's achievements with others. It will drive you crazy!"

Part of not comparing requires not comparing to how you "assumed" your family would be. One couple offered these thoughts on adjusting to their son's autism:

Wife:

"Everybody fantasizes about what their family is going to be like because little girls play house. This is not what my family was going to look like. I am a very good cook and my autistic son lives on noodles and butter."

Husband:

"And Chicken McNuggets and French fries—only McDonald's. Do you know what it is like having to stop every time you see a set of golden arches? You can't pass a McDonald's. If you pass a McDonald's, you have to go back because you cannot get to your next destination without a French fry. So we adjust to it and we eat at McDonald's, sometimes a couple times a day. Our son needs routine."

Wife:

"When you are dealt a bad hand, change your game."

It can also be painful to compare your child to others who have the same diagnosis. For example, with cerebral palsy, children vary greatly regarding when and if they accomplish specific motor skills. One mother offered this advice on appreciating your child on his or her own terms:

"Don't forget to celebrate the small successes. It is easy to get caught up comparing your child to other children with a similar disability. Worry more about doing the best you can for your own child."

[If you must compare, be thoughtful about how you compare.]

Parents find some careful comparisons to be helpful. Examples follow.

> **T**here is always a silver lining: My daughter has all her problems, but she is not out getting pregnant and she's not out smoking dope. My son's not out wrecking my car. The problems are different, not the popular problems."

> **T**his may sound odd but it works for me. Sometimes I think about all the children in the world together, not just those in my small part of the world. I think about what I have read in the newspapers. This includes the parents and children who died a few years ago (in the Philippines, I think) in an avalanche of garbage where they lived picking through the trash to get a means of subsistence. Believe me, this cures self-pity and pity for my child fast!"

As illustrated in the preceding quote, a common strategy is to compare your situation to someone who has it worse. It works, at least for a little while. Sometimes a little while is all we need to regain a bit of strength to keep coping.

Concluding Thought

As we bring this Introduction to a close, I wish to remind you of something that should be obvious but isn't always: Being a good parent does not always equate to being a good husband or wife. One father commented:

> **T**he roles and responsibilities of being a father and a husband often get intertwined, mostly for the bad. Overcompensating in one role usually means you're neglecting the other role. For a long time I didn't get it when my wife criticized me as a spouse. After all, I was doing more for our son than almost any father I knew. Eventually, I understood that I was doing a great job meeting my son's needs but not hers. One does not make up for the other."

The following chapters will provide you with a wealth of ideas for improving or protecting your marriage. We will begin by taking a close look at the foundation and structure of good, resilient marriages.

Chapter One

The Structure and Foundation of a Good Marriage

Laura E. Marshak, Ph.D.

"Even getting a dog changes a marriage if it had only been the two of you up to that point."
—comment made by the father of two children with disabilities

Children have a powerful impact on a marriage; children with disabilities often change the structure of a marriage even more because disability typically amplifies aspects of life. If the foundation of a marriage is somewhat "off kilter" to begin with, the unique pressures of raising children with disabilities may further alter the structure of the marriage. For example, a mother of a child with multiple severe disabilities described the impact on her marriage this way:

"We lost the bond we used to have because I only know how to give 100 percent, and my daughter is my cause."

Her comments, which reflect a fatalistic belief that deterioration of the marriage was inevitable, were characteristic of many expressed to us. There were also numerous exceptions, however, which we will identify throughout this chapter.

There is no reason why couples need to settle for a "second-rate" marriage because they have a child with a disability. However, couples do need to be especially careful to build a marriage that is particularly solid and resilient in standing up to strong forces. The story of the "three little pigs" lurks in the back of my mind as a good analogy for thinking about marriage. A good marriage rests on a strong foundation of trust and goodwill, and it possesses a certain structure that enables it to be an emotional, functional home for a couple. The structure of your marriage needs to reflect your values and personalities in much the same way a home reflects its inhabitants. Like a home, there are structural aspects that, if ignored, render it unfit for habitation or vulnerable to collapse. The focus of this chapter is on these aspects of the marital home that keep it standing and make it work as a shelter.

We will begin with practical considerations for marriages in general. This will be followed by a discussion of how a child's disability or illness affects the structure of a marriage. The chapter continues with special considerations for building a resilient marriage in the face of extra strong winds that may come along with disability.

The Most Basic Structure of a Healthy Marriage

A traditional healthy marriage, without children, is often conceptualized as shown here:

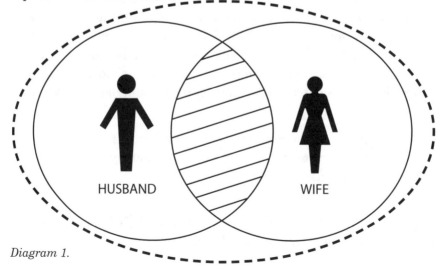

Diagram 1.

The arrangement of these circles depicts the very basic in-frastructure of a good marriage. The overlapping shaded space is shared marital life, togetherness. It is an essential ingredient for a marriage because it is the bond that helps people want to stay married to each other.

[
Children are an important aspect of shared marital life,
but they cannot be all that fills this marital space.
]

Along with a shared love for your children, there must be other elements of this shared space in order for it to function as a "magnet" that draws partners together. No two couples' marital "space" is quite the same. It may include: shared history, religious or spiritual practices, sexual intimacy, values, meaningful and pleasurable activities, physical attraction and emotional intimacy, and a genuine personal knowledge of the other. (We will call the art of maintaining this shared space *connectedness*.) As will be discussed throughout the book, connectedness is fostered in many ways including through time, communication, and sexual intimacy.

For a marriage to be sustained there needs to be enough connection through these non-child-related aspects of togetherness. While always essential, they are critical to a marriage when (and if) children are no longer center stage in life. Realistic concern over the absence of connectedness is apparent in the following comments from a mother who has two children, including one with Down syndrome.

"I sometimes worry that we're going to discover we don't have anything to keep us together as a couple once the kids are out of the house (or want nothing to do with us). But right now there are so many day-to-day concerns, it's hard to focus on the future."

Several people who contributed to this book cited useful examples of what they do to maintain connectedness despite enormous time demands. Strategies include:

☑ Emailing each other throughout the day;

☑ Making a commitment to have at least one conversation every day about their day (not just their children's day);

☑ Taking time off work when children are at school to be together.

The white space in each of the circles in the diagram on page 2 indicates that both members of the couple also have areas of life where they function relatively more autonomously or independently.

> There must be a measure of autonomy that enables you and your partner to retain your identity and some parts of life that don't need to be "negotiated."

Autonomy enables you to spend at least a little free time how you want to, to engage in activities you value, and to exercise your own prerogative in personal matters. These personal matters include things such as religious beliefs, how close you may want to be with your own parents, and how you choose to deal with strong feelings such as grief (as long as you don't take them out on your partner). Lack of autonomy in a marriage breeds problems.

If one or both members of a couple have a notion that they are supposed to become "one" through marriage, they will end up with a marital structure that does not work. The image of two flames of candles being joined into one flame is used in some marriage ceremonies. This image depicts a new entity that is created by two people, but it can be misinterpreted. It is healthy to be devoted to making a marriage work while remaining a distinct person with a separate identity. No one can entirely lose himself and continue to function without resentment. Some of the most unhappy marriages involve at least one partner who feels he has entirely lost himself within the marriage. He either stays in the marriage and oozes resentment or flees. Autonomy means that not all needs or desires are subjugated to family goals—a balance is imperative.

Examples of autonomy in marriage include:

☑ While respecting the family budget, each partner still has some discretion about how to spend a portion of the household money (whether or not they are the primary breadwinner).

☑ Each partner has a right to his own religious practices even if one partner feels a single choice is "better for the children."

☑ Each person has the right to pursue interests, further education, and career changes as long as he also carries an equal share of family responsibilities. (These pursuits may need to be limited due to time constraints but should not be entirely dismissed or subjugated to family needs.)

The third component of a healthy marriage depicted in the diagram (by the dotted line) is an awareness of "the marriage" as an overarching structure to be protected and nourished. People in healthy marriages typically carry with them a sense of "the marriage" almost as if it has a life force that needs to be nourished to keep it strong and vibrant. When faced with tough decisions, these people sometimes ask themselves, "What's best for the marriage?" They are attuned not only to their own needs, but to those of their partner and the marriage itself. They recognize that the whole of their marriage is greater than the sum of its parts (husband and wife). There is a "we-ness."

The image of a garden is a useful metaphor for a marriage. A beautiful garden can yield a bounty and serve as a refuge, but only if tended to over time. It requires nourishment and occasional ridding of noxious weeds and pests. The parallels are quite clear: neither a garden nor a marriage can thrive with total neglect, no matter how beautiful they once were.

The following comments of a mother of twins with severe disabilities illustrate an awareness of the overarching nature of her marriage; in her case it emphasizes romance:

> "It is almost as if we have two separate relationships. We have our relationship, our love affair. And then we have the relationship that we share as parents. We always agree in the love affair. (We usually don't agree in the parenting.) This has always kept us together at points when things got very tough."

Protecting and nourishing "the marriage" includes:
☑ Planning occasional romantic time for just the two of you.

☑ Finding times to prioritize the marriage above all else (relationships with your parents, children, and your career).

Healthy marriages do not need to conform to the proportions of this model, but couples with successful marriages do strike a good balance between shared and autonomous space, and an awareness of the marriage itself.

The "how-to" of changing marital structure begins with knowing the basic structure—the blueprint—of a healthy marriage. We recognize that you may need a set of tools to make needed renovations to the structure of your marriage. They will be provided in following chapters devoted to topics such as: changing roles, communication and conflict resolution, romance and sexual intimacy, and removing barriers to connectedness.

How Children Affect the Marital Structure

As discussed above, it is the connection between husband and wife that holds the marriage together. This connection needs to be strong, but not necessarily large. After all, a strong magnet does not need to be large in size. The connection can be sustained through many factors such as time spent together, physical and verbal intimacy, feelings (of love, sexual attraction, respect, trust, admiration), and common roots. However, even strong magnetic pulls can be interrupted by other forces. For parents, the strongest force is often the birth of a child.

The First Critical Transition

In the life history of all marriages, there are few transitions as momentous as when a baby enters the couple's life.

[It is important to make the transition to parenthood as a team.]

John M. Gottman, a well-known marital researcher, writes of the dangers involved at the point in the marriage when the baby enters the family. He writes that the greatest factor in determining whether the marriage continues to be satisfying is whether the husband also experiences the transformation of parenthood or whether he is "left behind." (This is the first critical transition.) If you are aware of this danger, you can take steps to keep it from damaging your marriage. Gottman notes that *some* husbands initially resent the losses of attention and the previous marital lifestyle and find it hard to embrace the transformed marriage that places the infant in a central role. Our own observations have confirmed this. For example, one woman (now divorced) said:

> "**M**y husband got less attention when these problems with our daughter came up. A mature man would have probably handled it. I wasn't married to a mature person. He acted like it was a competition a lot of times, and she was winning."

In her book, *Grown-Up Marriage*, Judith Viorst provides a blunt description of feelings husbands may experience due to the changing nature of marriage following the birth of a baby:

"Indeed while everyone knows that a new mother may suffer from postpartum depression, we may need to be reminded that a new father may have postpartum depression too, or certainly may experience a variety of distressing postpartum emotions. Maybe he's lonely because he misses the closeness that he always enjoyed with his wife. Maybe he's horny because he's deprived of sex. Maybe he's jealous—maybe he's excruciatingly jealous—because of all the attention his wife gives the baby. And maybe he's embarrassed and deeply ashamed of feeling jealous of his own kid." (See chapter references.)

This may be even more problematic if the spouse previously received a great deal of nurturing and attention. Suddenly the new mother may feel incapable of nurturing both. Although shifting her attentions may feel natural and right to her, her husband often experiences it differently. Feelings of abandonment may not be rational, but they are real and they are, nonetheless, forces to be reckoned with.

Negative feelings in marriages have a way of forming a vicious cycle. If the husband feels neglected, he may withdraw his attention from the new mother at a time when she may also be feeling needy, exhausted, and in need of support herself.

If a transformation is not made together, eventually one spouse may turn away from the marriage. As the husband and wife grow more distant, the mother and baby often become a tighter unit and the marital structure becomes more distorted.

Tips on Safely Navigating the First Transition

To successfully negotiate this juncture, remember that the goal is to increase spousal involvement. The following strategies can help you achieve this goal:

- ☑ Deliberately make room for your partner to share in and become comfortable with infant care from the beginning, even if this feels harder initially than just doing it yourself.
- ☑ Accept that your partner may not be as good as you at handling the baby at first. Fight the thought, "But I can do it better!"
- ☑ Refrain from blunt criticism. It is human nature to avoid activities that make you feel incompetent—be understanding if you want your spouse to be involved.
- ☑ Give helpful suggestions rather than only focusing on what is wrong. Refrain from comments such as: "I can't believe you are holding the baby like that!" or "Didn't you hear the baby crying? I thought you were going to watch him!"
- ☑ Don't critique every little thing your spouse does. Even positive suggestions can be problematic if you make too many.
- ☑ Be careful what you wish for. Although many mothers want to be regarded as the sole expert on taking care of their child, understand that there are negative, long-term consequences if this happens.

This last point is particularly important and merits elaboration. I am a firm believer that we often need to give something up to get something else. In this case, you may need to give up some control over how everything is done in order to get more partner involvement. Many times a parent assumes the role of the "expert parent." This role may feel comfortable and natural for a while. However, it is not optimal or sustainable over the longer haul of childrearing and shared marital life. The parent in the expert role often resents it over time and the other parent decreases his or her involvement. The gap then widens and may become so wide that it is not easily traversed.

The Second Critical Transition

[Make sure there is marital life separate from parenting.]

Typically, a baby becomes the main focal point of a marriage and initially consumes a couple's conversations and activities for awhile. Although there are very many marriages in which children continue to dominate center stage long after infancy, you eventually need to reclaim at least a portion of marital life that is not child-centered. Couples who have typical children generally begin to "shift gears" and reestablish other parts of their life after a few months, including the romantic aspects of their marriage. With support from others and many role models, the couple reorganizes their marriage into a structure that still contains shared marital space, some autonomy, and shared space with the children. Gottman views this as the second critical transition that can damage the structure of a marriage if not properly handled.

At this point, the marital blueprint, with children, should roughly approximate the following structure:

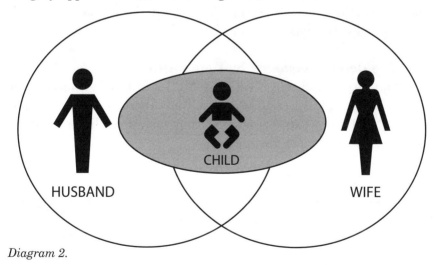

Diagram 2.

Differences When the Child Has a Disability

In the structure above, children have central importance but do not take up all of the marital space or all of either parent's autonomy. Achieving this structure is far more complicated when a couple has children with disabilities. One parent described this well:

> **"I** would compare the experience of having a disabled child to the experience of parenting during the first eight weeks of an infant's life—intense, exhausting, you are always on duty (vigilant). All other aspects of your life fade to the background, and you question yourself and your decisions. It's that intense, and the difference goes on for years."

It has recently been recognized in books and the media that our generation has gotten carried away with utter devotion to the needs of our children in general. A cultural shift in values now endorses the belief that everything that can be done to prepare children to excel in life should be done. Some experts believe this is in response to the recognition of how competitive society has become and anxiety over our children's futures. Meeting children's needs has risen to a priority above those of the needs of the marriage or either individual parent. Even families with typical children find themselves relatively consumed with their children.

Avoiding Being Consumed by Your Child

Families with children with disabilities or illnesses experience these same societal pressures, as well as others that further perpetuate total attention—so much so that sometimes little is left for anything else, including the marriage.

[If necessary, resist becoming consumed with a child because this is not good for anyone, including the child.]

Clearly, it can be a struggle to keep your child's disorder from consuming a disproportionate share of your time and energy, but many parents are able to do it. An example can be found in the reflections of this mother of a child with an autism spectrum disorder. She described herself as "homebound" with her son and involved in daily therapies with him. I was impressed with her proactive stance not to let her child's disorder entirely alter the shape of her marriage:

> "We decided that we were not going to let autism consume our lives. We would make sure that we had services available for our son but we didn't want to let it take over our lives and avoided getting involved with a lot of support groups. Some call it 'denial,' but I think that we are coping mentally with the problem."

As much as this woman recognizes the role of selflessness in parenting, her self-sacrifice does not include sacrificing her marriage.

Sometimes there is no alternative but to spend almost all of your time on a child. For example, if your child has a precarious medical condition, it may demand a crisis-mode type of response in which virtually everything else is "dropped." Healthy couples seize the moments between genuine crises to replenish their marriage.

Some individuals and couples operate as if they cannot attend to their lives until their child is fine—in other words, they are consumed with their child's needs. Although self-sacrifice has a role in parenting, well-adjusted parents also set a boundary to protect some personal life and shared marital life.

There are two circumstances when it is hard not to be consumed when you have children with disabilities:

1. When you are in the earlier phases of grappling with the diagnosis of your child's illness or disorder.
2. When you feel internal and external pressure regarding the importance of early intervention. As one parent stated: "There is that sense that if we 'do it right' early on, *he* will be all right."

We are living in a time when, thank goodness, the importance of early intervention has been well publicized. However, this emphasis creates more anxiety for some parents. I have worked with parents who see the window of time for intervention to be narrower than it is. With this in mind, they find it intolerable to pass up *any* opportunities. And yet, the quest to improve a child can become all-consuming to the point that potential treatment gains may be offset by the development of problems within the family.

> Guilt, self-blame, and other problems related to adjusting emotionally to a child's disorder may cause an unhealthy devotion to the child's needs.

One father shared his observations of another couple whose child had the same disorder as his own:

"He is basically bringing home a paycheck and that is his function and she is out in California for months with the kid. They just bought a house and have no furniture in it because they have stopped living. They are sacrificing their marriage and themselves; they are blaming themselves because of that child. And they are repenting and punishing themselves by totally giving up their love to make this child whole again. They don't go out, they don't go on vacation, and they don't talk to each other. They are spending every nickel that they have and every waking hour thinking about how they are going to fix their kid and they forget about themselves. That, I think, is a choice that you make."

In general, there is a law of diminishing gains. This type of absolute focus usually doesn't help the child. With only the exceedingly rare exception (such as life-threatening circumstances), saving a bit of yourself for other parts of life will not diminish your child's care. It is absolutely necessary to take care of yourself, other family members, and your marriage.

I have devoted my career to maximizing the abilities and quality of life of people with disabilities. Yet I firmly believe that we cannot lose sight of the fact that the lives of other family members also count. Each life is valuable and important. I believe in devotion and self-sacrifice but not to the point of entire negation of self or marriage.

Parents, particularly the primary caregiver, often become part of a relatively informal support network with others who may be equally consumed. This network may be formed through contact with others over the Internet or parents involved in a specialized treatment. As helpful as these supports are, sometimes they fail to include role models of mothers who meet their children's needs yet strive to focus on other aspects of life. It is then easy to feel guilty when you do not go to the nth degree in pursuing treatment for your child.

[Raising a child with a disability is like running a marathon, so you need to pace yourself.]

A parent of a child with cerebral palsy shared her insight:

"During my son's first year, I quickly descended into burnout and depression. I sought help from a psychologist who, over about three years, taught me many important things, including: 1) I want to be there for my son over the long haul. Therefore, burnout is not a viable option and I have to take care of myself. 2) Despite the importance of early intervention in the first three years, my son will have many chances to learn over the course of his lifetime."

[Don't assume your partner is consumed voluntarily— he or she may simply need more help!]

A word of caution for readers who feel their partners are consumed: the causes are rarely clear at first glance. Spouses who find themselves in this position need to question whether what appears to be "voluntary consumption" has actually occurred because there are just too many activities that genuinely need to be done. Especially in traditional marriages in which roles are strictly divided, one partner may not understand the magnitude of childcare demands and that being consumed is sometimes not by choice or is driven by problems with adjustment. The strategies to deal with this depend on the structure of your marriage, as discussed below.

Common Marital Structures Involving a Child with Disabilities

Two common marriage structures often develop when a child has large needs due to a disability or chronic illness:

1. Utilitarian,
2. Parent/Child enmeshment.

Although it is easy to see how these structures develop, neither is conducive to a satisfying marriage over the long term. Identifying whether you are in one of these types of marriages, however, may be the "wake up call" you need to begin to make changes in your marriage. I have known many couples with these types of marriages who have successfully rebuilt their marriages and gone on to enjoy happier, healthier relationships.

Utilitarian but Separate Structure

The *utilitarian* marital structure is very common in marriages that have at least one child with a disability. It is motivated by a "divide and conquer" attitude in the face of a massive amount of family responsibilities. The following diagram represents the basics of this structure.

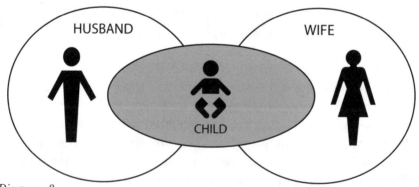

Diagram 3.

You can see that the only connection involves children. Both spouses may be pitching in equally, but their own lives don't often intersect unless it involves children-related matters. One parent generally does the vast majority of caring for the children and the other assumes the role of financial provider. Both may be working exceptionally hard for a common family goal. This marital structure reminds me of two engines running back and forth down parallel tracks. For example, a mother of two children with autism spectrum disorders said:

> "We have no time for each other alone; we are often more like 'parent partners' than husband and wife. There is no time to dedicate just to us."

This approach is efficient for childrearing. However, although it tends to "get the job done," it can lead to two very separate lives for the husband and wife. Sometimes this threatens the viability of the marriage itself. One mother of two children with disabilities spoke of how good intentions led to a loss of connection (and in this case, an affair).

> "He worked day and night to get the business up and running. We were on two separate tracks. He was working even on weekends and I did mostly everything else to keep the family running. I felt that by giving my husband the time needed to establish a business I was helping, but we were drifting apart."

A marital structure that is primarily utilitarian may feel (or be) unavoidable. If this is the case, it is important to make modifications so there is more connection between the husband and wife. One couple we interviewed organized their marriage largely in this manner but made sure there was time together no matter how busy they were:

> "The only time we have to be alone together is in the mornings. So we get up very early. I get up around 5:15 or 5:30. I make coffee and get things ready. And eventually, I'll get her to get out of bed, and we'll have coffee together before the kids get up. We sit down and talk, then we know what we need to do for the rest of the day. I'll make her breakfast or she'll make me breakfast."

Partners in a utilitarian structure also need romantic time together. Whereas it is important in all marriages, it often needs particular attention in marriages with this basic structure. One mother of a child with multiple disorders suggested:

" **M**y best advice is to make time for each other no matter what and do not feel guilty about having time to yourselves. Get a babysitter or respite care—don't try to be super parents and not go out or away. It will make you better parents if you do go away."

See Chapter 5 for strategies that may help you reclaim some of the romance in your marriage.

Parent/Child Enmeshment

The second common marital structure that incorporates children with disabilities also involves problems with connection and is invariably unhealthy. Enmeshment means there is not enough differentiation between the two lives of parent and child; it is as if they are "one." As is depicted in the following figure, the child's life becomes the parent's life. Generally, there is also a lack of connection between husband and wife.

Diagram 4.

Parent/child enmeshment can occur in any family but seems to occur more often when there is a disability. Causes include:

☑ Strong problematic feelings about the child's disability, including guilt, anger, or attempts to "mask" the disability by trying to head off *all* potential problems so the child will appear to be functioning well;

☑ A preexisting lack of connection between husband and wife;

☑ Non-disability-related adjustment issues for the enmeshed parent—that is, he or she finds it is easier to focus on the child's life than on his or her own life.

Laurie Ashner and Mitch Meyerson's book, *When Parents Love Too Much*, provides additional insights into why a parent may be overprotective, overinvolved, overly controlling, and/or overly nurturing. They note that parents who "love too much" almost invariably have memories of being failed by a significant figure in their own childhood. Regardless of the reasons, the impact on a child may be the same. These authors note that parents who don't let their children take risks as a result of "overparenting" raise children who have difficulties articulating their needs, problems with initiative, and feelings of undue entitlement. In addition to harming children, enmeshment often harms the child's relationship with the other parent.

The concept of a mobile is a classic analogy that is often used to describe family functioning. When you touch one part of a mobile, its movement has an effect on all other parts of the mobile. This analogy conveys the dynamic relationships between couples and their children. For example, the quality of the emotional relationship between husband and wife has an impact on closeness with a child. If unhappy, a parent may turn more to a child. (For purposes of illustration, I will put the mother in this position, although it could be either parent.)

As the mother-child relationship draws closer, the gulf between the spouses often widens and the father often becomes more distant from that child. This, in turn, may lead to the mother "overcompensating" for the husband's distance by forming an even closer alliance with that child. The mother's devotion and fulfillment literally centers on the child, which detaches her from her spouse. On a more positive note, attempts to decrease distance with your spouse bring the configuration back to a healthier arrangement.

During my years as a marital therapist, my impression has been that enmeshment arises more often in marriages where there is a child with a disability. Given that parent and child usually spend more time together in the first place, it is not such a great leap for the parent to discuss more and more of her thoughts and feelings with her child. In addition to the emotional burden this creates for the child, he or she is often drawn into arguments between parents. (This is one more reason why it is important to address marital problems if they exist.) This structure is particularly bad for young adults who may want more freedom from their home. This naturally difficult separation process is made more difficult by a few factors. The young adult does not want to emotionally abandon his or her parent. Furthermore, the child may fear that the marriage will end when he is out of the house and no longer provides a buffer.

Research by Elizabeth Essex on the relationships between older husbands and wives who have adult children with mental retardation at home reached several important and practical conclusions. She found that the emotional relationship between spouses had an impact on the father's closeness to the child and that fathers tended to have more difficulty carving out a caretaking role when a child has a disability. This underscores the importance of tending to the marital relationship and making sure that there is enough space for both spouses to become well involved with the child.

In order to avoid enmeshment:

☑ Do not confide your marital or personal problems to your child. True, this is tempting if you feel lonely and there is no adult in sight to talk to. You must recognize, however, that no matter how mature a child is or how close you are, it is not healthy for a child to fill your needs for companionship and/or emotional support.

☑ Be careful not to greatly "overcompensate" with a child if his or her other parent is distant. A little makes sense; too much makes matters worse.

☑ Understand that no matter how involved you are with your child, you cannot shield him or her from all negative experiences and that being ever-present or over-involved in other ways will not prevent all distress.

☑ Make sure you have sources of gratification in your own life that are not related to your child.

Building a Strong, Resilient Marital Home

Good will toward each other helps shape a resilient marriage despite heartfelt differences, aggravations of daily life, and your partner's personality or habits. Good will can only exist if both of you experience relatively equal power or influence in your marriage. Power balances can go astray in a variety of ways. One troublesome way is to assume that the major breadwinner should have more power in decisions without taking into consideration the non-monetary contributions of the other partner.

> If there is a significant imbalance of power, people simply resort to more covert ways to combat feeling powerless in a relationship.

People find ways to gain power in dysfunctional ways such as through passive-aggressive behavior. In this case, a person may superficially consent to decisions made by the more powerful partner, but then undermine the decision through subtle lack of cooperation. For example, someone may superficially agree to his spouse's firm decision to educate the children in a religious school yet undercut the religious education in a variety of ways.

> People rebel when they feel powerless and will get their share one way or the other.

Lack of overt power is one of several causes of emotional tyranny. When people feel powerless in decisions, they resort to making their feelings extremely well heard in other ways. The tyranny comes into play when it colors the emotional climate of the home. In essence, you are saying: "I will do what you say but make you miserable in the process."

Roles and boundaries are inseparable from power. The boundary defines *who* is in charge of *what*. Fair and functional role division is so important (and complicated) that we devote Chapter 6 to it. For now, let it suffice to say that roles need to be negotiated, be somewhat flexible, and be renegotiated over time when they no longer fit. As people and lives change, roles need to change. For example, a mother might have happily agreed to be the primary caretaker of two small children. She might have enjoyed having the home front be her entire domain and even have been territorial about it. If one child develops a severe disability, however, this arrangement might change and feel intolerable. She might also become angry and resentful that her husband is at work all day, leaving her alone with the kids.

Tolerance of Differences

Your spouse is not you. People often act as if they wished they had married themselves. They think their spouses should be like them in terms of how they spend their time, how they choose to express themselves, how they look at their children, how much sexual intimacy they want, how they choose to handle their emotions, and how they think overall. This is one of those situations where we might be very unhappy if we really got what we wished for. Generally, the differences between spouses are eventually beneficial. They create a "whole" that is greater than the sum of the parts, and the differences have the true potential to add balance if they are not viewed as simply maddening.

Tolerance of differences is made easier by paying attention to other aspects of building a strong marital foundation. Start by respecting your partner's autonomy and his or her right to be different from you.

Realistic Expectations

Realistic expectations also help form a basis for a resilient marriage. These include realistic expectations for your spouse, marriage, and love.

☑ ***Expect your spouse to be flawed.*** If you are typical, you married your partner for both the right and the wrong reasons, and it is very likely that your partner will have some flaws that go beyond merely being different from you. These don't have to be fixed for a marriage to be relatively good; in fact, many are not fixable. People learn to work around them.

☑ ***Embrace a realistic notion of "love."*** Love is not only a feeling, although *passion* is an important part of a marriage. It is also a decision to love someone despite flaws, disappointments, and struggles.

Genuine Teamwork

[Remember that you are on the same team.]

An awareness of being on the same team helps couples keep from getting too divided and fosters resiliency. It is easy to identify aspects of teamwork by considering relations within childhood sports teams:

- ☑ They accommodate for members having disparate strengths and weaknesses.
- ☑ They work together for the larger goal.
- ☑ They look out for each other, don't always have to have their own way, and cheer each other on.
- ☑ They pull together when faced with hard times and celebrate better times.

Many parents speak of teamwork (explicitly or implicitly) for handling concrete tasks as well as emotional challenges. For example:

"**I**f one of us is getting stressed working with our son, the other one jumps in and takes over."

"**W**e give each other hugs, lots of hugs. You are both going through it, not just one person. It takes teamwork."

"**I** tend to be angrier than my husband, but he lets me vent when I need to. I think he's more accepting and I try to be more accepting based on his thoughts and ideas about our son's disorder."

Components of a Healthy Marriage

The following chart presents essential components of a healthy marriage. None of them are *entirely* dispensable, although some good marriages do have weaknesses in a few of these areas. The absence of any of them makes a marriage unlivable (like a home without a bathroom, kitchen, or place to rest).

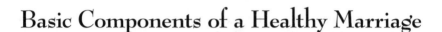

Basic Components of a Healthy Marriage

- Connectedness through time, affection, verbal and physical intimacy

- Skills in communication and conflict resolution

- Tolerance and respect for each other despite flaws

- Basic fairness in the distribution of power and responsibilities

- Being a team and being adaptable to changing circumstances

- Commitment to the marriage

An additional characteristic seen in some marriages is important to consider even though I can't say that it is unequivocally essential: prioritizing your marriage. This goes beyond nourishing and protecting your marriage, which clearly is essential. Realistically, many couples can have a good marriage without making their marriages number one. However, many couples do follow this philosophy:

"Hold and care for each other **first**. And don't lose it. Then care for your child or children. That may sound terrible, but we believe that's the answer for us. We come first. And I don't mean material things at all; I mean caring for each other."

The following comments were shared by the mother of a boy with serious behavioral problems due to autism, mental retardation, and AD/HD. Her approach to marriage does include prioritizing it. Her comments on her marriage, provide a candid and valuable illustration of a healthy marriage:

"Our child's behavior was so out of control that our lives were in many ways a living hell. The stress we endured was indescribable; however, somehow it never affected our marriage, our love for each other. The worse our son's behavior was, the more stressed out and depressed I would be. I don't think this affected my relationship with my husband that much, though. He wished that I wasn't so stressed and depressed and we both wished our lives weren't so miserable, but our ability to get along with each other and our closeness to each other helped."

Other couples, too, have prioritized their marriages despite severe stressors related to childhood disability and illness, as well as feeling their partner was not the perfect parent at all times:

"Realize that husbands and wives react differently to learning their child has a disability. In our case, I threw myself into trying to help our son, and my husband distanced himself from the situation. I wish my husband would spend more time with our son, but I try not to push him too much on this as I know how sad he is about our son and what a hard time he is having dealing with his limited abilities. We have always been very affectionate on a daily basis and each of us knows we are number one to another. I once felt like we lived in a prison; however, my husband and I were a refuge for each other."

These marriages are not exceptions. We will share comments from many similar marriages throughout this book.

The final element listed as an essential component of a healthy marriage is commitment. As discussed in the Introduction, some people make the mistake of prioritizing commitment to their children *or* commitment to their spouse. Both are vital.

The elements identified in this chapter help couples maintain a gratifying marriage despite being faced with the many and often unique stresses of parenting children with disabilities. In the next chapter, we demonstrate how components such as respect, tolerance of differences, teamwork, and connectedness enable couples to handle intense emotional demands that often occur when faced with the waves of emotional feelings that may accompany having a child with a disability or illness.

Chapter Two

No Longer Cruising Down the River:
The Early Stage of Adjusting to Disability

Laura E. Marshak, Ph.D.

The focus of this chapter is on the *initial* adjustment of learning of a child's disability. Often the greatest emotional challenges lie during this period when life feels irrevocably changed. This may be experienced by couples learning that their newborn has Down syndrome, cerebral palsy, or many other disorders that are diagnosed shortly after birth. This phase also pertains to the period of time shortly after parents of older children learn that they have a disorder such as progressive deafness, brain injury, or autism that is likely to have a major, lasting impact on their lives.

We recognize that some parents have little or no problem adjusting to the diagnosis of a disability. Many others struggle and find it impossible to imagine that anyone could cope, much less keep their marriage intact. One particular couple we met provides a particularly good example of what is attainable in individual and marital coping despite what appears to be overwhelming odds. In brief, this couple fell in love and started an idyllic marriage and life together. They overcame problems with infertility and were delighted to learn they were expecting twins. As a result of gross medical malpractice, they found themselves with twin newborns who had mental retardation, cerebral palsy, and seizures. One was also blind. An understanding of the extent to which their lives changed is best found in their own words:

Wife:

"During the time when my husband was this internal optimist, I shut down. He was telling me that everything would be all right and I was mad at him because I didn't believe him. We were bombarded by bills. When the twins came home, the final bill from the NIC unit was $1.1 million for one child and $1.3 million for the other. We were being told that insurance would cover 80 percent and we had to come up with 20 percent. Do the math. I had just lost my job. My husband's business was fairly new and it was just at the point where it was taking off. Up until that time in the marriage I had been the major breadwinner. We had put everything we had into the house. I was so overwhelmed, and, because I came from a position of great responsibility, I was frustrated that I could not even grasp what was happening to me; we were battling like crazy."

Husband:

"I saw what was going on with her. And then the bills were coming in. A million calls from clients, hospital, and doctors. On top of all that we had a million people running around our house, perfect strangers living with us twenty-four hours a day. We had things beeping in the night. There were times I used to say to myself, 'Where the f---- am I? Did I go to that subterranean place? Where did all these people and things come from?' Let me tell you there is no one stronger than me, but...."

When we met with them, three years had passed since the birth of their twins. They had survived as a couple, although they had gone through a time when this did not appear likely. This couple had used a variety of strategies and resources in order to cope. They reached a point where their deep love and enjoyment in each other were apparent, and the romantic feelings they thought were dead were rekindled. Like many other couples, they found a way to regain their equilibrium by working through a crisis without breaking apart. The following discussion of handling strong emotional responses includes their strategies, as well as those of other successful couples.

Do You Need to Read This Chapter?

This chapter was written for parents who are having trouble coping with the emotional challenges of raising a child with a disability. You may not need to read it if you and your partner have both met the following goals:

- You are managing grief and depression well enough that you can enjoy your child.

- You have adjusted expectations so you neither deny the effects of the disorder nor let them overshadow your child's potential.

- You have not succumbed to guilt or shame.

- You roll up your sleeves to address, rather than avoid, problems.

- You have preserved a sense of self and a connection with your partner.

- You are not coping with strong feelings of anger or bitterness that life is unfair or that you have been betrayed by God.

- You are able to meet the basic demands of daily life roles at work and/or home.

While some people have no difficulty accomplishing these markers, others spiral into personal crises. If we use the metaphor of a marriage being like the two of you going down the river in a boat, this phase of life represents the rapids in terms of the speed and intensity of forces that may crash into you. Many of those who do experience a rough ride make it through as a strengthened couple. Some are relatively unaffected as a couple, but others sustain damage that threatens to swamp or destroy the marital "boat." The main danger involves breaking apart from each other as a couple. This is often due to a failure to understand or accept differences in emotional coping styles. This lack of comprehension or tolerance in such a stressful emotional time often results in alienation and a widening gap between spouses.

Differences in Emotional Response

[*It is crucial to accept that your partner will deal with
his or her emotions very differently from you.*]

Husbands and wives who are coming to grips with a child's disability often expect their partners to respond to the emotional challenges as they themselves do. Many find differences in emotional response disturbing—mostly because of how it is interpreted. For example:

> "I know when our son was diagnosed I had terrible guilt feelings and I felt that my husband didn't really care. The diagnosis didn't seem to faze him at all. That made me feel like the feelings I was having were not important or not warranted."

Before we pinpoint strategies to deal with this type of situation, it is important to understand why you need to expect that your partner will respond *differently* from you. Rarely are couples "in sync" with each other throughout the adjustment process. The reasons for this can be found both in gender differences and in the psychology underlying aspects of mate selection.

Gender is a large factor in explaining why husbands and wives often initially respond so differently to the early stage of learning of a child's disability or illness. One wife who understood this provided excellent advice:

> "I think it is very important to remember that moms and dads react very differently to the diagnosis. The journey to acceptance is a grieving process. Moms often blame themselves for the child's disability, while the dads are more removed."

Her observations are consistent with observations on this topic by professionals such as Deborah Tannen and John Gray. These experts clearly describe the ways that men and women respond differently to problems and emotions. For example, in general men are more prone to withdraw or attack problems pragmatically rather than with emotional expression, whereas women place more value on talking about their feelings.

The second main reason we need to expect—rather than resist—differences in emotional response and coping styles is that opposites attract. We tend to become partners with people who have qualities we desire but lack. We are initially attracted to these differences and intuitively seek them as a kind of balance to ourselves. Unfortunately, we often subsequently have a growing discomfort with these same differences. For example, the man who represses his own feelings yet chooses an emotional wife may discover that her expressiveness churns his own emotions up in a way that he can't stand.

Although spouses often wish to change how their partner handles emotions, this is relatively fruitless and unnecessary. What helps?

[First, accept differences in coping style without drawing conclusions about what it means.]

Trying to read your partner's mind often leads to hurt, misunderstandings, and alienation. Mind reading occurs when we assume that we know what is in our spouse's mind. My experience has been that husbands and wives, even in the closest marriages, are often so mistaken about the depth of their partner's emotions or the content of many of their thoughts. For example, you may feel distressed by your partner's lack of overt emotion, but it may simply represent his or her attempt to cope, to conform to gender role expectations, or to keep from falling apart emotionally.

[Second, aim (high) to embrace the emotional difference.
If you are unable, aim for nonjudgmental tolerance.]

Tolerance means understanding that differences are valid and to be accepted. Embracing emotional differences means finding value in the differences rather than finding them unsettling or merely tolerable. When couples are able to assume this mindset, they can pool their strengths and benefit from a diversity of emotions and coping styles. Examples from three couples follow:

"We don't see eye to eye on a lot of things. When I grieved for a very long time about our daughter's disability, my husband (who grew up on a farm in Kansas), just shrugged his shoulders and said it changed nothing. He just loved her and did whatever he had to do for her. Only when I get him all liquored up can I get deep emotions from him, but even then, he is very calm and at peace with her condition. I've always commented that farmers take everything in stride—a tornado, hail, drought—they don't get upset, they just go back to work. That seems to be his motto in life. I guess this is good because I am a hot-tempered Irish woman who emotes, cries, laughs, gets angry, yells, and hugs with great abandon. **Maybe I did the feeling for both of us, while he held down the fort.**"

"I think my wife was generally more optimistic at first. As a physician trained in treating psychopathology, lots of different diagnostic possibilities went through my head, most bad. She, on the other hand, immediately saw a baby who needed nurturing. Part of this related to her belief that things often happen for a reason. This kind of orientation helped her rally at a time when she (we) really needed to get in gear and take care of this baby. I think this helped me come around more to a nurturing, problem-solving perspective."

"I would say that husbands and wives need to give each other the freedom to cope with and express feelings differently. My style of coping is to gather as much information as I can about the disability and treatment. At first, when my husband didn't behave the same way, I thought he didn't care. Now I realize his focus is more on how our son is like other children. I think this gives our son a healthy balance."

Many people have to work at embracing rather than resisting such differences in coping. Although you may need to exercise conscious control over your mindset, the outcome will be worth the effort this may take.

The Challenges of Adjustment

Although some couples handle the emotions and existential questions that arise as a result of disability together, many husbands and wives struggle with these issues on more of an individual basis. Parents who have recently learned of a child's disability initially employ whatever strategies help them to manage their emotions and to make sense of and try to control what has occurred so suddenly in their lives. Some individuals plunge into information gathering, some direct anger at God, some try to seal emotions off tightly, and others feel the need to talk about their feelings often and at great length. Others become immersed in grief and mourning. Some need to dwell on the worst case scenarios, while others need to be filled with hope and inspiration. Some attain solace in their partners. Many learn that coming to emotional terms with a child's disability requires them to find the answers within themselves at their own pace.

The remainder of this chapter will focus on understanding and handling aspects of the adjustment process both on an individual level and as a couple.

Understanding Grief and Mourning

Many people experience a period of mourning as part of the adjustment process. There are several important points to bear in mind regarding grief and mourning.

[Give yourself and your partner permission to grieve.]

Mourning is actually a natural way to come to terms with circumstances that appear impossible to accept. Grief has a way of being satiated through tears and time and normally leaves the mourner better able to "move on" in life. Some people brace themselves against mourning even when they feel grief welling up because they equate it with weakness, succumbing, and loss of emotional control. Some parents feel ashamed of their grief because their baby survived significant medical risks and they are painfully aware that other parents they met in neonatal intensive care units lost their children.

Many parents grieve with the same emotions and intensity often experienced when a loved one actually dies. This intensity of grief is normal, because parents often are mourning the death of the child they envisioned having and the dreams attached to that child. The mother of the twins with multiple disabilities (described earlier) recalled her grief:

"**M**y babies were alive but my vision was dead. I'd thought I was having a Gerber baby. So I had to switch my head from the Gerber baby to these two-pound babies who were vented and mainlined with tubes, wires, and contraptions beeping and buzzing. Others knew how to care for them better than I did. And that was a horrible thing too. I couldn't make them better. Mommies are supposed to kiss it and make it better. I couldn't. So I was mourning all of that."

[Understand that grief doesn't mean you won't or don't love your child.]

Grief over the loss of the child you dreamed of does not invalidate any love you may have for the newly born or newly diagnosed child. Parents may feel deep love for their actual child yet be overwhelmed with grief for the loss of life as they had known it or wanted it to be. Others may be in such distress upon the birth of a child with a disability that loving emotions are indeed blocked until grief is better resolved.

[Don't use the presence or absence of grief as a barometer of love.]

Parents vary tremendously with regards to the experience of grief related to disability. Some experience none or very little while their spouses may be overwhelmed with grief. These responses have no intrinsic meaning. Over the years I have met many wives who have mistakenly interpreted their spouse's lack of grief as meaning they don't really care about their child. This can be a very costly misunderstanding.

[Remember that your losses are not the same as your partner's.]

Loss is very personal. Your partner's grief may be very different from your own. Therefore, it may be experienced more acutely or for a longer period of time. Examples, focusing relatively more on the experiences of males, follow:

"It is hard for my husband to be around typically developing kids. He feels that loss more than I do."

"We will never be grandparents and my husband will never have a child who carries on his name."

"I had hurt pride. That male perspective that I had the 'best genes' compared to other males hurt. My genes were faulty. This is the only major difference between me and my wife. She probably wondered about genetics at first, but understood that this would probably have happened with or without the best genes from either one of us. I took a little longer because of pride. All men want to be the stud who can 'fertilize the fields best.'"

[Mourning is not necessary in order to accept a child's disability; people need the freedom not to grieve if that is their inclination.]

All too often a worried spouse assumes that something is wrong with her partner if he does not go through a mourning process. There is a common but erroneous assumption that a mourning stage is a prerequisite for adjustment. Professionals may also make this mistake, although research has *not* substantiated that mourning is an essential step in the adjustment process.

[Watch out for guilt.]

Guilt is both pervasive and damaging if left unchecked over time. Most parents experience some self-blame when a baby is born with a disability, no matter how careful they were during the pregnancy. Mothers may second-guess themselves: "Did I work too hard, exercise too much, or was it the glass of wine I had before I knew I was pregnant?" Men in their traditional role as family protector often blame themselves for somehow having failed. Many parents also have to fight the feeling that somehow they did something that merited "divine punishment" because of the common belief that good things happen to good people and bad things happen to bad people. The tendency for parents to experience depression during early adjustment often causes such thinking to become even more convoluted but to feel personally logical.

If guilt persists, it is important to find someone to help you or your partner reality-test your guilty feelings. Talk to a healthcare provider or knowledgeable and trusted friend. People often wait far too long to share their fears that they are to blame, which then grow far out of proportion. I have met many people who harbored these secret painful beliefs and fears for years. Most find that when they summon the courage to talk to someone, it is a tremendous relief. Unrelieved guilt is one factor that can derail mourning and cause it to develop into a full-blown depression.

[Spare your spouse from your blame and anger.]

Anger is often part of the mourning process and it is often directed at spouses, no matter how irrationally. One wife who generally had a very loving marriage described how her thoughts turned to blaming her husband for her losses:

> "You are looking to blame someone in the early stages of diagnosis. So for me, the logical thing was that I had twins, and if I hadn't had twins, I would not have gone into premature labor. And if I hadn't gone into premature labor, they wouldn't have had all these issues. If they hadn't had all these issues, they wouldn't have been brain damaged. If I had just met someone who was my age who had healthier sperm, I would have delivered Gerber babies like other moms."

When faced with a crisis, we may subconsciously expect our spouses to somehow make everything all right, perhaps as our parents seemed to do when we were little. When they don't pull through like heroes, we resent them.

Irrational feelings of anger and blame will dissipate and it is usually better to ride out the emotional storm. Venting an emotion does not necessarily make it go away and some things are better left unsaid. Also bear in mind that comments made during the adjustment stage often cause great harm and rarely bring the desired relief.

There are many ways to refrain from saying something harmful. For example, you can:

- vent to a friend,
- write your thoughts in a private journal,
- leave the room, or
- exercise until the impulse to lash out passes.

[It is important to realize how lengthy the adjustment process is.]

Most people don't understand how long it takes to come to grips with a child's disability.

"When we first realized there were problems with our son, we both dealt with it differently. We eventually felt a real strain in our marriage; we had some long talks (late at night) and slowly started working together. It took us about three years to fully accept our son's special needs. Since that acceptance, our relationship has grown stronger."

This couple's experience was not unusual; it is typical for the initial adjustment process to take a few years. This may seem disappointingly long to you, but on one hand it is actually good news. It means that even if your spouse seems to be having trouble adjusting now, he or she may very well be on a normal timetable for coming to terms with the diagnosis. The mother of a five-year-old with Down syndrome provided further insight on the role of time in resolving painful adjustment and marital problems following the child's birth:

"I've been married for seven years. My husband has a fifteen-year-old daughter from a previous relationship and I can't help but accuse him of favoring his older child over my child. He doesn't spend any time with my son. Just last week, for example, my son received an award at school for 'Student of the Month.' My husband drove us there and sat in the car until the ceremony was over. It was his loss because when they called my son's name, he ran to the front of the room to receive his award and took a big, gracious bow. Everyone got a kick out of him and said he was so cute. He showed his award to everyone in the place.

"I started crying because they also told me that I am doing a good job and it showed through him. When I asked my husband why he sat in the car and told him I was mad, he made up some dumb excuse and said that he didn't realize that it was going to be a ceremony. He said he just thought that he was going to the school to pick up his award. I know for a fact that when he was with his daughter's mother, he went to all of her school functions. Why not for my son? Don't get me wrong: I know my husband loves me and my son, but I don't think my husband had time to grieve and really accept the situation. You know how fathers feel about having their first boy."

A while later, I received this follow-up note from his mother:

66 **I** was reading over my thoughts that I sent to you regarding my family situation and realized that I left out something important. I don't want you to think that my husband doesn't interact with my son at all. He plays with my son and they jump on top of each other and they roll around on the floor and my son loves it. I just think that my husband just doesn't have patience and maybe something happened in his childhood that makes him believe that the mother should take care of the kids and the father should be able to put his feet up and watch TV.

"It's great because now that my son can talk and really knows what he wants, he will go to his father and make him play with him. Sometimes I try to make them have time together, so I tell my son to take a book to Daddy. When my son brings a book to him and tells him, 'Daddy read book,' my husband just melts and reads the book to him. I think as he's getting older, my husband is spending more time with him. My son is talking more and every day he's saying something new, and my husband is now realizing that the situation is not as bad as he thought it was going to be. He is realizing that our son isn't too much different than any other child. We just have to wait a little longer for him to progress and **every day gets a little sweeter.**"

It is important for husbands and wives to accept that they may also have greatly different time frames for experiencing grief. There are people who grieve once briefly and rarely revisit these emotions. More commonly, mourning is revisited in more of a cyclical manner. It is not unusual for certain milestones or small but symbolic events to result in resurgence of mourning.

One mother of three children with disabilities whose disorders greatly affect their communication abilities said:

66 **W**e initially grieved for the loss of our dreams but now we are grieving the lack of communication. As every stage of our life comes up, we will have new

things come up. It is almost like it is a never-ending, evolving grief. And you have to accept that because if you fight it, it is just going to drain you."

A father of a young boy with cerebral palsy described his grief as it was revisited:

"When our son was born, my wife bought me one of those wonderful backpacks from LL Bean that the kids go in. Eight years later, we still have it. Our son doesn't have the strength to sit up. I found the backpack last summer, and I started to think about walking again. And I broke down and cried because this is what I have lost. That's what the tension is. My role has been taken away and her role has been taken away. And we are put in this other role of being caretakers of an eight-year-old baby."

> Understand that some sadness may simply not be left behind. Find ways to manage it and to accept your partner's ongoing sadness, if necessary.

Feelings of grief, enjoyment, and pride in your child are not, for the most part, mutually exclusive. For a few reasons, handling ongoing periods of sadness becomes a task to be worked out individually to a great extent. First, a spouse is more likely than not busy handling her own reactions. Perhaps more importantly, what works for one person does not for another. Coming to terms with a child's disorder requires finding and following a very personal path. As the father of a child with cerebral palsy expressed:

"A lot of time, I think that an individual in a marriage needs to learn how to take care of sadness and discouragement on their own. Take a walk or talk to a confidant."

What helps you cope may feel very distancing to your partner. Some differences in coping that may feel particularly divisive will be the focus of our discussion below.

Clashes in Coping Style

Denial

Although the general public uses the term "denial" in a general way to describe the refusal to accept the seriousness of a situation, denial is a defense mechanism. This means it is a primarily unconscious strategy people use to "protect" themselves from anxiety and from awareness of external threatening circumstances. As a defense mechanism, it can temporarily provide necessary protection ("buy time") until life circumstances feel more manageable. This is less common than denial-like defenses in which a spouse more consciously refuses to acknowledge the impact of a child's disorder. Refusing to accept the presence or impact of a disability occurs relatively more frequently with disorders that are not visible, such as AD/HD, learning disabilities, Asperger's syndrome, or bipolar illness. Denial-type responses are also more prevalent when a diagnosis has not yet been formally made, even if there is abundant evidence that something is wrong.

Problems with denial are complicated, have the potential to be very divisive, and must be handled thoughtfully in a marriage. The following is an example in which a couple differed yet were able to work as a team:

> "I came out of denial about our son's disability before my husband did. That made deciding what to do about evaluations and treatment a challenge at first. Getting the diagnosis itself was not easy. There were school evaluations, neurological exams, blood work, and private educational testing. Deciding how far we were willing to go with our time and money was a challenge for us. I'm grateful to my husband for continuing when he didn't think it was necessary, but I did. We had to learn to agree to disagree and then finally compromise."

Many of the following strategies and concepts are useful for dealing with both denial and denial-like responses:

[Remember that denial can be helpful under some circumstances or detrimental under others.]

For example, denial as a genuine defense mechanism may enable a parent to continue to cope and care for a child who has a terminal condition. In this situation, refusing to believe the prognosis for a while may be helpful as long as it does not interfere with appropriate care and support. Sometimes the best course of action is to simply give the situation time until your spouse can face the situation more gradually. The use of defense mechanisms most often diminishes naturally as you become more able to withstand the reality of an extremely painful situation.

Some questions to ask yourself at this point if you believe that your partner is in denial and it is upsetting to you:

☑ Are services and treatment being put into place even if your partner does not agree with the seriousness of the situation? This is the number one consideration.

☑ Are your spouse's needs for psychological self-protection beneficial even if they are disturbing to you? For example, your spouse may feel that your child's prognosis is actually far better than what the doctors indicate. In this circumstance, your desire not to feel alone with your grief or fear is not a compelling enough reason to try to affect your spouse's defenses. After all, she is likely to work through her feelings naturally once she feels strong enough to face more of reality without such a buffer.

> [If denial is problematic, make sure your partner receives
> information from sources other than you.]

There are several ways to accomplish this:

1. Encourage your partner to meet with your child's healthcare professionals and to ask them questions. This is particularly helpful if you have previously been the one attending most appointments. It is easy for your partner to be dismissive of what the professional says when removed from the situation. (It is also possible that your spouse has some very legitimate questions that need to be asked to help her determine the extent of your child's problems). It is not unusual for

spouses to accept the veracity of information they have heard from their partner only after also hearing it from a professional.

2. Ask your spouse to attend a conference with you pertaining to your child's disorder or illness.

3. Arrange opportunities for your spouse to be directly faced with your child's needs. For example, a parent who denies the severity of a child's cognitive problems might benefit from time helping that child with homework. The more knowledgeable parent often assumes this role because she feels more equipped to meet the child's needs. Over time, however, this shields the spouse from exposure to the seriousness of the child's problems. This strategy worked (but too late) for one wife. She wrote:

"**M**y ex went through and is still going though a lot of denial when it comes to our children's disabilities. I think now that he actually has to work with them by himself, he is finally seeing the severity and complexity of it all."

What these strategies have in common is that they relieve you of directly imparting information to your spouse when it is clear that this no longer works. The information needs to be made available through a new source, no matter how knowledgeable you may be.

> Remember that time is a factor with denial and that situations often improve greatly even when they look hopeless for a fairly long time.

We are aware of many couples who struggled with denial to the point that they questioned the viability of their marriage, only to find that the problems were eventually very well resolved.

"**A**t first, my husband refused to believe me when I expressed my concerns that our son may have autism—because my family didn't believe me. I felt alone and grieved without support. My husband made me feel ashamed that I would 'think such an awful thing' about our child. After our son was diagnosed, the stress eased a little and my husband agreed to any help I thought our son needed. I felt like we were a team then, with a united cause to fight for."

Denial does not need to ruin a marriage unless it results in emotional harm over time to family members. This generally occurs only if one partner denies that there is a disability and instead attributes problems to character flaws of the child or the other spouse. For instance, one mother of a child with Asperger's syndrome who was eventually separated from her husband wrote:

"It greatly affected my marriage. His father chose not to accept of any of this and decided that our son was 'just bad.' As our son has gotten older, he has matured, but because his father will never understand him, there is no way to relate to my spouse."

[Respect hope and don't mistake it for denial.]

People have a right to choose how they view a threatening situation. The process usually involves finding a way to view the situation that reduces anxiety and makes it more manageable. The father of a son with Asperger's syndrome provides an illustration:

"I think men get a bad reputation for not accepting disabilities. We may respond differently, but every father I have spoken to knows his child has issues. We are just as hurt and traumatized by the knowledge when we learn about it, but are expected to take strong roles and not react strongly. Part of this is to keep balance, I think. I have always accepted my son's diagnosis; I recognize he has problems, but in my eyes he is not disabled. He is, I think, 'differently-abled' and needs help relating that to the real world."

Hope may also be part of your chosen stance and how you choose to process what you're faced with.

Pride vs. Shame

Because most of us are raised in a culture that denigrates disability and prizes competition and "perfection," some people initially feel ashamed of their child due to his or her disability. These parents are also often "ashamed of being ashamed," yet these feelings continue for awhile. People need varying lengths of time to come to grips with these feelings. Some spouses need to get used to situations they feel will be embarrassing. For example, many parents fear the first time they need to be in public, such as the mall. One mother of a child with Down syndrome described how she had to learn to get used to people seeing her child's face because she thought many people would stare. It is a learning process and one that may be far easier for you than your partner.

Emotional Intensity

The extent and intensity of each partner's emotional expression is another difference that can become a serious source of conflict and alienation. The following is an illustration provided by the mother of a child with multiple disabilities:

"We stayed strong together while our daughter spent ten weeks in the NICU. We had different coping styles, though. My husband would go into military mode, and I just wanted to cry. He always got irritated because I would cry every time we had to leave the NICU and our daughter. One night after a really hard visit, I stopped to cry because I couldn't take it any more. My husband stopped too, so I put my arms around him for comfort. He would not even hold me because people were walking by. I was embarrassing him!? If we had been alone he would have held me and stroked my hair, and talked to me until I felt better. This is an example of how coping skills are different and that alone can shake a solid marriage."

People need to choose for themselves how to handle their emotions. One wife stated that she would have felt so much better if her husband had also cried over their sons with multiple disabilities. Her husband spoke of his belief that crying would dismantle the "emotional structure" he built for coping. He commented: "The structure I have built is holding everything together, and I'm not going to pull my finger out of that dike."

Coping through Distraction vs. Immersion

Parents differ in the extent to which they immerse themselves in matters related to their child's disorder. Some plunge in to gather as much information as possible. In addition to the direct benefits of an improved knowledge base, the act of gathering information is a coping strategy. For some, it helps reestablish a sense of equilibrium and is a way to begin to gain a sense of control over a fearsome situation. The Internet, other parents, and support groups supply endless opportunities for knowledge. Some parents (more often mothers) become completely absorbed in learning about the disorder and potential treatments

Conversely, some parents try to avoid anxiety by not dwelling on their child's condition. They appear much less involved and gravitate toward distractions. The distractions may take the form of throwing themselves into their jobs, hobbies, or activities that draw them outside of the home. For some, it is an effort to maintain their strength and reduce the impact of their children's serious problems.

These contrasting coping styles are both valid attempts to deal with emotional distress and upheaval. Over the years I have met far more couples in which the husbands adopted a style that attempted to preserve normality and the wives were immersed in the disorder.

Accepting Differences and Adjusting Together

[Agree to work toward achieving the midpoint on a continuum if you and your spouse have divergent coping styles.]

As much as I believe that many different coping styles are natural and adaptive, I also believe in moderation of coping styles. Time alone brings many people closer to the midpoint of the continuum so that they can engage in necessary discussions and collaboration with their spouse, even if they initially avoided them. A father of a son with cerebral palsy described this for us:

> " There was a time close to my son's birth that a lot of really strong feelings about his needs came up in our conversations. For me, things like realizing that his intimate physical needs will always need to be attended to were very upsetting at first. Now that I am more aware of just what it means to be in my son's situation without the emotional shock, the discussions don't seem as difficult."

Sometimes, working toward the midpoint has to be more deliberate and part of a negotiated agreement between spouses. Sometimes couples can achieve this themselves; sometimes a therapist helps. An example from therapy illustrates how this kind of compromise can be achieved. One couple I worked with had a child with a life-threatening medical condition, requiring vigilant monitoring. The future felt as frightening as the present. The mother was immersed in gathering information about her son's relatively rare disorder and thinking about the future. Her husband sought normality and was very involved with work both at the office and at home. He acknowledged discomfort with his wife's strong emotions.

I described the wife as being like the kind of smoke detector that goes off at the hint of steam (much less smoke). The husband admitted that he was like a smoke detector that did not go off until a roaring blaze was going. My advice was for both of them to move somewhat toward the middle of the continuum. The wife needed to limit her utter involvement because she had reached the point where immersion in professional literature and "what ifs" can undermine daily coping abilities. (Parents of medically fragile children do often need to eventually learn to set fears aside for bits of the day and to adopt more of a day-at-a-time approach about the future. That does not mean that they should not line up and utilize resources, but rather that they should not dwell in all future possibilities.) For his part, the husband needed to learn to better tolerate the emotions connected to his child's condition. This would help him cling less to a sense of normality so that he could respond better to very real dangers and his family's changing needs. He agreed to engage in more discussions with his wife and to learn more about his child's condition.

How to Make Talking Less Distressing

It is often the mother who feels an unremitting need to talk about her grief and fear. This is one useful path to coming to terms with what has happened and to processing it emotionally. On the other hand, men may be attracted to other paths for coping with sadness or stress, such as attempting to move on and deal with other matters. This does not mean that their grief is not equally gripping.

Sometimes husbands try to help their wives with grief by suggesting ways to contain it or seek solutions. Women do not generally experience this as helpful and are likely to feel more alone with their grief. As the husband feels his efforts are impotent in alleviating her suffering, he increasingly avoids his wife and home. The cycles then intensify with more despair, anger, and helplessness. A friend shared her strategy for handling her husband's reactions to her need to talk. She begins intense discussions with, "I don't expect you to fix this, but I need to talk about...."

No matter how long you have been married, you sometimes need to teach your partner what you need rather than get upset when he or she doesn't intuitively anticipate your needs. If you need your spouse to simply be close and listen without offering "solutions," clearly explain this. If you have already done so, do it again and again if necessary. When it comes to marriage, there is little "one trial learning." As a marital therapist, I have found that spouses often feel as if their partner doesn't love them if he or she has to be told how to do something—as if the teaching invalidates the action. One could easily argue that it shows as much love to allow oneself to be taught.

Husbands and wives may need to learn how to talk to each other about their grief at the same time that they understand the need to respect each other's style of grieving. As with other elements of a successful marriage, there are times for compromise. It may be useful for you to learn to listen to the outpouring of your spouse's emotion while your spouse learns to honor the fact that you can only tolerate immersion in so much grief (or vice versa).

If coping with grief is causing difficulties in your marriage, it may help for you and your spouse to set aside a limited period of time several times a week to talk about your situation. The time could range from fifteen to thirty minutes, long enough for a person to express herself and ventilate fully but not so overwhelmingly long that the other partner will feel swallowed up in interminable grief. Spouses can become less frightened by their partner's grief. More spontaneous discussion is eventually the goal.

How to Help One Another Cope

[Respect differences in coping while (if necessary) gently and persistently encouraging coping.]

This approach involves encouraging your spouse to face what he or she fears dealing with, but in manageable doses and with support. This tends to reduce avoidance or strong denial-type responses. For example, I have seen good results when a wife has introduced her husband to another man with a child with a similar disorder. Inviting a spouse to attend a support group for a single session sometimes works as well. If your partner is too immersed, it is reasonable to ask him to take breaks with you which involve activities that have absolutely nothing to do with your child—for example, an evening out when discussing children is entirely off limits.

[If your partner struggles, don't let him or her drift beyond reach.]

As much as I emphasize the individual nature of adjustment, I do believe it is important that spouses try to find a means to keep one another from drifting beyond emotional reach. There is an art to maintaining a connection with your spouse when you are both bombarded by life. The key is to sincerely try to help your partner rather than criticize her for her difficulties coping. Three examples from parents follow:

"For so long we were just surviving and my husband went into his 'cave.' But I kept (nicely) saying, 'Hey, come out of your cave, come on.' That was my way of saying, 'I love you enough to want to be with you.' He saw that. A couple days later he would come back to me."

"I operate from a theory that the more someone pushes you away, the more they need you."

"When I am having a freak-out, he steps his support up a notch. I think you have to look beyond words. My husband's reaction to freak-outs is: 'What can I do to help?' He realizes that he doesn't freak out because he has a job to go to."

[
Set limits to your spouse's behavior if his or her behavior
is clearly damaging to your child.
]

Some matters stemming from adjustment problems require a much more heavy-handed approach. This includes physical abuse, emotional abuse (such as name-calling), lack of essential treatment, and repeated rejection. As we discuss in detail in Chapter 10, there are times when a child's basic needs must be prioritized over survival of the marriage.

When to Get Professional Help

Serious marital problems may be related to untreated emotional problems that are not identified for a variety of reasons. These include clinical depression and substance abuse. Depression is the most common of these, and according to the National Institute of Mental Health, almost 10 percent of adults in America are affected in any given year. Both depression and substance abuse pose risks to the individual and the marriage. Both require professional treatment if serious enough.

Depression

Grief and the mourning process are not the same as clinical depression. Both grief and depression can include pervasive sadness and tears, but there are important differences.

Clinical depression is different from sadness, grief or "being down." It is more accurately considered to be a whole body illness that affects mood, physiological processes, and thoughts. For parents of children with disabilities, its impact can be insidious because you may be so busy with caretaking that you initially disregard the alterations in your functioning. Because depression affects thought processes as well as mood, the depressed person may lack insight into the causes of her negative thoughts. As a result, the depressed person often feels a lowered self-worth, may struggle with guilty ruminations, and hold a hopeless view of the future. It is easy to mistakenly feel that these are normal reactions to difficult situations that may surface when parenting children with disabilities or illnesses. Clinical depression may limit resilience in the face of difficulties. When in doubt as to whether you or your spouse are indeed depressed, seek a professional evaluation.

Classic symptoms of depression include pervasive loss of interest and pleasure in almost all activities for at least two weeks. In addition, many of the following are commonly seen:

- pessimism and hopelessness;
- decreased energy and a marked sense of fatigue;
- increased or decreased appetite, manifested in unintentional weight changes;
- insomnia, hypersomnia (excessive sleep), or early-morning wakening;
- difficulty with concentration and decision-making;
- feelings of guilt, hopelessness, and/or worthlessness;
- decreased sex drive;
- thoughts of death and/or suicide;
- anxiety;
- irritability.

It is important to note that men sometimes manifest depression differently, and for this reason, their depressions may be missed. Men are less likely to admit sadness. In addition, symptoms such as feelings of helplessness, worthlessness, and hopeless-ness are not as prominent. Instead, depressed men often increase their use of substances, seem irritable, and withdraw through ex-cessive work or pursuit of activities outside of the family. I have seen many depressed men ward off their feelings by compulsive behaviors such as gambling, viewing of Internet pornography, or unrestrained spending.

Depression and prolonged stress can change brain chemistry, so some people may need medication to feel more like themselves again. Before I recommend that someone seek an evaluation for medication, I generally wait to see if she responds to counseling. Naturally, there are exceptions when symptoms are severe. If medi-cation is deemed necessary, I usually find that counseling is also helpful in addressing the problems that have led up to such difficul-ties. Let us turn to the poignant words of one woman who described her lowest moments, as well as the help she found. Comments from her husband are also included:

Wife:

"I was alone with the twins for a couple of hours. One began having what we used to call his 'blue phase.' He was blue and wouldn't breathe, and I was screaming at him to try to get him to breathe. The other was this helpless infant who was crying in need. And they were hungry—normal baby stuff on top of all the other stuff. I realized that I was either going to kill them or I was going to walk away. I put them in their individual cribs, I raised the sides, and they were screaming...I mean screaming. I walked out of their room. It was surreal. I walked into our bedroom, which is our safe haven, since no one comes into our bedroom except us. I closed the door, went into the walk-in closet, and closed that door. I got down on the floor and I just rocked. And I fell apart. I heard them screaming and I just thought, 'Oh my God, they are going to die because I can't take care of them and I don't know when anyone is coming home.' I was paralyzed on the floor. I heard my husband come home and I heard him calling. And I still couldn't move. I heard him go to the babies...."

Husband:

"**I** hurried down and I remember going into their room. They were still crying but they were okay. Then I went into the closet and she was sitting there. And I remember getting down on the floor with her. I remember holding her, trying to get her to calm down. We obviously knew that we had to deal with the situation at that time."

Medications such as antidepressants don't solve problems, but they can be invaluable in helping someone dig out of a hole well enough to begin to solve problems. Depression alters perception and obscures the ability to see any positives or opportunities to resolve problems. Antidepressants are not used to instill a false sense of well-being; rather, they are intended to help diminish the symptoms such as hopelessness, overwhelming fatigue, and indecisiveness, amongst others, that interfere with functioning and coping.

As noted earlier, many depressed parents find the help of a therapist particularly useful. (By "therapist," we mean a psychologist, social worker, marriage counselor, etc.) The mother of twins, who described her agonizing depression above, made the following comment about getting help:

"**I** nitially I was not willing to talk to anyone. I was certain that no psychiatrist, no matter how well trained they were, could understand. I had been in therapy before, so I was not opposed to therapy. I was just absolutely positive that no one could understand what I was going through. So I was reticent."

In addition to finding a psychiatrist who *did* understand, she found other sources of therapeutic help:

"**B** ut truthfully, my greatest source of help has been the social worker from our early intervention program. My husband and I have a weekly appointment with her. Because we know she's coming every week, there

are times we don't express things to each other all week
(positive or negative); they will suddenly come out because
she is in the room. If it is something that might have
snowballed and become an issue, it is diffused because we
talk about it. And that is the greatest service."

Substance Abuse

Some people develop substance abuse problems as they attempt
to blot out stress and distressing emotions. As with depression, this
exacts a price for the individual and the marriage. Often these problems take the form of excessive reliance on alcohol or prescribed
tranquilizers or painkillers. What had been appropriate use sometimes mounts to the point of substance dependence or abuse. If you
suspect that your spouse may have a substance abuse problem, it is
important to share your concerns with your partner. Although this
can be a difficult issue to raise, the alternative path is running the
risk of helping a partner deny a growing problem. Pay attention and
curtail the substance use.

Moving Ahead (and Picking Up the Pieces If Necessary)

It is human nature to adjust over time. Many strategies can
help you and your spouse find your ways and help you to think and
feel differently about your child and your lives. Some unfold naturally; others occur through interactions with others or helpful life
experiences that could not be planned or predicted. Mourning sub-
sides, new dreams are created, and couples generally find ways to
bridge the differences that result when childhood disability brings
about upheaval.

In closing this chapter, we share these valuable reflections of a
mother of a son with cerebral palsy:

"Our son's birth and the new demands it created
exacerbated some very distinct differences between
my spouse and me. For example, I wanted to face the

challenges head-on, getting all the therapies started and learning everything I could (with hopes of reversing the problems, of course). My husband, on the other hand, had a 'wait and see' attitude, and said he was not sure our son needed all the help I had lined up. While I was studying everything about our son's condition and making lists of all the things we had to do, my husband seemed to go about parenting and other aspects of his life in his usual way. While his 'business as usual' approach was comforting in some ways, at times I would get very upset because he did not share the pain and anxiety I was having. I would get particularly upset when he would go outside and tend to his thirty-plus bonsai trees. Watching from the kitchen window, I would stew over how he could spend more time tending the trees than he did tending me.

"It was at least three years before I came to understand, through marital therapy, how his hobby helped him feel grounded and to cope with our stressful situation in those early days. Before I came to this understanding, 'the trees' had become the emblem of my dissatisfaction with our marriage. When I witness the dynamic between my husband and son, it brings up a memory from my son's first year. There were many moments when I was so crushed by grief that I could barely look at my son. His disabilities were so apparent and critical to me. While I was busy learning about the disability, my husband would simply be holding our son, talking to him, just hanging out. Then and now, it is clear to me that the differences between my husband and myself are complementary. My son's birth brought our differences into very sharp contrast, but we managed to grow into our new roles and stay together. I believe that our marriage will last if we can move to a new level where we can appreciate each other again as individuals, not just as parents."

Chapter Three

Practical Solutions to Practical Problems

Fran P. Prezant, M.Ed., CCC-SLP

Many of us experience increased stress due to the nature of life as parents of children with disabilities. Ordinary situations and challenges in the lives of other families may suddenly become the straw that breaks the camel's back in your situation. (It is like adding that last block that topples the stack in the game Jenga.) Fatigue or mental exhaustion, juggling taxi service for kids, bill paying, grocery shopping, therapy, finding the right daycare provider or school program, or somebody making the wrong comment at the wrong time, can all be that final straw. Sometimes the issues mount to the point that they affect the dynamics of the entire family, so it is important to find ways to conquer and divide the multitude of everyday problems. Otherwise, they can cumulatively overwhelm you; it is kind of like being nibbled to death by tiny duck bites. This chapter addresses common problems and suggests practical solutions.

Creative Problem Solving

Although we will share many useful solutions to commonly experienced problems, it is simply not possible to be all-inclusive.

So, we offer insight about how people may devise creative solutions and wield overlooked strategies for solving problems. One of the best strategies is based on the principles of brainstorming. The point is to jot down as many ideas as possible without thinking (yet) about any of their limitations. Quantity breeds quality. Even a list of far-fetched ideas often contains potential gems that can be polished up to practical solutions. As you generate a free-flowing list, initially withhold your judgment about their relative merits. It is too easy to get caught up in the flaws of each of them. After generating a long list, go back through the list and identify a few of the best ideas. Then these can be shaped up.

As you will see in this chapter, sometimes unconventional solutions work very well. In addition, it may help to recognize that these problems have been solved by many others. Try to pick people's brains and enter problem solving with the positive attitude that you can find a way to manage the problem. Perhaps try something to see if it works, and remember that compromise is important. Sometimes there is no perfect solution, but there are many ways to improve a situation. Don't fall into the trap of discarding all strategies because none of them are "perfect" or solve a problem entirely.

Common Problems

In our survey of several hundred parents, we identified some of the most common practical problems that added stress to their lives and marriages. These became the basis for this chapter, and include problems stemming from:

- Lack of diagnosis,
- Information overload,
- Financial issues,
- Time constraints,
- Mental and physical fatigue, and
- Dealing with the reactions of others.

Problems Due to Lack of Diagnosis

If parents know there is something wrong with their child, but do not yet have a working diagnosis, it causes significant problems in daily life. This state is hard to live with and may be protracted if your child's symptoms are vague or intermittent. So many parents grapple with finding the information they need. Lack of diagnosis compounds problems. This is illustrated by one couple we know who had an infant who cried and screamed uncontrollably for most of his first few months. Doctors suggested that it was colic, so the parents tried to alter diet, routine, and everything else to see if it made a difference, but something was still very wrong. This was their first child and they wondered why other parents would have more than one child if their experience was typical. They questioned whether the problem was simply due to their own parenting style. Their relationship became strained because of the uncertainty layered onto the already stressful changes associated with becoming first-time parents. Eventually, the child was diagnosed with severe sensory integration and learning problems.

Getting a proper diagnosis is often a lengthy process, but key strategies can help you.

[Honor your instincts and follow your gut feelings.]

Many parents "sense" there is something professionals are missing about their child's problems. If you have nagging thoughts about your child, check them out to confirm or rule out your suspicions. Investigate suspected problems with appropriate specialists, getting second opinions if necessary.

I can't tell you how many times I have heard family members (including spouses) or professionals mistakenly advise, "Don't worry; you're just exaggerating," or, "It's nothing; he'll grow out of it." Examples of misjudgment include the mother who was convinced her son had a severe attention deficit disorder. After she described the worrisome symptoms to a physician, he minimized the issue by saying, "Boys will be boys." When the doctor failed to give the mother's concerns credence, she became concerned about her own parenting capabilities, and in the end, her child had to fail several times in school before being diagnosed with exactly what she had reported.

Other strategies to bring you closer to a diagnosis include:
1. Read about symptoms.
2. Contact organizations that specialize in early development.

3. Talk to knowledgeable parents—particularly ones who have had to search for answers.
4. Contact your local Child Find office. Through the federal special education law IDEA (Individuals with Disabilities Education Act) these offices are required to cover diagnostic assistance for children from birth to three years old. If there is a problem, therapeutic services and parent training may be provided in your home or early childhood treatment centers.

Resources at the back of this book include several federal parent programs specifically designed to provide support, connections, and referrals to parents seeking information.

Managing Information Overload

[
Remember that there is a limit to how much information you can process at once.
]

Too much is too much even if it is relevant. This is particularly true when information is intense, unexpected, and has major life ramifications for your family. You can manage the problem of information overload by being in charge of the pace with which you are expected to absorb it. Rather than miss important information, tell the information givers that you need to take time to process what they are telling you.

Consider the experience of another parent who was told after an evaluation that her daughter had a severe progressive hearing loss due to a congenital deformity in the auditory system and that it would probably result in deafness. Although the doctor continued to provide technical medical information for the next ten minutes, she never heard a word of it—she was stuck on the prediction of impending deafness. The physician could have exclaimed that the building was going to blow up or that she had just won the Nobel Prize. It wouldn't have mattered, because she was in information overload and couldn't process any more information at that point.

Our brains are only capable of processing so much information before we go into overload and stop processing. On a day-to-day level, people break down information into manageable chunks. "Chunking" is a recognized term that describes the breakdown of verbal information into segments that can be processed. (This is why phone numbers and Social Security numbers are broken into hyphenated sets.) Most numerical series we are expected to recall do not exceed seven numbers because people can't process more. Most people can't remember their credit card numbers, bank account, or loan numbers because they exceed our storage and recall limits. Similarly, there is a limit to how much we can take in, absorb, and process at once—especially when the information may be critical or have major ramifications for our child.

We can also experience information overload if we receive conflicting information from specialists, parents, and family. This can provoke more angst rather than capability to deal with the situation logically.

If only one partner is being overloaded in this way, the burden can be amplified. On top of feeling overwhelmed by the sheer amount of information, he may feel that he cannot understand or convey the information. Resentment that the other partner wasn't there to get the same information builds.

Some practical suggestions to minimize information overload are:

- Remember, two heads are better than one. If it is possible for both parents to attend meetings with medical or educational professionals, both of you could get the same information at the same time.
- A second best alternative is to get prior permission to tape the meeting so you can play it back and share it with your spouse.
- If neither of these options is possible, ask a friend, family member, or advocate to attend important meetings with you. Sometimes having a more objective person hear the information is helpful when it comes to summarizing it for yourself and your partner.

[Ask for clarification if you don't understand.]

- Don't be afraid to ask medical or educational professionals to repeat information or to explain what it means and what the ramifications are for the future. Professionals tend to use jargon frequently, and may assume that if you don't ask, you understand the language they are using. Many parents I advocated for told me that they didn't ask questions at meetings for fear of appearing ignorant when everyone else seemed to understand.

- It's okay to remind the professionals that you need clarification of terms or information presented in a different way or that you have questions that they haven't answered.
- Professionals should not be offended if you want a second opinion and you are perfectly within your rights to ask for one. In fact, some insurance plans require that you get another opinion for some procedures.

Handling Financial Issues

Money isn't everything, but it sure has a way of tripping us up at times. You may not consider financial issues as a primary threat to the inherent qualities in marriages like trust, honesty, love, and understanding. However, the complications of financial issues caused by disability status can snowball into actions and situations that affect those very qualities. This is particularly true for couples who have children with extraordinary medical conditions. The financial stress can cause people to take second jobs, relocate, borrow money, find unconventional ways to get money, sell homes, or bring extended family members into the mix. Strong emotions naturally accompany these transitions.

Before we get into practical strategies, we want to share an admittedly extreme case of a couple in Florida who are trying to get national attention for their incredible plight. They exemplify *thinking outside the box.*

Their daughter was born with multiple severe and life-threatening disabilities that required over sixty operations within the first four years of life. In addition to physicals, test procedures, surgery, and hospitalization, she required feeding pumps and related equipment for basic survival, nursing care, and disposable medical supplies. Their health insurer initially paid claims for the feeding pumps but would not pay for any of the equipment or supplies necessary to use the machine. The insurer also refused to pay for necessary nursing care, claiming that it wasn't medically necessary. Additional claims for services and equipment were similarly denied, although necessary.

When the family's medical insurance policy came up for renewal, their premiums were suddenly doubled and benefits were reduced, including removal of prescription drug coverage. The family, already financially strapped, had to decide between accepting woefully inadequate medical care or give up their incomes so they would be eligible for Medicaid (which would cover more services than their private insurance did). There were no guidebooks that could have prepared the couple for these excruciating circumstances. Their united instincts to save their child convinced them to go on Medicaid—but this was only the beginning. According to the wife, her husband's sense of worth was affected and he felt like a failure due to his inability to provide for his family. By profession he is a nurse, so as a caretaker, he felt even more responsible for understanding the system and knowing how to maneuver through it.

The strategy they decided on to assure continued Medicaid coverage, which paid about $10,000 monthly for basic home nursing care, might be considered extreme. They sought formal separation and now live in separate domiciles, while the mother remains unemployed. They also sued the insurance company. Does this sound like a dysfunctional and aberrant solution? On the contrary, given the circumstances, perhaps it was more functional and creative than it seems.

According to the mother's report, living separately has actually improved the situation and she and her husband see each other daily. In the meantime, they are trying to attract press coverage to highlight the fact that there are numerous families in similar situations and that current practices are destructive to health, life, and family stability. They are also exploring relocation to another state whose policies are more medically friendly and all the while, warning other middle income families who run into extraordinary medical situations to "look out." The wife's advice to other parents is that if they have it within themselves to challenge a system that doesn't make sense, do it and make sure the things you fight for will make a difference in children's lives.

Hopefully, you will never find yourself in a position where you have to choose between your marriage and paying for your child's medical expenses. In any case, this story exemplifies the fact that being in a certain financial bracket doesn't negate financial problems and the need for solutions. For parents of children with medical disabilities, hospital social work staff should be able to provide resources and financial information that may be helpful. If you need this help and aren't getting it, ask.

Financial issues can also be a major management challenge for parents whose child has no medical needs but severe learning needs. One family we know was told by a school district that their deaf child could not attend an appropriate public school in a neighboring town because the home district refused to pay the $15,000 transportation fee even though the child needed the program there. The couple had already moved and rented a home (although they owned one somewhere else), so that their child would be eligible for area services. After the mother hooked up with advocates at the IEP meeting, she discovered that transportation costs are to be paid by the school, not by the family (which was news to her but shouldn't have been to the special education director).

Here are some strategies to consider when you face unmanageable medical or educational expenses related to your child's disability:

- Increase your awareness and gather information about insurance, social service, and educational systems and regulations. This information may be available through social service agencies, hospital social workers, or school counselors and therapists. Also, every state has offices that can send out information on regulations and procedures including appeals and arbitration.

- Speak to other parents who have gone through similar situations (particularly ones that involve medical insurance or hospital and therapy expenses). This can save you unnecessary steps as well as angst. It can help just to hear another parent who's been through it tell you that a claim rejection isn't necessarily final and how to get to the next step.

- Be assertive, knowledgeable, and persistent. This was a solution for one family with insurance issues and denials resulting in non-payment of bills, letters from collection agencies, and added stress to an already stressful situation. This family designated the wife as the contact with the insurance companies and medical providers each time a large claim was denied for reasons that didn't make sense. When a $10,000 claim for medically necessary procedures was denied by insurance, and the family was expected to come up with the cash, she used a combination of information gathering and assertiveness for a resolution. Using the very information that insurers provide, the wife:

1. Wrote a letter of protest requesting that a physician rather than a clerk make a determination of what is "medically unnecessary" (and suggesting that the supervisor on this case try the procedure himself outside of a hospital and determine it to be medically unnecessary);

2. Asked for a review or formal appeal;

3. Noted that the insurance appeal forms stated to be enclosed in each denial were never enclosed; *and*

4. Therefore, an additional request for outside review and arbitration was being made as well. The letter indicated several political and medical administrators at the state level who would be receiving a copy of the letter.

Result? The couple received immediate notification that the procedures in fact should have been covered and should no longer be a source of stress for them to be concerned about.

The Lesson? Persistence coupled with good investigative skills often pays off. (Just a bit of anger at being victimized by a system that is supposed to help you can be productive if channeled the right way. For instance, think of the clerk making decisions about your reimbursements for medical procedures by looking them up in a code book to decide if they were medically necessary.)

Remember, "No" is not always a final response. One parent advises, "When they say no, go to the next level and if necessary, go to the people with the purse strings and say, 'This is the situation. What can you do to help my child get the treatment he needs?'"

Not all financial stress is due to insurance or medical and therapy costs. Because of inordinate time requirements and other issues like housecleaning, finding childcare for siblings or after school care may be necessary. Other financial problems may result from the need for special classes, summer programs, or private schools; moving to a neighborhood where services are available (and housing may be expensive); and transportation costs—not to mention that employment may be compromised as a result of any of these changes.

One couple who had jointly decided that the wife would be a stay-at-home mom while the child was young was forced to change their minds when their son was found to have significant learning and attention problems as well as neurological issues. The best option described to them involved placing their child in a specialized private school in an area that had no transportation services and came with a price tag that exceeded tuition at the nearby state university. In addition to depleting the money they had used to begin the child's college fund, the couple had to devise a creative way for both of them to work and have the flexibility to provide transportation to and from school. Strategies included finding a carpool and having dad drive the child to school several mornings a week on his way to work, even though "on his way" meant driving twenty miles out of the way.

Other strategies that may work for you include:

☑ *Prioritizing and examining expenses.* Deciding which expenses are most critical is sometimes necessary. Good spending practices include paying major bills like rent and utilities first, restricting credit card use and paying off debts to avoid penalties, and looking for sales on food and clothing items. One parent stopped to add up the cost of her daily morning stops at Starbucks for coffee and a scone, and found that the $3.59 she spent each work morning totaled close to $1000 a year!

☑ *Finding ways to share expenses with others.* For instance, using co-ops, sharing child care costs, or using rotating play dates can save on child care fees. Ridesharing, a practice encouraged in many metropolitan areas to ease traffic, saves on transportation costs. Some communities such as Berkeley, California, have co-ops for more than food. Tool co-ops are established so anyone who needs to do some repairs to their home may borrow rather than purchase costly tools. Trading expertise sometimes pays off. I would gladly cook dinner for a friend who would come to fix my computer so I didn't have to call in a repair guy.

☑ Taking *second jobs, changing jobs, or relocating.* Some families have tried to pick up second jobs or have moved to higher paying positions. The one caution to consider is that both of these options layer on other issues like less available time for family if you take another job. Also consider the costs of relocation and changes in your standard of living if you move. These options may benefit some families, but should be scrutinized carefully to make sure the cost benefit is positive.

Managing Time Constraints

> Time is of the essence.
> It's a limited commodity and once it's gone you don't get it back.
> Use it for what you have to and try to save some for yourself!

Another major source of problems is lack of time. We aren't talking about time to do extras like play tennis or get our nails done or go on a second honeymoon for a month each year. We're talking about time to pay bills, cook meals, talk to teachers, help with homework, get to therapy and tutoring, see doctors and lawyers, clean the house, locate child care, taxi kids around, and find time for siblings. The time requirements involved in raising a child with a disability may leave little time for other responsibilities such as having a job, a family with their own needs, perhaps aging grandparents, and, of course, a marriage to sustain. As one parent observes:

"It is extremely stressful to attend to my child, give her the constant attention she needs, and then accomplish even daily chores on a limited amount of sleep."

The key is to recognize that you can't do it all and then decide which things are more important, which things can be delegated to someone else, which things can be done in less time, and which things can be tossed. Also, not feeling guilty will help to lighten your load.

[Learn how to ask for help and how to accept it.]

Some of the most efficient and "together" people I know are the ones who always ask others for help. They just do it in an assertive rather than a helpless way. Asking for and accepting help is difficult for many of us to do, but perhaps might solve some of our own time issues and simultaneously make someone else feel good about being useful. Letting go of your need to "do it all" sometimes means that you need to accept someone else completing a task in a less proficient way than you would. For example, if your kids make their own beds, let them do it even if it doesn't meet your standards. You've just saved ten minutes!

Additional suggestions for managing time constraints:

- ☑ Take advantage of opportunities that may already exist such as carpools or neighbors who are going to the store anyway.
- ☑ Schedule activities at less busy times of the day. It may not sound like much of a solution, but one parent saves a lot of time by doing all her grocery shopping after 11 p.m. when the stores are empty.
- ☑ Use respite care or babysitting. Numerous social service agencies or nonprofit disability-specific organizations will provide respite by sending in trained professionals or dedicated volunteers for a few hours a week to stay with your child so that you can get out, do errands, or take a nap. Some will even drop off meals. If you're uncomfortable with having a stranger or paid professional come in, the concept of respite can still be used with friends or parents as the respite workers.
- ☑ Maintain a routine. A byproduct of not having enough time is that family members are always running in different directions. Attempting to maintain a family dinnertime, if not regularly, then at least a few times a week, helps to preserve a routine and assure a gathering place and time for sharing and reconnection.

☑ Monitor your time on different tasks by keeping track on a weekly worksheet. Forcing yourself to count will increase your awareness of how much time you spend doing different tasks and will usually help you monitor your time better.

☑ Take advantage of modern technology. Current technology has not only enhanced our access to a world of information at high speed but also makes it easier to act and respond on our own time. For example: email messages and telephone answering machines save incredible amounts of time by allowing us to screen messages, delete trash, answer when we want to, and get off when we want to. Cell phones allow many of us to take care of business when we are away from our home phone, stuck in a line, or in traffic. The Internet provides opportunities to shop online for books, clothes, food, and more. Look for disability-specific technology that can reduce the amount of time you need to spend doing things for your child. For instance, the child who has a reading disability can now transform speech to text through voice-activated computer software to do homework or email a friend. Adaptations such as captioning on TV and in movies now may mean that children who are deaf or have auditory processing problems can get information in different ways without you having to re-explain.

Dealing with Physical and Mental Fatigue

When children's disabilities require constant attention, the result may be exhaustion for one or both parents in a day filled with therapy appointments, tutoring and homework, counseling or medical appointments, social interventions, and trying to attend to other family members. One stay-at-home mom discussed her physical exhaustion after spending all day trying to tend to her screaming child who rarely napped. As soon as it looked like he might sleep, she would force herself to lie down and physically try to separate from the rest of the environment and alter her mindset. She stuffed cotton balls in her ears and when that didn't quite do the trick, she finally found that exercise helped her to not only feel better but sleep better as well.

Take Turns Being Tired

The father of a child with cerebral palsy says that transferring his son from chair to toilet to bath and bed were physically fatiguing. On a nightly basis, his son lost covers, slipped out of bed, or moved his feeding tube into a bad position and needed attention. A lighter sleeper than his wife, he would end up being the one to get up several times nightly. Their solution to this problem was to take turns being tired. Short of hiring someone else to come into their home, one of them had to get up each night. He found that when he wore ear plugs, his wife woke up first, so they agreed that he would use ear plugs a few nights a week and know that on those nights his wife would wake up.

The mother of three children with fragile X syndrome had this to say about exhaustion:

"**M**y sleep is extremely important to me. I call it my etch-a-sketch nap. My brain gets all filled and I need to shake it, and wake up to have a better day. My husband knows this, so when I need a nap, he watches the children for me."

Find Respite Care

Respite can be available through formal or informal networks. Informally, trading off childcare with another parent is a workable solution for some parents. When my first child was a toddler, I became involved with a group of four professional women who all had children in the same age range. None of them had returned to work full time but each needed to carve out a little time each week to take care of personal and professional issues. We created a rotating play group and each mother took a morning to "host" all five children for about three hours. That provided each parent with twelve hours a week on their own. On a more formal level many social service organizations offer formal respite services for families of children with disabilities. See information in Chapter 9 on Respite Locator services.

"Teach Them to Fish"

Perhaps you have heard the adage, "if you give a person a fish, he will eat for a day. If you teach a person to fish, he will eat for a lifetime." As with this old adage, teaching your children to be more independent will decrease unnecessary dependence on you and therefore give you more time. For children who are able, teaching them to pick up after themselves and help out with basic chores will be productive for both of you and support growing independence.

Dealing with the Reactions of Others

How others react to our children with disabilities, though usually not intentionally or consciously negative, can be problematic for us. Reactions may be ignorant or may represent limited views that can affect our child's daily activities, friendships, achievement in school, and actualization of his potential today and in the future. Sometimes other people's words or actions lead to conflict between husbands and wives who choose to respond differently to "offenders." I have worked with many couples who argue over this issue and don't even agree on what is damaging, and whether to do something about it or not.

The reactions that we are referring to usually fall into these categories:

1. identifying the disability rather than the child,
2. stereotypic notions and social stigma,
3. pity or overt curiosity based on ignorance, and
4. rude comments.

A few examples are:

☑ The teacher who assumes that your child's label *epilepsy* means that he cannot be intelligent; therefore, she will have lower expectations of your child and your child may not progress as much because of it.

☑ The guidance counselor who says that no one with a learning disability should go to college may affect what your child decides to do as an adult.

☑ The customer in the grocery store who outwardly expresses pity for your child with a physical disability and for you as a "courageous parent" can be damaging, despite her good intentions.

Husbands and wives often must decide how or whether to respond when people make comments about their child with a disability. There is no recipe for how we as parents choose to respond, but it is important for husbands and wives to discuss their shared opinions on this issue or their differing feelings in order to minimize the impact of this problem on the marital relationship itself. Below are examples of scenarios with possible solutions.

Identifying the Disability Rather Than the Child

At a school meeting about his eight-year-old son with cerebral palsy, a father was told that his child would do fine at this school because there was another kid just like him who had spina bifida. A common and damaging reaction is one that assumes that all children with disabilities are more like each other than like other children who don't have disabilities. This occurs because people tend to identify the disability as the predominant characteristic of the child rather than consider that he might be a math whiz, love to listen to jazz, or have a great personality.

Solution: Talk about your child by name and focus on his strengths and characteristics that make him unique aside from disability. Be sure to always discuss what he can do, his interests and choices, and likes and dislikes without always focusing on what he can't do. The disability should be discussed only as needed in order to determine learning accommodations.

Handling Reactions Based on Social Stigma

"It bothers me that nobody questions you if you have a child with mental retardation or blindness. But when you have a child with a mental health diagnosis, people look at you differently and don't understand why you can't do something to influence their behavior."

This parent of a young adult with a mental health issue expressed her concern about how the reactions of the public to mental health disabilities differ from reactions to other disabilities. She found that reactions always seem to overflow onto the parents, almost in a suspicious way, as if either the parents have a "black sheep gene" that they have passed on or as if they had intentionally done something (for example, abuse of some type) that caused the disability and is a reflection of family character. Although this mother thought she was being singled out for social stigma, this feeling is certainly not limited to mental health issues and also affects parents of children with intellectual, physical, and other disabilities.

Solution: Provide awareness information to parents, friends, and community members to help educate them about your child's disability. Mental health and disability organizations frequently have fact sheets for teachers. For instance, a mother of three children with fragile X syndrome gets cards from a fragile X organization that explain "my loved one has fragile X syndrome" which she hands out to gawkers with a smile. Again, focusing on strengths that your child does have is important.

Another parent shared that it was a source of stress in her own house when other parents discouraged their children from playing with her child who had a significant disability, telling them that they should pick other friends, or that they might "catch something." She and her husband disagreed about how to handle such reactions. One wanted to confront the "offenders," while the other wanted to let it slide and restrict their child's potential contacts instead.

Solution: If it is at all possible to talk to the neighbors on friendly terms to identify what their concerns are about your child, there might be opportunities to increase awareness and convince them to view your child as a child first, just like theirs. Sometimes this may be difficult if they have been unfriendly to your child in the past. Sometimes getting them to relate to you as a person is a beginning.

Handling Pity/Curiosity

Sometimes reactions that may actually be well-intended fall short and anger us instead. The "Oh, you poor thing," or "How brave you are to deal with all of this" comments can almost sound patronizing. After all, parenting a child with a disability was probably not something you decided to do because of your courage or bravery as a person.

Solution: A number of parents do not react to this as a compliment but turn it around to let the speaker know that they just did what any good parent does. Some have said that it was choosing to become a parent that was the brave decision!

Handling Offensive and Rude Comments

“**I**never realized how frequently and loosely I used the term 'retard' to describe everything I did wrong, until a parent let me know that her child had mental retardation and those comments were hurtful.”

There are many terms that are very derogatory and invoke varied reactions from parents of children with disabilities, yet are frequently not even on the radar screen of people who freely use them. Walk onto most high school grounds and you are bound to hear students joking around by calling each other "retards" without a clue about the potential damaging impact of the term.

Solution: Tell people that common usage of a word doesn't make it appropriate, or explain why a term is offensive. Keeping your cool is important if you want to actually change people's behavior. In fact most of the time, people haven't ever really thought about how that word is used. I also tend to ask, "How would you feel if your brother had mental retardation and your closest friends used the term 'retard' to insult each other?"

A mother of a child with Down syndrome shared the different approaches she and her husband take in response to rude or ignorant comments:

“**W**hen we get stares, my guard goes up and I must admit, I am not always pleasant to people. My husband, on the other hand, is pleasant when people ask ignorant questions like, 'Do you know how smart he is going to be yet?' My response would be, 'Have they determined how smart you are going to be yet?' He gives the polite clinical response.”

Changing the reactions of others takes time. After all, some attitudes based on misconceptions are deeply embedded in our society, which places such an emphasis on being the best, brightest, and most beautiful. Providing instructive information in a positive way may be helpful if the circumstances are right. Providing opportunities for people to interact with your children in ways that allow them to see the person rather than the disability can help. Enlisting the support of well-informed and empowering teachers, friends, and colleagues can help create many teachable moments for the people we are trying to educate.

Conclusion

In this chapter, we have covered examples of some common problems and practical strategies that can be applied as solutions. You might be surprised to learn that some of the best strategies are some you have already applied without really thinking about them. Talking to other parents who are dealing with some of the same issues may also yield some undiscovered solutions for you.

Chapter Four

Communicating and
Problem-Solving as a Couple

Laura E. Marshak, Ph.D.

A child's disability often requires parents to discuss many emotionally charged topics and to make some very difficult decisions jointly as a couple. A mother of a child with cerebral palsy illustrated these challenges. She recalled being asked by the occupational therapist how her three-year-old son would get around in the future. She welcomed the suggestion to obtain a wheelchair because she felt as if previous professionals had sugarcoated the likelihood that her son would never walk. On the other hand, her husband felt very differently:

> "I thought getting a wheelchair was a great idea. My husband didn't want to hear it. The occupational therapist got some guy to bring a wheelchair to the house. When my husband came in, you could just see it on his face. He didn't know how to take a wheelchair."

A comment from a mother of a child with autism further illustrates how difficult some child-related decisions are to resolve when they are bound up with emotions, dreams, and fears about the future:

"I want my son to learn to sign. My husband says that if he learns to sign, he will not learn to speak."

Not only are there harder issues to discuss for parents of atypical children, but there is often less time to discuss them. Being busy, however, should not be an excuse to avoid handling problems with spouses. It is a compelling reason to learn to communicate and handle problems more efficiently and effectively. In fact, many incredibly busy parents of children with disabilities say that they actually began communicating with their spouse more because circumstances demanded it.

A friend once confided how her deep disappointment and anger with her husband was destroying her marriage. When I asked what her husband said about her feelings, she surprised me by saying, "We are working our way toward a conversation." Like many others, she felt that silence was preferable to the perceived dangers of communication. Silence may feel like the "lesser of two evils," but if partners are not able to talk to each other, the demise of a marriage may be less volatile but every bit as likely.

The goal of this chapter is to make talking and conflict resolution more effective and less painful. You will find numerous strategies to improve your communication and problem-solving style. My advice is to initially work on implementing one or two that seem to have the most potential for you. When you succeed in incorporating the first few ideas, add a few more. Over time, you will substantially increase your skills.

Essential Communication Skills

Many people tell me their spouses only talk when they are in a marital counseling session. This is because a climate is established in counseling that makes it safe and rewarding to talk. Many of the guidelines I have found successful in marital sessions with couples are incorporated into this chapter and will have good benefits if used at home.

[Say things in a way that can be "heard."]

This principle may be easier to understand if you think about hand-writing. The quality of your handwriting does not matter much when you are jotting down something for yourself. When you leave notes or directions for someone to follow, I imagine you take more care that they are clear and legible. You modify your writing so that it can be read. Verbal communication needs to be modified in a like manner. There are three main components to saying things in a way that will be *heard*.

1. Minimize your partner's defensiveness or desire for avoidance.
2. Be clear about your feelings and thoughts.
3. Demonstrate an understanding of your partner's viewpoints.

In this manner, you are trying not to add static that makes it harder for your message to get through. This is part of the "efficiency" I wrote about earlier. If you feel it is phony or have too little patience to modify how you talk, I would add that I am not asking you to alter your heartfelt messages. Just say things in a way that has the best chance of working. We will discuss many strategies that will help along the way and begin with a very important one: the use of empathy.

Respond Empathetically

[
Empathic responding paves the way to talk about difficult issues.
]

Empathic responding is discussed in almost all books on in-terpersonal skills and a host of training programs for professions that require "people skills." Amongst its many benefits, empathic responding has a way of diffusing resistance and negative emotions that present obstacles to communication. That is why it is a core skill in activities ranging from parenting and customer service to crisis in-tervention. Many people use this skill naturally; others need to learn to use it more consciously when interacting with an upset partner.

We will begin with an example of its use by a mother of a son with severe sensory integration problems. These problems largely precluded him from enjoying many activities that require motor skills. Instead, he mostly enjoyed playing by himself and involving himself in playing with lavish costumes.

“In the earlier days, I probably felt sorry for my husband because he couldn't have the typical 'Dad/ son things.' Our son couldn't play ball. He was always unsettled, and he was always pretending with his costumes on. It wasn't a very 'guy-ish' kind of Dad/son thing. And bless his heart: My husband is a little more pragmatic. I felt bad for him. I would look at him and say, 'I'll bet this hurts. I'll bet this hurts you because you'd rather be out there playing wiffle ball or out on the front deck (we have a basketball court out there), wouldn't you?'"

There are many ways this woman could have approached the situation. She could have said to herself (or her husband), "We both have it hard." Or, she could have simply ignored how her husband was feeling because she certainly had her own hands full. Both would have been reasonable. However, she chose to reflect on her husband's feelings and to put those reflections into words. This process, empathic responding, is powerful. In this case, it had the potential to help her spouse deal with his mourning a little bit more and it also could have helped defuse potential anger over their son's choice of activities. In addition, her empathy may have made him a little less likely to feel shut out of mother/son activities.

The steps to empathic responding follow. If you practice this skill when you are not upset, it is easier to draw upon when there is more conflict or high levels of emotion. It is not easy, yet the results are worth the challenge.

1. Listen to your partner.
2. As you listen, suspend judgment and don't think about whether you agree or disagree.
3. Don't think about what you are going to say next.
4. Paraphrase what you hear your partner saying without adding *any* commentary. You might begin with a phrase such as, "It sounds as if you are saying…. " Or, "Let me see if I fully understand what you are saying…."
5. Remember that emotions need to be captured along with the words.
6. Check whether you have understood your partner well; if not, ask what you have missed and genuinely try again.

The hardest part of empathic responding is the necessity of refraining from commentary. This is not the time to debate the validity of what your partner expresses. A principle in interpersonal relating is that you need to see the world through the other's point of view before you can even think about changing his or her perspective. So, making a good attempt to reflect in words what you think your partner is saying is a very helpful strategy.

Reflect Back What You Understand

[There is absolutely nothing to lose and so much to gain by conveying that you accurately understand what your partner is saying.]

Many people are hesitant to use empathy with their partners for fear that if they listen carefully and reflect back their accurate understanding of what their partner said, it will mean they are somehow endorsing their partner's viewpoint. Professionals who routinely work with people who are often very angry and volatile, however, know that clearly conveying an understanding of where the person is coming from is useful for deescalating the situation. Empathy helps discussions move forward rather than run in circles. Furthermore, conveying an understanding helps the other feel less alienated and better able to remain engaged in interaction.

David Burns, a well-known psychologist, researcher, and author, suggests people use the acronym EAR to remind themselves that a combination of empathy, assertiveness, and respect is a way to greatly improve communication. Empathy is a key ingredient. The second component, assertiveness, is a willingness to share your thoughts and feelings. Assertiveness is also important because if you don't take the initiative to express your thoughts, you may both end up in silence, and this sets the stage for estrangement. Assertiveness may require you to take a risk to express yourself even if you are unsure how it will be received. The third component, respect, is not always present because people have a way of subtly putting each other down. Even anger can be expressed with respect, however, if words are chosen thoughtfully. The following section should help with the issue of maintaining respectful communication even if you are quite angered.

Avoid Dangerous Comments

[Certain comments are minefields that cause useful conversations to explode.]

Often, in the name of communication, people engage in comments that almost guarantee that their valid points will get lost in the argument they set in motion. A list of some of the main verbal behaviors that cause such problems follows.

☑ *Blame*. Blame results in defensive behavior or a counterattack. "You do this…" results in, "But, you do *that*!" This certainly does not mean that you can't share a perception that is negative. It is better to describe what you see happening or what you would like. Develop the habit of statements that begin with *I* versus *You*. Compare the following statements:
> *"You make me watch the children every weekend while you take time out for yourself."*
> vs.
> *"I'm feeling as if I am doing too much of the child-care on weekends; I'd like you to pitch in more."*

Clearly, the latter has a far better chance of working. The problem is that blame often results in counter blame. Although sometimes blame is useful for alleviating self-guilt, it is not good for much else.

☑ *Labeling*. Labeling is essentially a form of name-calling: "you are crazy"; "you are irresponsible"; and "you are such a nag," for example. It is destructive to any ongoing discussion. It often leaves a residue of ill feeling and pessimism that your partner will see you for who you are or listen to your concerns. Although we often try to retract things we have said in anger, names have a way of sticking. We tend to remember them as if that is what our partner really feels about us. Words spoken in the heat of anger are sometimes more permanent than the mood that triggered them.

☑ *Global statements*. More often than not, people are less than perfectly consistent in their behaviors. Global statements such as "you always…" or "you never…" simply invite argument as the other points out exceptions to your blanket condemnation. It also makes your partner feel that you will disregard her improvement unless it is total. Total change may be unrealistic.

☑ *Being the bearer of the "truth."* Some statements are made with such a weighty self-righteousness that it's surprising that they come from a mere mortal. Rather than state things as absolute truths, it is better to say something like: *"From how I see it,* I am responsible for almost all of the childcare on weekends while you are off at the gym."

☑ *Predicting the future.* "You'll never change." For more than one reason, this type of statement often leads to a self-fulfilling prophecy. You may undermine your partner's efforts to change by making her feel that it is indeed, either impossible to change or impossible to please you.

☑ *Invalidation.* These include statements which serve to dispute what someone feels. "I can't believe you feel that!" or, "You don't really mean that!" You may disagree with how your partner feels but it needs to be accepted as real.

These minefields are momentarily gratifying. Expressing yourself without restrictions (especially if you are angry) feels powerful and is cathartic. At the same time, it most often defeats the purpose of getting through to the other person. So, when you find yourself heading into some of these behaviors, it is important to ask if what you are doing will make things better or worse. Chances are, the answer is "worse." In that case, remind yourself that the goal is to be heard, rather than simply express how you feel. When necessary, strong words are compatible with the guidelines presented above.

While writing this chapter I had two marital sessions in the very same day during which husbands volunteered that they were "scared" to talk to their wives. The wives in both instances were very committed to making the marriages work. One husband stated that when his wife is upset, he feels the best thing he can do is "stay out of her way so I don't make matters worse." The other husband spoke of a belief that whatever he said would be "wrong." I have worked with many others whose anxiety over expressing themselves is disproportionate to any realistic risks.

Sometimes a partner is indeed punitive and fear is realistic. However, many times this fear occurs within relatively supportive marriages. The foundation for self-expression is laid in childhood to a large extent. During childhood, many develop the belief that it is not safe or is futile to express oneself. This occurs when children's comments are routinely either ignored or criticized by people they are emotionally dependent upon. In addition, boys are often socialized to hide their feelings. It is possible to unlearn the childhood lesson that it is not safe to tell someone what you really feel, but it takes a supportive partner who is careful to listen respectfully to your comments no matter if they disagree with them.

[Practice nonthreatening communication every day.]

Getting into the habit of talking a little each day, while being mindful of the basics we have already covered in this chapter, goes a long way toward getting around communication obstacles. It is a desensitization process as well as one of the best ways to keep a marriage strong. This is far better than saving up issues until there is a backlog. This leads to both partners bracing themselves for a "big" talk, and the buildup often leads to undue pressure that makes communication far more difficult.

Some couples find it helpful to meet in the kitchen nightly after the kids are in bed to talk and have tea, a glass of wine, or dessert together. The setting and activity make talking less threatening. Knowing there is always tomorrow night enables you to open up a topic without necessarily having to "get it all out" in one fell swoop. In my home, my husband joins me for morning coffee before I set off to work (even when sleep is tempting) and I sit with him at the dining room table after the children have scattered. Sometimes we talk about mundane details of the day, but this routine also makes the time and space for more substantial communication as well.

I suspect that some of you feel you don't know where to begin to make conversation with your spouse because it feels awkward after not being in the habit. You can always get into the easy habit of saying, "What was your day like?" Then again, I have worked with some couples who found talking so anxiety-provoking that more creative solutions were necessary. Some have found that taking a walk together is the best time to casually talk because the exercise has a way of quelling anxiety.

If your household is very active, it is still possible to creatively find time to talk. For example, one couple advised talking during a drive, assuming the kids generally fall asleep on car rides.

I believe in finding a "good time" to talk about sensitive issues, but this is often taken too far. There are no perfect times and couples often play a game of saying "this isn't a good time to talk." It is not unusual for me to meet with a couple who has not been able to find a "good time to talk" for weeks and even months. It is more practical to avoid the worst times to talk rather than search for ones that are just right.

More often than not, it is the wife who feels the need to initiate "a talk." Over the years, I have heard so many women express their resentment that their husbands didn't take this step. This is one of those problems that does not necessarily need to be resolved in order for a marriage to be satisfying. Yes, it would be nicer if you both took on this role, but it is not likely to change and does not jeopardize a marriage. The important point is that it does not matter who initiates communication as long as it occurs. John Gottman, a marital researcher, notes that about 80 percent of the time women have the role of raising sticky issues while men try to avoid them; he adds this holds true in happy marriages as well.

[Make it easier for your partner to talk.]

"**S**ometimes I can't communicate to my wife. But she is understanding, and she helps me get it out. She will say, 'This is how I see it. Maybe this is what's going on.'"

This is one of many ways that partners can help rather than criticize or become totally resigned to partners who don't communicate well. Actually, it is fairly routine for me to hear women describe their husbands as looking like deer caught in the headlights when they tried to speak with them. Typically, they attribute their spouse's lack of response as indicative of not caring about them. Gottman describes this deer-caught-in-the-headlights look in more professional terms, "flooding" and "stonewalling." They are useful concepts to understand in order to get around roadblocks to talking with your partner. Both are responses to anxiety over communicating.

Stonewalling is a sustained "tuning out." Flooding is also anxiety-based and occurs when the listener is so overwhelmed with the prospect of her partner's harsh comments that her efforts are all directed at avoidance and emotional detachment. This is one of the reasons Gottman recommends "soft startups" when discussing topics that are likely to arouse strong emotion. He views the easing into a discussion as a way to combat physiological arousal that prevents the anxious partner from being able to remain engaged. This is different from the proverbial walking on eggshells that may be necessary when someone is volatile. Walking on eggshells avoids discussion, whereas soft startups can be thought of as warming up a car engine before embarking on a drive.

"Pursuers" vs. "Distancers"

Another reason to work on easing communication for your partner is that this helps avoid the trap of assuming the classic roles of "pursuer" and "distancer" within a marriage. The pursuer repeatedly initiates discussions with her distancer partner. Research has shown that this pattern is common amongst couples who eventually divorced. The pursuer starts out wanting to address perceived problems, and the distancer often wants to avoid discomfort or a potential fight. Unfortunately, both generally end up getting the exact opposite of what they desire. The pursuer's frustrations often build to the point that she says things she regrets and this makes future discussions less likely. And the distancer almost guarantees the conflict he wanted to avoid by frustrating the pursuer.

If you are the pursuer, this is one of those situations where the most control you have is in changing your behavior—in other words, your part of the marital dance. It is a basic principle that people engage in behaviors that are rewarding and avoid situations that are aversive. All the strategies identified so far are effective at helping distancers find it easier to communicate.

Several book participants underscored the importance of communication and shared how they work with their partners to help them talk. The following quote demonstrates many good characteristics. You will notice that this woman takes the lead in opening up discussion even though her husband is reluctant to talk. She uses empathy to reflect on her husband's recent dissatisfaction with her and is careful to avoid finger pointing:

"You need to communicate and not just let the door shut, stay shut, and let the animosity towards each other grow. You need to nip it as quickly as you can when you see that things are not right. My personal way (and I am the communicator) is to say, 'We need to talk about this.' And I sometimes force it until it happens, whether he is ready to talk about it or not. And sometimes I say, 'I notice that you are not happy with me. I can tell that you are unhappy.' I don't threaten him with 'You've made me feel this way, or you've done this....' I express to him what I'm seeing, and I try again to communicate to him what I see and how I feel he is reacting to me. Then we can start an honest dialog without blaming someone."

This woman offered some excellent advice on what to do with a withdrawn spouse:

"What I have found helps with a withdrawn spouse is to always speak the truth from my heart and to never threaten or to make him feel that he has done something to make this whole thing a mess. It is always both of us--we each have a part in why we are arguing about our son or mad at each other."

A husband and wife had these thoughts on easing communication in their marriage:

Wife:

"First of all, we have a desire to communicate and to not lose track of one another. I think I am very creative. So, periodically I come up with different tools that facilitate conversation. For example, I will buy a supermarket book about men and women and read a passage, and we will talk about it. I will read a page and say, 'What do you think about that?'"

Husband:

"If you don't do something like that then you are just talking about the same thing over and over again. That will dull a relationship very quickly."

Intimate Communication

Quantity of communication is not quality. Most experts in the field describe women as more easily able to communicate in a relationship. Some have cited physiological explanations such as that the *corpus callosum* that connects the right and left hemisphere is larger in females. It has been suggested that this enables women to have more access to the emotional nature of the right hemisphere alongside of the verbal abilities that tend to generalize to the left hemisphere. However, if you think about the true nature of intimate communication, talk alone does not breed intimacy. My favorite definition of intimate communication is found in Lillian Rubin's *Intimate Strangers*. She writes that intimate communication is "…the wish to know another's inner life along with the ability to share one's own."

As a marital therapist, I have seen many wives who speak very freely in sessions and appear to have fewer barriers to verbal intimacy. However, on closer look, many are indeed more verbal but are equally guarded against intimacy with their partners. If you tend to be verbal and impatient with a less verbal partner, consider whether your comments move you further toward intimacy or not.

Returning to the definition of intimacy, it is evident that the definition does not say that all communication must be verbal. Nonverbal intimate communication is not to be overlooked or devalued. A good sexual relationship provides one invaluable form of intimate communication. Within many couple relationships there are individuals who are more comfortable with one mode of intimacy rather than the other. Ultimately, helping each other to be comfortable with verbal *and* nonverbal intimacy nourishes the marriage because discomfort is often at the base of avoidance of either mode of expression.

[If you want your partner to communicate, make sure you don't jump on his or her comments and squelch them.]

A final thought about increasing communication: try to make communication rewarding. I have seen many people who really want their partners to express themselves, but inadvertently "punish" their partner for her comments. It is important to reinforce communication even if you are not happy with what you are hearing because the alternative is worse.

Conflict Resolution and Problem Solving

It is not the presence of problems and disagreements that weakens a marriage; it is how they are handled. Marriage, life, and problems are inextricable. Gottman speaks of "perpetual problems" in the majority of marriages. He defines perpetual problems as due to fundamental differences in personality or needs that are fairly integral to you. He differentiates these from "solvable problems." He adds that perpetual problems don't necessarily need to be solved and that the majority of conflicts fall into this category. Gottman has written that in his long-term follow-up of marital couples, he found that they argued about the same issues year after year. I think this finding is important because it clarifies that not all problems need to be solved for you and your spouse to live together well. In my own life, I have identified several perpetual problems that don't threaten the basis of my marriage and are pointless to argue about further. The image of a couple's futile arguing about the same issue for the lifetime of a marriage has worked as a good motivator. Why bother? However, I absolutely believe in solving conflicts and problems that need to be addressed.

One of the most basic yet important skills in conflict resolution is the ability to articulate your needs in ways that maximize the likelihood that they will be understood and responded to.

[Make sure you are asking for what you want rather than complaining or criticizing.]

Requests for what we really want are often expressed through criticism. ("You never want to spend time with me.") Or sometimes desires are expressed so vaguely that they are hard for our partner to discern. ("I just don't feel close to you anymore.") The likelihood that a spouse will know what to do about this is quite low. One woman shared several examples of how she used to try to get her husband to help her.

- "Can't you see I'm so damn tired that I don't want to make dinner tonight?!"
- "Why can't you see that I don't want to stand here another five minutes?!"
- "Why can't you pick up your own damn cereal?!"
- "Would it ever occur to you to do the laundry?!"

She described how she changed this pattern (with her husband's input)."He would call me on it. He'd say, 'If you want something, tell me what you want. I am not here to feel guilty or to feel angry. If you are feeling frustrated, tell me what's going on.' He helped me grow up."

Notice the husband's manner of stating his criticism. He spelled out, in noninflammatory ways, the change he would like to see his wife make. In this manner they both got more of their needs met.

Some additional useful strategies to consider:

- Don't overwhelm your partner with too many requests at a time at once. One at a time is more effective even if there are many that you feel very strongly about.
- Don't make your partner try to read your mind. You may believe he or she should know what you want by now, but if this were the case there would have already been evidence of such clairvoyance.
- Don't assume that just because you made the requests months ago, it does not bear repeating (and repeating).
- Remember that a demanding tone tends to breed opposition to even very reasonable requests.
- Develop the habit of catching yourself when you are complaining. Then identify whether there is a request you could make that would be more constructive.
- Don't fall into the trap of thinking that if you have to ask for what you want, it doesn't count when you get it.

Strategies for Conflict Resolution

Compromise

The first technique is so simple that I am often embarrassed when I need to suggest it to couples. It is simply the art of the compromise—something we all learn in childhood. Couples tend to over-look it, and I have routinely found that couples can achieve a compro-mise solution even on emotionally charged topics in a relatively short period of time. For example, I recently had a couple find a resolution in about thirty minutes to a conflict over accusations of "enabling" versus being too hard on an adult child living at home. My job was simple; it consisted of asking a few questions, keeping them focused on hammering out a compromise, and keeping the discussion from getting off track or too heated.

Two simple questions form the basis of discussion aimed at reaching a compromise:

1. What does each person want?
2. Where is the middle ground?

Parents think of compromise as basic skills when raising chil-dren to get along with each other. We tend to underutilize it our-selves, although it is probably the backbone of conflict resolution. Simply saying, "Let's find a compromise that will work for both of us," begins the process. It begins the process of instilling some good-will into the argument. If you can't reach a middle ground, a com-promise can also take the form of a reciprocal give-and-take on more than one issue.

Both partners need to be willing to give on some issues even if they don't agree. A good example has to do with the need for servic-es. It is not unusual for the husband to feel that his wife is acquiring excessive services for their child (often because he sees the child's problems as relatively less severe). I have heard from several con-tented spouses who spoke of how their partner went along with their pursuit of services despite disagreeing over the necessity.

Some of the most tedious marriages I have seen are those in which every issue is debated at length because neither spouse will agree to do anything they don't personally think is best. In contrast, consider this subtle and beautiful example of a meaningful compromise:

"When our daughter was first born, the doctors gave her very little chance of living. My husband and I handle stress differently. He goes into shock and can't remember what is going on. He just shuts down. I start going into action immediately. I was very clear to everyone who spoke to me, 'This kid was going to live.' And my husband was shut down. He was not going to name her in the synagogue (with a Hebrew name), because if she died, he did not want to have a name attached to her. I had already picked out a name for her when she was in utero, though, and I was already talking to her with her given name. I told my husband that it was important to me that she be named in the synagogue. We talked to the rabbi and arranged it so that the baby naming was incorporated into the Torah reading quietly. So unless you were standing right there on the bimah, you did not know that a baby naming was occurring."

"He did this response for my need. This is one of the hallmarks of our relationship. An awful lot of what we do in our marriage (and we have been married thirty years) is out of respect or concern for the other person's sensitivities. We don't always agree with each other. Certainly we have our arguments but in the end, when decisions are made, it's to accommodate each other."

Be Flexible

Try something 180 degrees different from your typical problem-solving style.

The concept of trying something different underlies some of the more effective techniques for problem resolution. Michele Weiner-Davis, an author of books on restoring troubled marriages, urges people to try anything but more of the same old approaches that have not worked in the past. This includes being brave enough to do something that is 180 degrees different from what you typically do and then observe the results. Weiner-Davis illustrates it with a vignette that is particularly relevant to this book. She describes a couple fighting because the wife feels her spouse is overly critical of her daughter (his new step-daughter). Their typical positions in this conflict were for the wife to defend her daughter against what she considered her husband's unrealistically high expectations. The more she did this, the more he criticized her daughter and the more the wife soothed her daughter's feelings. When a therapist urged trying something 180 degrees different, she began to support her husband when he verbalized his criticism of her daughter; this, in turn, diminished his criticism.

Is there a guarantee that doing the opposite of what you usually do will work? No, but if your approach has not been successful after a great deal of use, there is almost a guarantee that it will not all of a sudden become effective. Many of you have undoubtedly been using the same approach for five, ten, or more years without a positive result. Doing something different can be as simple as touching your partner during an argument rather than becoming more distant.

In keeping with this spirit of flexibility, letting go of "being right" is also the foundation of other productive approaches. People implement this principle in different ways. You could:

☑ Stipulate that there is always truth in the other person's position and be intent on finding it ultimately.

☑ Remind yourself that the best solutions will be a product of combining your mutual points of view.

☑ Let go of the need to "win" the argument.

☑ Remind yourself that even if you are the one who may have more knowledge about your child's disorder, you still will not always have the best ideas.

This last strategy is one that I am fond of. As a psychologist and professor of rehabilitation and counseling, I am used to coming up with suggestions for others and am professionally and personally very immersed in being informed. I must admit that my husband, a salesman in the building trades, has sometimes come up with some of the better ways to resolve problems related to our son. Whereas I used to think I knew best, it has been a relief to relinquish this need to always be right. Dr. Phil McGraw has called being right the "booby prize" in arguments and asks, "Would you rather be right or solve the problem?"

Another approach that I use is one that I regard as "planting the seed." When I am patient, this often works. In essence, you speak of your viewpoint without being so assertive that you polarize your partner's position. A good example is provided by a father of a young boy with cerebral palsy:

"**M**y wife was petrified about inclusion. She rarely acknowledges this (we have been married for 28 million years) and one of the things that I realized was that if I plant a seed in her mind now, in two months she will come up with this brilliant idea and say, 'I thought of this.' I used to get very annoyed about this but it is how it works. So I was going to all these workshops about inclusion, coming home and talking about it, and she was saying, 'No, no, no.' And then one day she said, 'You know, I have an idea.' So, we sort of arrive at it differently."

Last but not least is the principle of "agreeing to disagree." This can't always be done due to the nature of some conflicts. However, sometimes a decision does not need to be made at a specific point in time. A good example of this strategy:

"**Y**ears ago my husband and I set a rule in our marriage that we would never go to bed angry at each other. For the most part, we have been able to follow that rule and when we did go to bed angry, we usually worked it out the next day. This has helped when we agree to disagree about issues with our children, special needs and not."

Keep Arguments from Escalating

Many arguments and fights are preventable. Couples have different thresholds for how much fighting they can tolerate. Some are best described as "conflict avoidant," a style that trades off discussion of problem areas and conflicting opinions in order to avoid open discord. This style often stems from earlier life experiences which left the belief that conflict is dangerous.

It generally is safer for the health of a relationship to be able to tolerate an argument as long as you have the proper skills to keep it from escalating.

There are couples who cannot be called conflict avoidant but simply decide that arguments are not worth it.

"We have decided not to argue—we both feel that too much time and energy is wasted on arguing. We have so little extra time and energy. Why waste it like that?"

Sometimes one or both partners pick fights as a way to vent other frustrations:

"Our son's oppositional and acting-out behavior can, at times, play havoc with this marriage. We work hard for this not to happen but are not always successful. I work very hard to stay calm and not return my son's sometimes tireless provocation. Often I am very pleased with my self-control only to find that, moments later, I start an argument with my husband. At first glance, it looks rational. But in my heart of hearts, I know it is just because I feel about to burst because of controlling my anxiety and frustration with my son."

One way to diminish arguments is to screen out those that are not over genuinely important matters. You can learn to stop many of these and ask yourself what you really are angry about. Is this a genuine problem that needs to be resolved? Will you even remember this problem in six months? If it is a genuine problem, are there alternatives to an argument?

Some matters that couples argue over have very little to do with the substance of the conflict. I will use generic As and Bs to describe this dynamic. If one person argues for position A, then the other makes a case for position B. If the first person changes and wants B, her partner would invariably not be happy until he got A. This type of behavior occurs when the underlying problem has to do with unresolved struggles in their relationship. The underlying issues vary but can generally be summed up under power struggles. Sometimes they are related to the marital structure, such as the perception that a partner has too much power in the marriage. Sometimes they stem from unresolved issues earlier in life with such as having grown up with an overbearing parent or a bad and lingering case of sibling rivalry that results in competing rather than cooperating with one's spouse. Being honest with yourself, if these are some of your motivating factors, can enable you to refrain from engaging in these types of arguments.

Fight Fairly

Arguments can be constructive rather than destructive if a few rules are followed to provide structure that makes communication safer and more productive. With regard to productivity, remember that the goal of the argument needs to be arrival at a mutual agreeable solution that is likely to involve compromise and flexibility from both of you. Several important guidelines follow:

☑ Make a rule for absolutely no name-calling and no character assassinations. As one woman said, "Words are never retracted."

☑ Agree to stay focused on the topic at hand rather than piling topic upon topic ("Well, what about...?"). The argument can be redirected by saying something like, "I would be glad to set a time to talk about that later; let's resolve this issue first."

☑ Don't dredge up the past. Some people bring up the full history of grievances that they have filed away over the years. Others do this to try to establish a pattern of behavior. Six months is an admittedly arbitrary but reasonable cut-off point in terms of defining what is the "past."

☑ If tempers are flaring, agree to call a "time-out" to cool down. As part of this, it is important to set a specific time to continue the discussion. As a rule of thumb, it should not exceed twenty-four hours.

Handle Your Anger

Anger is useful as a signal that a situation needs to be changed. What you do with your anger is another matter. The manner in which women, in specific, have been taught to handle their anger has changed dramatically over the years. We went from an era where women were cautioned to repress their anger to an era where we were exhorted to express it. In fact, both men and women were taught that it was important to "get out" our anger.

In retrospect, psychological research has found that the more one expresses anger (after a point) the angrier one feels. Neither extreme is helpful. Certainly anger should be used as a "red flag," a warning that something is wrong and needs to change. However, free expression of anger tends to simply breed more anger.

The most powerful strategy for controlling your anger is understanding that it is your responsibility to control prolonged or frequent outbursts. People need to identify strategies to cool down. Mine include removing myself from the scene of the argument, jumping on a treadmill or taking a walk, putting a cool washcloth on my face, or checking the flowers in the backyard. There are numerous ways to distract yourself from anger so that you can return to the issue later in a more productive way. Anger is often fueled by stress and the repetition of thoughts that fuel the anger ("I can't believe she said that to me!"). Dwelling on an "injustice," though, is like pouring fuel on a fire.

We have included in the Resources one of the best books on handling anger: *When Anger Hurts Your Relationship,* by Kim Paleg and Matthew McKay.

Make Repair Gestures

John Gottman writes a great deal about repair gestures and their importance within a marriage. He describes them as essentially a "turning towards each other" after conflict in a conciliatory way. A willingness to make and accept repair gestures has a large bearing on the health of a marriage. Once again, an excellent illustration is provided by a parent we interviewed for this book:

> "If we are nit picking on one another, I need to give him the benefit of the doubt. I say, 'I know this person loves me and is maybe just having a bad day.' Then it is not so much about what he is doing. I always know he is trying and that he loves me. These basic things are the foundation...the rest are details."

Other good advice from parents includes:

☑ "Pick your battles. This is a very big thing. Decide what is most important and focus. Be understanding of your spouse's feelings."

☑ "Try to talk no matter how mad you are. Say you're sorry for all the stupid stuff."

☑ "Your spouse feels every emotion you do about all your children. Even if you are not a good communicator, be open at least to listening actively to your spouse process the problems and feelings they are having. Just like we have to meet our children where they are to go forward, we have to meet our spouse where they are to experience the journey together. Both parties need to be active participants in the journey, though."

Chapter Five

Romance and Sexual Intimacy

Laura E. Marshak, Ph.D.

It would be hard to find a more beautiful illustration of romantic and intimate bonding than in the following comments shared by a woman who has been married for twenty-two years. She is the mother of five children, including one with Down syndrome and one with autism:

> "**M**y husband and I have a Friday night date night. Cooking is my passion, so I cook us a gourmet meal every Friday. Oftentimes, we each have a child on our lap, but we still sit together with lighted candles and a glass of wine."

This couple's style epitomizes an approach that prioritizes the marriage, understands the importance of romantic intimacy, and is creative regarding how to work around ever-present complications. Unfortunately, this couple's ability to keep the romance alive in their marriage seems to be relatively rare among parents of children with disabilities. Romance and sexual intimacy were common casualties in the marriages described by participants in the book. More common were rueful comments such as:

>   "I continue to wonder why we have lost this intimacy. I sometimes think that the lifestyle that accommodates disability requires so much attention, persistence, and giving that there is little left to share with my husband. Most of the time I desire a peaceful night of sleep rather than sexual intimacy or even romance. What a shame."

The absence of a romantic and sexual life is not a problem exclusive to parents of children with disabilities, but raising children with disabilities poses relatively more obstacles to romance and physical intimacy. Often a child may be up throughout the night or require periodic attention. Medically fragile children may require vigilance both day and night, with parents never really feeling "off duty." Lack of time for yourself adds to the mix that may already include other problems described in earlier chapters. One or both partners may feel that spending time alone or asleep is far more precious than engaging in sexual intimacy at these times. Some parents of children with disabilities, feeling the need to prioritize where they put their energies, end up practically eliminating romantic and sexual aspects of their marriage. This is rarely done intentionally and some don't fully consider all the consequences of this loss.

Without romance and sexual intimacy in a marriage, the partnership may more resemble "best friends" or "parent-partners." Certainly friendship and genuine partnership are more important than romance and intimacy, but one should not preclude the other.

There are times when we truly can't worry about romance and physical intimacy, but ongoing disregard is very different. A near complete absence of romantic and sexual intimacy generally exacts at least a small price in the relationship. Depending on the individuals involved, the cost to the marriage may be far greater. For most people, romance and sexual intimacy cannot be replaced entirely by other strengths in the marriage.

Why Bother?

Romance

The benefits of at least a little marital romance can be subtle but, nonetheless, meaningful. Romance can give us a "breather" and a way to step out of our day-to-day roles. Romantic gestures from our partners are important because they communicate that we are not invisible; they signify that our partner views us as attractive for qualities other than our abilities to care for children, bring home a paycheck, or clean the house. Romance also signifies that our partner thinks we are worthy of having some attention devoted solely to us. This also lends the spark to the relationship that is sometimes a prerequisite for physical intimacy.

Sexual Intimacy: It's Not Just about Sex

It is not accidental that people have the capacity to form sexually intimate bonds that extend far beyond their procreative years. The benefits of sexual bonding have been written about from various perspectives including religious, physiological, and psychological. In some religions, sexual bonding in marriage is viewed as imparting holiness into a union through a merging of souls. Researchers into physiological processes have discovered that sex leads to endorphin release, enhancing bonding as well as relieving stress. Marital researchers and therapists have written at length about the ways that sexual and marital satisfaction are intertwined for many. In addition, only within a sexually intimate relationship can we experience some aspects of touch that have mostly been lost since infancy (aspects of kissing, touching, and holding). The power of touch in a relationship is not replaceable.

As a marital therapist, I want readers to consider a few additional reasons to maintain sexual intimacy. Perhaps most importantly, even if sexual intimacy is not particularly important to you, it is likely to be more important to your partner. One father we interviewed commented that many parents he meets in support groups have given up their romantic relationships with each other and pour all their time, energy, and resources into their child. He sees this as a mistake and views the sexually intimate bond as essential especially when faced with children who will most likely continue to face serious problems throughout life. He commented:

> "Everyday we need to be in touch. We need to say, 'I love you.' You need it particularly when you are going through a crisis. Some people get along without intimacy for a year or two years or three years, but there comes a point that you can't do without it. And you either look for it somewhere else or you just can't exist and you crumble...and you still can't fix your child."

There are many good reasons to think about your romantic and sexual bond with your partner in spite of daily stress and perhaps loss of interest yourself. Additional reasons to *bother* about romance and sexual intimacy, despite a stressful, busy life include:

☑ Compromising about the frequency or nature of sexual intimacy is absolutely reasonable. Asking a partner to sacrifice this aspect of living almost entirely is not reasonable.

☑ Many partners find that sexual intimacy paves the way for more good will in the marriage and find it is beneficial even if they personally are not aware of their own sexual desires.

☑ Sexual intimacy is not only about sex. It is a means of connection between two people that is unique from all others and often very symbolic.

☑ Lack of sexual interest by one's partner is often experienced as a personal rejection.

Parents who participated in this book offered personal thoughts about the meaning and unique value of sexual intimacy within their marriages and how it goes far beyond sex itself:

> "I think one day you realize, 'Someday I am going to be old and feeble. If he isn't touching me now, is he going to care for me physically when I am old and falling apart?' I know my husband will be there caring and nurturing me. It is extremely important, that comfort."

"It is a way for us to connect in a way we can do with no other. It is an unspoken language to each other that says, 'I'm always here for you.'"

"When we come together for sex I know it is his way of saying, 'I still want you and I still love you.' Even if he doesn't say those words, I still hear it when he is touching me. I call it 'soul talking.'"

Here is how one mother underscored the value she places on her romantic and sexual relationship with her husband, especially during times when their child's behavior has the potential to be divisive:

"Our child's psychiatric disorder results in very hostile acting-out behavior that can go on for hours. Sometimes my husband and I fight with each other out of sheer frustration and because of our son's attempts at divisiveness. Sometimes, I think proactively and decide to solidify my bond with my husband. Romance and making love strengthens our bond to weather the next day with good feelings for each other. It reminds me of the game Red Rover, Red Rover in which you hold hands knowing someone is going to come crashing in to divide you."

[Some partners, especially men, find that they are better able to express tender feelings within sexual intimacy than they can at other times.]

For some men who may have relatively more difficulty with words and vulnerability, sexual connection provides a vehicle for emotional expression and closeness. This is often misunderstood by the partners of quiet men, who may resent bids for sexual intimacy if they are not preceded by verbal intimacy. However, one could argue that both are equally valid forms of connection and communication. Of course, a relationship that includes a good balance of both verbal and nonverbal communication is much better.

Protecting Romance and Physical Intimacy

Protecting your romantic and sexual life requires handling potential problems stemming from too little time and too much guilt.

Too Much Guilt

The type of guilt that poses a common threat to the romantic life of parents of children with disabilities stems from two main sources. First, as discussed previously, it can result from the belief that *all* your energies should be devoted to the wellbeing of your children. Second, guilt often is related to what is known as "survivor guilt." The essence of survivor guilt is clear in this mother's comment: "Romance and passion are pretty nonexistent. I feel guilty when I enjoy myself."

Survivor guilt, as discussed in more detail in Chapter 3, involves a struggle to embrace life when we are acutely aware of someone else's loss. The fallacy in this emotional reasoning is that by our not living fully, we can help the other. In the case of parenting, survivor guilt weakens us.

Some parents find that if they decide to take more time out for the two of them, other parents of children with disabilities disapprove of their plans. Given that many parents feel isolated to some extent, disapproval from the network of other parents of children with disabilities may be especially problematic because they often represent a very valuable source of connection and support. A mother of two children with multiple disabilities commented: "Many of those parents make us feel guilty because we have a life. Because we are opposite of most people."

A mother with a son with an autism spectrum disorder described the importance of romance in marriage as well as the disapproval she felt from others:

"What was really a big help to us was that I earned a trip to go on a cruise. My husband and I had not been on a trip for eight years. Actually, we never even went to movies because we couldn't afford it and because of the kids. But when I won this trip to go on a seven-day cruise

I said, 'I'm out of here.' (Of course, I made arrangements with my mother to care for the children, prepared food, and left money and a car.) There were so many criticisms even from people within our autism society. One family that had two children with autism could not understand how I could take off and do this. I said, 'My husband and I need our second honeymoon and we need a break.' It was a way to finally let our hair down and I didn't have to worry about autism or anything. We needed that."

Too Little Time

> Many parents of children with disabilities see "date nights" as the best way to protect romance from competing time demands.

As described previously, we had the input of a few hundred parents of children with disabilities while writing this book. When asked what they do to protect romance and passion in their marriages, they most commonly cited establishing a "date night." Intimacy requires feeling like "a couple," whether planning a shopping trip and movie every two or three weeks or having dinner out once in a while without conversations related to the children.

"We try very hard to get out once every two to three weeks by ourselves to go to a movie, dinner, etc. It helps us to be a 'couple' again and not just 'Mama and Dada.' It's very important to remember we were once 'us.' Not that we would ever trade being parents!!"

"At least twice a month we go out...dinner-shopping-movie and try not to talk about our child."

Potentially successful strategies sometimes look impractical. In this case, you may be thinking that this sounds like a good idea *but* it won't work because you won't be able to find the requisite energy or a babysitter. I strongly suggest that you try, anyway. I have heard many initial objections from people who subsequently reaped the benefits. If you are one of the few with extraordinary circumstances and absolutely cannot obtain babysitting or respite care, the alternative is dating at home:

"We tell each other when we need time together. Before my husband leaves for work I'll tell him that we are having dinner together after the kids are in bed. He then knows we need a night of romance."

Some couples report absolutely no time or energy to devote exclusively to each other, despite creative efforts. For instance, one declared:

"We are often too exhausted to care. We co-parent, we just happen to be married."

If a *total* lack of couples' time persists for more than several months (and your child is not in medical crisis), consider the following:

☑ This is a red flag to dispense with some other activities that may appear indispensable.

☑ You may be mistakenly placing all of your children's needs above your partner's. Some families have benefited from fewer child-related activities in order to find breathing room for the parents themselves. In the long run, it benefits the children, but even if it didn't, it would be entirely justifiable.

☑ Is the problem really one of avoiding intimacy? Where there is a will, there is a way to find some time—except during intermittent crises.

One father we interviewed spoke with regret about not having taken the steps to protect his sexual relationship with his wife. He also said:

"I was angry in the beginning when it was happening but became less and less angry and now it's gone. If you are in a similar situation, I would say you should work very hard at it. I think if you parallel it with regular parenting, when the kid is born you need to make sure that you still have a date. You need to make sure that you have a babysitter just to go for dinner, coffee, or a movie."

Making the Transition to Sexual Intimacy

For many reasons, women often have relatively more difficulty than men making the transition back to sexual intimacy. In contrast to men, stress greatly decreases libido in women. Many men view sex as a way to relieve stress, while women often feel sex will only be one more thing to contend with.

Women often describe hectic days during which they feel as if much of the work and childcare is on their shoulders. When evening comes and their partners all of a sudden become romantic, they are often not in the mood. The bridge to sexual intimacy is not in place. This bridge is made up of both personal and relationship elements. It is not reasonable to expect sexual intimacy to develop well without a foundation characterized by goodwill and basic trust. Although this is the foundation of a sexual relationship, it is not sufficient. Many women regard sexual foreplay as beginning outside of the bedroom earlier in the day. On a *daily* basis, there are three factors that contribute to this foreplay:

1. a little time and attention,
2. affection,
3. (non-sexual) touch.

Many parents who participated in this book incorporate these elements into their daily lives, despite experiencing major stress. Their examples and advice follow:

"Our intimate life suffered more out of exhaustion than anything else. We were so exhausted from the hospitalization and the emotional pain. Even if you can't get to the point where you have the strength, energy, and inclination to have sex, I think part of the daily routine has to incorporate affection."

"We make time for each other on a daily basis, even if it is just twenty minutes over a cup of coffee, talking about the day."

"We call each other during the day when we are at work. We do the things for each other that say, 'I love you' and 'I care about you.'"

"We touch each other when passing."

As a marital therapist I have heard all too many women complain that their husbands only touch them when they want sexual intimacy. Simply kissing good morning and goodbye can go a long way in the relationship if this is not already part of your daily life. Daily touch is very helpful in making sexual intimacy a natural part of a marital relationship and is part of simply staying connected in other ways.

Getting in the Mood

It is so easy to think that your partner should get you in the mood that it is easy to overlook your role, responsibility, and control in kindling your own sexual desire.

[Expect your sexual desire to need to be nurtured by you.]

☑ Make an effort to remember you are both a parent *and* a sexual being. Men and women sometimes have problems integrating these two roles, partly because they may not have regarded their parents as sexual.
☑ If you are a woman with a sex drive that barely whispers, listen to it carefully.
☑ Increase activities that make you feel more sensual.
☑ Exercise; libido is positively affected by blood flow and general fitness.

[If you feel a lack of desire, it is important to explore the underlying factors and be proactive about rectifying them.]

Identify what you need and work toward getting it. Maybe you need at least a little time alone before you can even think about physical sharing with your partner. Perhaps you need more non-sexual couple's time together. Remember, you need to ask for what you need in a clear, positive manner that can be heard.

Loss of sexual interest can be related to depression as well as to the use of several types of antidepressants. Some antidepressants result in relatively fewer side effects that cause sexual dysfunction, so physicians can often diminish or rectify this problem. Sometimes sexual desires are suppressed due to fear of a pregnancy; this occurs with greater frequency when a couple has given birth to a child with congenital disabilities in the past. Other medications, hormonal changes, and medical problems such as thyroid dysfunction all have the potential to inhibit sexual desire. For these reasons, a physical exam and discussion with a physician are essential to rule out these problems. This relatively broad array of obstacles can usually be re-solved if you communicate about the fact that a problem exists and seek appropriate help.

[Establish an evening routine that helps you stop thinking about daily stresses and ongoing problems.]

Establish a habit of doing something relaxing after the children are in bed. There are many options, even if time is at a premium. For example, relaxation and transition could be eased by watching a favorite show side by side with your partner, a glass of wine, a warm bath, or "slipping into something more comfortable."

[If your partner needs help getting in the mood, don't overlook his or her suggestions.]

I have heard so many wives say, "If only my husband would arrange a sitter for a night out, I'd be more receptive." If you have heard this from your partner, simply act on it. People often know very well what will work for them. It is a common mistake to dismiss these suggestions by rationalizing that they won't make a big enough difference.

[Avoid the most common, predictable power struggle over sex.]

There is a common power struggle over sex that commonly occurs with couples. In brief, women often say that they would be interested in making love *if* they received the emotional support and closeness they desire from their spouses; meanwhile, husbands often assert that it would be easier to be supportive and close if sexual intimacy was not such a struggle in the relationship. As women get more upset over lack of emotional support, they often become more physically distant from their spouses, with the result that their partners often get more irritable and distant. Both express valid viewpoints and are acting in natural, understandable ways; unfortunately, it does not resolve the dilemma. It is resolvable if a couple avoids rigid "you go first" stances.

Does this mean that you should consent to lovemaking no matter how you feel? Absolutely not. But it does mean that sometimes it is useful to be generous about making love when you are not *entirely* in the mood. After all, we do many things in a marriage for the other person. Sometimes making love fits in with this framework when you are not actively opposed but not feeling all so amorous yourself. It is an investment in good will and part of the give and take that characterizes many a happy marriage. The art of the compromise is relevant here because there is truth in both viewpoints regarding sexual intimacy and marriage.

"If I waited for a time when my husband did not do anything that I could consider insensitive, we would never make love again. I try to find a balance where I honor my feelings while realizing that sexual intimacy is generally followed by increased closeness and harmony. I try to be somewhat practical about it because it does soothe the rough edges sometimes."

"I truly believe that people who start obsessing and controlling and do this power stuff around sex drain themselves of energy that they could be putting toward something else. I don't have a notebook where we keep score with stroke marks. There is none of that."

[Don't wait for the perfect time to make love.]

Sexual desire can become dormant if you have not made love in a long time. It may be better to go ahead for your own sake than wait for the "perfect time." You will most likely find that this kind of "jump-starts" your desire in general. A change of feelings may then very well follow a change in action. Couples vary greatly in terms of the frequency of lovemaking. However, experts suggest that a couple that makes love less than ten times a year is considered barely sexual.

Finding Opportunities

There is an art to finding both the privacy and time to make love when there are children in the home, especially when they have disabilities or medical needs. The art actually mostly involves developing an attitude that is flexible and welcomes opportunities as they arise even if they are not ideal. Following are a few good examples of how others have solved this type of problem:

"We try to make the most out of the time we have when the kids go to bed. Yes, it may mean staying up late and being tired the next day, but it's worth it."

"We spend afternoons together when the kids are in school, stay up after the kids go to bed, and have conversations about ourselves or things that bother us."

"**T**ypical times to make love are often just not available to us due to our children's sleeping problems. However, we developed the attitude to take opportunities when they present themselves, like when the kids are out. It may not be ideal, but it can also be romantic if you let it be—kind of like being teenagers again."

Your privacy may also be restricted if there are healthcare providers in your home:

Wife:

"**W**hat we don't have in the house is the intimacy of a normal marriage. Because we have a million people here. And so we can't make out in the kitchen. We can but we would feel foolish."

Husband:

"**W**e have a nurse on the other side of our wall twenty-four hours a day in two shifts. You even learn to make love differently."

Some privacy concerns can be rectified with fairly easily. For example, some couples use the hum of an air conditioner. Sound masking ("white noise") machines can also be bought quite inexpensively.

Sleeping Arrangements

For parents of children with disabilities, a fairly common obstacle to intimacy is thinking that one or the other of you need to sleep in the same room with your child.

"**W**hat romance? I have to sleep with my child, as she is afraid at night and will look for me if she awakens and I am not there."

"**O**ur son still sleeps in our bed because our room is downstairs and his room is upstairs. If he gets uncomfortable, he can't do a thing about it. So, he would cry and cry and it was up and down and up and down, and so we finally just brought him back to bed. This means that the majority of nights I either sleep on the couch or upstairs. Obviously, that has put a big rift in the marriage and changed its whole focus. We are sort of trying to work back into sleeping together, but it is difficult. The silly thing about it being difficult is that our son is on my side of the bed. Is that a major issue? No, but it's an issue. We have grown physically further apart. Much further. There has been no intimacy for years. I think we have grown apart because of it."

An occasional night with a child is one thing, but setting the precedent is another. I would caution you against sleeping with your child out of convenience (for example, to be there to attend to needs throughout the night). With a medically involved child there may be no end to this in sight, and, as described so well above by the last parent, it may indeed have a compelling effect on the nature of your relationship. Instead, consider making yourself available to your children at night by using a sensitive monitor. Along these same lines, I also believe that parents should have a lock on their bedroom door for occasional use. Without one, sexual intimacy is improbable.

If you are truly compelled to sleep with your child in the same room, then plan for how and where you can maintain a sexual connection with your partner. Don't leave this simply to chance without a strong commitment to find a way.

Rekindling Romance

There are times in life when it is enough to simply make it through each day, and sexual intimacy is completely disrupted for a lengthy period of time. Resuming this aspect of the relationship may feel very daunting because of the intensity of competing emotions such as grief and or fear. People have to find their own path to reclaiming the sexual aspects of their marriage. One illustration is found in the following comments of a mother we interviewed, who described the aftermath of her daughter being born prematurely at twenty-five weeks, with small odds of living:

"During that time our daughter 'coded' a few times. So it was very, very stressful. We just maintained the routine. My husband went to the office when he could. When he was too emotionally drained, he was in the hospital, and sat in a rocking chair either stroking her or sleeping next to her. I went down every day too. I don't remember doing much talking except for saying, 'This is what the doctor said today'—very, very focused on her physical and her emotional wellbeing."

If you met this woman, you would see a confident, multi-talented person with a very strong intellect. I underscore this because of the depth of her feeling of inadequacy for not being able to carry this baby full term. She continued:

"The marriage was never put 'on hold' but sex was, because I didn't feel good about who I was and my body. I was very upset that it was my body that failed...so I didn't feel sexy. I didn't take off the baby weight for a long time. I didn't dress well. I didn't get my hair cut. I never had my nails done. In pictures of me from that time, I was either wearing a black sweater or a maroon sweater every single day. I let my person go. My husband was really very stressed. He was trying to support us and his work and we had the two younger children. And sex was on hold. Intimacy was not."

This couple made a successful transition to reincorporating sex into their marriage. She graciously shared how they achieved this with us in the interest of helping others. We found her description to be a wonderful example of working to sustain your marriage in respectful, loving ways:

"We held each other a lot. We'd walk on the streets and hold hands. We'd cuddle in bed, cradling and spooning. There was never any demand on his part that we resume sexual relations. When we did, it was very slow and tentative. It wasn't great passion. It was not, 'Oh my

God, we've rediscovered each other!' It wasn't calculated.
It wasn't 'I'm going to buy her flowers and seduce her
tonight.' Moving from casual petting, to cradling, and
spooning to having sexual relations. There was nothing
abrupt and there were no demands on it."

Taking vacations together is another way parents can both re-
kindle and protect their romantic and sexual relationships. Many couples we interviewed described trying very hard to get away, without
children, even for a night or two each year. For many it was not easy
due to worries over money and childcare, but well worth the effort.

Personal Strategies from Other Parents

While preparing this book, we specifically asked couples to discuss how they protect their romantic lives in the midst of caring for
their children. We received several good strategies to share with you.
Bear in mind that couples develop strategies that fit their personal
style. So, regard these as ideas that demonstrate creativity and can
encourage you to come up with your own strategies that best suit
you and your partner.

"We make fun of our bizarre lot in life. We leave
dirty e-mails for each other and see who can get
the nastiest. We call each other once or twice a day and
share our frustrations, our disappointments, our joys. We
talk about meeting each other in the closet for sex even
though we both know that we usually fall asleep before it
reaches fruition. We constantly tell each other it's going to
get easier, maybe tomorrow. When we do get those times
alone we don't waste a single second."

"We set dates with each other, even if to be in bed
by 10 o'clock. We make sure we say at least three
loving things to each other each other each day and we
keep time alone."

"We make sure a part of each day is for just the two of us; it can be done."

A final word of wisdom from a husband and father of two children with severe disabilities:

"Intimacy and closeness sort of work hand in hand. If you never are close, the odds are that you are not going to be intimate."

Chapter Six

Negotiating and Implementing Livable Roles

Fran P. Prezant, M.Ed., CCC-SLP

The roles we take in our marriages and families are multiple and varied. Some we freely choose, and others we end up with by default. As life changes and we change, roles may sustain and support healthy marriages or become a source of discomfort, contention, or resentment. All marriages are susceptible to role-related problems. However, in marriages where there is a child with a disability, the issue can be a source of even more resentment because the childrearing and financial demands are relatively greater. Parent input for this book underscored how often role problems occur and can rob a marriage of its goodwill. One such example follows:

"**M**y husband tends to turn it all over to God, who he thinks will handle everything. But then I feel I am the only one doing all the actual work of tending to our daughter's needs and playing with her, helping her to stand, doing therapy, etc. He will spend fifteen to thirty minutes in actual one-on-one play, then hand her back to me because he's tired now. Meanwhile, I have been caring for her all day. My husband comes home from work about 4:00, goes hunting till about 7:00, comes home again, makes a couple of phone calls, takes a shower, and wonders why I'm in a bad mood."

Ending Up in Roles: For Better or Worse

The marital partnership begins with a couple whose primary role is to support each other. The spouses come to the marriage with certain commonalities and work out the details of the role each will play within the marriage: financial support, maintaining a home, daily chores, etc. When children enter the family, those roles need to be changed and renegotiated. Just as role transition is part and parcel of moving from single life to married life and then again to parenthood, the introduction of a child with a disability usually requires additional transitions because of the additional care, tasks, relationships, and service coordination. Some of the transitions occur without our realization, and parents may be dissatisfied or resentful when they recognize that the transition is not what they had planned.

"When we first got married, it was fun to prepare multi-course dinners for the two of us. It was almost an extension of 'playing house.' Shopping and cleaning were initially shared responsibilities. I had a job while my husband was pursuing his studies, and had to spend many hours a week working. I continued to do the cooking, and began to do the shopping and pay the bills. Then I went back to school myself but continued to do the other things.

"When our child was born, we did a little flex time in terms of her care but I was the one who took a three-month leave from professional life and then only went back to work part-time. From then on, the professional part of my life was compromised. Nobody told me it had to be, but we both felt strongly about not wanting full-time daycare, and my profession gave me a little more flexibility. The fact that my professional training was related to education was a benefit but also a detriment because of the assumption that I should be more involved with school issues. Eventually, I found myself being not only the chief cook and bottle washer but also the education coordinator and social overseer as well."

The "working" spouses are often trapped in a different world. Many are not happy with their jobs, work long hours, and feel increased financial responsibility. When they arrive home, they are often met by an upset partner who wants them to pitch in immediately. Many working spouses argue that this is like a second job. One husband's comments exemplify this point of view:

> **I** come home from work in the evening and have full childcare responsibility, also on the weekends. The only way to get anything done is to take time off while the kids are in school, and then that tweaks my wife because she claims never to have any time like that."

Factors That Shape Our Roles

Gender

Gender underlies many of the assumptions about what role we should fill in a marriage. The roles our own parents played tend to color our own assumptions about who should be the breadwinner and who should take care of the home. These are often intertwined with our beliefs about how to be an adequate man or an adequate woman and then are further complicated by economic need and cost of living, geographic location, and other family obligations.

Roles may have been more easily defined in the United States in the 1950s and 1960s, when nuclear families were the norm, most mothers stayed at home and assumed responsibilities for the home and the children, and fathers were usually responsible for supporting the family. Despite dramatic changes in the roles of women over the last several decades, women who work or have careers often continue to take on (whether by choice or by default) the lion's share of the responsibility with children and home.

Some might say that this role division has persisted as a result of genetic or evolutionary roots related to women's function in bearing offspring and nurturing children to independence. (Women, if you think your situation is overwhelming, then you might be interested in *Blaberus giganteus*, a large cave cockroach which mates once, retains the sperm, and is pregnant for life! Then there is the

Surinam toad whose 60 to 100 eggs are fertilized and deposited on the female's back, absorbed, and embedded into the skin for 12 to 20 weeks until they push out of the membrane to escape!) Others may say that old habits die hard, and, although women have made great strides in securing a more egalitarian status in society, for many this has been an add-on to what they have already been doing rather than a re-shifting of what they do.

Competence

Competence is a second major factor that drives role division. Very often one partner assumes a role because he or she is better at it:

> **"H**aving a child with special needs has been very difficult. The responsibility was mainly mine. Her father basically said, 'I can't do this the way you can.' I was eventually the only caregiver."

This also holds true for non-childcare roles. Spouses who are the primary breadwinner sometimes end up being the one worrying about the bills. Because they are in charge of finances, they also often feel alone with troubling problems such as where to come up with the money for expenses. If they need to work longer hours or oversee family spending habits, they are often seen as unavailable or controlling. They often carry the emotional burden of worrying about job insecurity and potential loss of income. This strikes at the core of their major role, sense of adequacy, and manner in which they contribute to care for the family.

[Be aware of the problems that may develop from extreme role divisions.]

Role divisions based on competence can breed their own sets of problems. The competency gap gets wider, marital connections may weaken, and the opportunity for teamwork in parenting diminishes. In addition, roles that may have been freely chosen become sources of bitterness. There is also the related problem of *skewed problem ownership*.

Skewed Problem Ownership

Whether the result of gender-based division of labor, differences in expertise, or other factors, it is important to watch out for skewed problem ownership. This occurs when one spouse shoulders all or a disproportionate share of the responsibility for a given task.

> It is fine for one parent to take a leadership role or primary responsibility for some specific tasks or functions, but be aware that it may end up becoming that parent's exclusive role.

Either spouse may end up having skewed ownership for any set of problems. For example, many spouses feel that they are the only ones worrying about and handling child-related needs. One mother voiced the following precautions:

"Don't take complete responsibility for the care of your child. Involve your husband in the different aspects of raising this child with a disability—doctor appointments, IEP meetings, goal setting, physical care, etc. Insist that your husband educate himself about the disability so he can make informed decisions as part of your child's team. Share in the responsibility. Burn-out can come quickly to someone who is raising a child with a disability along with other children, possibly working a full- or part-time job, along with taking care of other responsibilities."

When one parent is either a medical, therapeutic, or education professional by training, she may easily become "designated caretaker" of these (medical or educational) issues. Medical or educational knowledge is certainly an advantage if it allows you to have necessary information about the issues, get a head start on advocating for your child's unmet needs, and understand "how the system works." However, in these situations, the nonexpert spouse may say, "You go to that meeting for us because you understand this and you know what to say and ask for," and slowly that partner withdraws from those situations. Although the justification for having a "knowledgeable" parent take on a more active role in meetings may have some merit, the absence of the other parent can raise numerous problems.

" **M**y spouse assumes that I will attend all of these meetings and do and say the right thing, and come away with all the solutions just because I have a background in this field. The idea that we might have different perspectives on an issue or that important information about our child may be discussed is lost on my spouse, who just opts to delegate me to be the one to figure things out or make me feel guilty if I don't want to shoulder the responsibility for this role."

Some parents voice resentment when told by a spouse, "Well, you take care of this. You're the expert after all," or, "You should know the answer to this. This is your field, not mine." There appears to be a fine line between recognizing and trying to capitalize on the knowledge level of an informed partner and partially abdicating your own responsibility. When this happens, the "nonprofessional" parent may become more removed from discussions about the child's present or future, and be absent when there are significant and important interactions or decisions that need to be made with medical and educational professionals.

Spouses ideally must agree on role responsibilities in order to get the most bang for the buck. The two scenarios below contrast how this works well in some families and how it doesn't in others.

Scenario 1. The father of a young child with life-threatening medical disabilities was a nurse by training. According to his wife, his knowledge of medical practice, hospital procedures, and navigating health insurance was invaluable during the course of his daughter's birth and lengthy hospitalization. She was happy to have him be the leader (but not solo participant) in this role, and he felt good about it. She viewed his knowledge and expertise as a strength that should be capitalized on, yet she did not abdicate or delegate all responsibility to him. They still made important decisions together, once they both had all the information and both understood all the options and ramifications of their decisions. During this time, this couple negotiated their roles well in a way that made sense, seemed equitable, and was designed to facilitate best possible outcomes for the child.

Scenario 2. On the other hand, a teacher who was the mother of a child with a severe hearing loss resented the fact that her husband never learned anything about the educational needs of their child, school options, or legal entitlement. Instead, he assumed that she would take care of these issues. He never participated in educational meetings because he never bothered to acquire information. His insights as a father might have been helpful in bringing another perspective to the table, but he needed a basic level of information, a sense of ownership, and an interest, in order to make any contributions to discussions. Instead, he assumed that everything would be taken care of without his participation.

There is a major difference in the above two scenarios. In the first situation, there was mutual agreement about the value of the husband's medical training in making informed decisions about treatment. His role as information conveyor and facilitator was key, but both parents continued to be jointly involved in obtaining new information and making decisions. In the process, the husband taught his wife what he already knew. They agreed about the position each one played on this field. In the second scenario, the mother's training as an educator was also an advantage when it came to understanding school procedures, placements, and educational laws. But the father opted out, assuming that the mother's knowledge meant that she should participate in meetings, decisions, and follow-ups without a need for his involvement. There was no mutual agreement about roles and responsibilities here, and, over time, the mother ended up feeling increasingly resentful.

Striving for Fairness in Role Division

Major resentment is one of the main red flags that signal the importance to open up discussions regarding role divisions in your marriage. It is important that roles are perceived as equal and *relatively* fair in terms of several major factors:

☑ Element of choice: It is important that role divisions be subject to re-negotiation or modification over time.

☑ Equality of work load

☑ Equality of time demands: Roles should be relatively equal in terms of providing a little discretionary time

☑ Equal in terms of power for major decisions that affect you or your children
☑ Not skewed to the point that you feel alone with parenting or financial problems

As noted earlier, roles naturally may need to be modified over time if they cease to function well in a marriage. For parents of children with disabilities, this need is often greater because initial role changes related to the child's disability factors may have been abrupt and sweeping. For example, parents with careers often resign from their jobs in order to be able to devote the time and care needed to meet their child's needs. This may work very well for years. However, sometimes once a parent feels that childcare is under control, this role may become problematic. This is especially true for people who gave up careers they loved. There are also plenty of parents who have loved staying home with children but are faced with spouses who want them to return to work. Others want to retain certain roles but not *all* the responsibilities that come with them.

[Major problems can occur in a marriage when a partner insists that roles are engraved in stone.]

Many unhappy couples fight over a spouse's decision to continue to stay home after the children are in kindergarten rather than return to work. These fights often refer back to agreements made earlier in life. Both partners may feel betrayed. One spouse may feel a promise was reneged upon. The other may feel betrayed that their strong and current desires are disregarded.

Changing Social/Psychological Roles

The Introduction includes the view that changing a marriage is possible to a sizeable extent by changing how one functions within the marriage. We noted that a change in one partner tends to result in changes in the other. Much of this reciprocity has to do with roles that are assumed; the roles we are referring to are often unarticulated but very real roles.

[Sometimes we have a large hand in controlling the roles that we live to resent.]

If we are not aware of our own part in the problem, sometimes our own actions (or lack of action) result in our assuming roles that we blame the other person for putting us in. Two pairings of roles that often cause problems are:

1. *authoritarian/child,* and
2. *overfunctioner/underfunctioner.*

We will describe both of them briefly as well as explain how both can be modified greatly if the dissatisfied partner takes the lead in these role pairings and recognizes the power she has by changing her part of the marital dynamic.

Authoritarian/Child Marital Roles

One woman, who is representative of many others, recounted how she believed she married the wrong man. She described her husband as overbearing, and described her inability to carve out a life for herself that resembled what she wanted. As the mother of several children, including one with a disability, she loathed the idea of a divorce and saw her fate as one of needing to settle for her "lot in life." She described her marriage as one in which her husband called the shots and portrayed him as very selfish.

She agreed to concentrate on her behaviors in the marriage and to try new behaviors herself even though she believed the root of the problem lay with her husband's personality. Over time she discovered that she had a great deal of latitude in changing this marriage by changing the roles that perpetuated many of the problems. Although she said she was "scared" to speak up to her husband, there had never once been an incident in which he physically threatened her, so she agreed to push herself out of her comfort zone. She felt that she had to be a "buffer" between him and the children. She exhibited the pattern of assuming the role of a little girl who interacted with her husband as if he were a stern father.

As much as this wife resented having an authoritarian spouse, we found that she reinforced this role. She asked permission to engage in activities that she believed she should not need permission for. Initially, she accepted being scolded for many small matters and tried to do things her husband's way to make sure that he would not be displeased with her. After some time in marriage counseling, though, she told him how upset she was with some of his behaviors that she felt jeopardized family functioning and she agreed behave more like a grown woman and wife, rather than somebody's daughter. She started off slowly, knowing that the other often resists changes in one partner even if they are eventual welcome changes. A different side of her husband became visible quite quickly. When she expressed her requests in a respectful, adult manner, he most often responded to them cooperatively. Her husband was surprisingly cooperative on matters that she said he'd never agreed about. These changes were most likely also due to the fact that he felt some relief in not having to play the father role, even if it initially seemed to suit him.

As this woman worked to relinquish the daughter role and act like an adult woman, the quality of marital life improved for both of them. In an adult role, she did not have to struggle with resentment over her husband's authoritarian behaviors, and this resentment no longer prevented her from expressing affection for him. The rewards for changes in his behavior were natural and satisfying. She no longer felt he was selfish and understood that it was natural for him to disregard her needs if she rarely asserted them and prioritized his above her own. An added and very important benefit was that his parenting improved; she gained the freedom of leaving him with the children more often without feeling she had to be there to soothe hurt feelings. As she stopped regarding him as the big, scary "Daddy figure," her children also became much more comfortable with him. In fact, in terms of role changes, she needed to get used to the children wanting his involvement rather than hers.

Overfunctioner/Underfunctioner Marital Roles

This role pairing is seen especially often in marriages with children and even more so when children have disabilities. It is the lack of balance that is problematic, and the only way out is to work to restore the balance. For example, if you are married to a spouse who does not contribute enough financially, continuing to add on work hours yourself, while resenting it, will only result in a further lack of balance. The more you take over (grudgingly or not), the less your partner will share the responsibility. This is part of the problem. As long as one partner "overfunctions" in what should be a shared endeavor, the other will generally "underfunction."

This pattern can occur in all kinds of shared couple responsibilities, such as helping children with the homework, managing finances, earning income, and housekeeping. As discussed in Chapter 1, this is especially problematic when a new baby is born. Over a fairly brief period of time, the couple starts assuming that the overfunctioner has the official role of being in charge of the responsibilities he or she assumed by default. Certainly there are some activities that you can't help but continue to assume—such as the many aspects of baby care. With other activities, you have more discretionary room to change. For example, if you overextend your work hours in order to buy extras for the family and you resent that your spouse is not pitching in financially or watching expenses, you can get out of the vicious cycle. In this case, cutting back so that you have more livable work hours and can cover living expenses, but not some luxuries, will result in initial discomfort. Yet, it sows the seeds for your partner to respond to this change by either cutting back unnecessary expenses or getting some additional income. "No pain, no gain" is a motto you have probably heard, related to physical exercise. It applies to this area of modifying roles as well.

When it comes to role modification, you need to accept that your partner may not perform responsibilities as you would if you retained a role. For example, if you want your partner to help the children with their homework, she needs to do it *her* way without your intervention or supervision. Otherwise, she will resist and feel like a disgruntled delegate, and will have little sense of role ownership.

Sorting Out Roles

In sorting out roles, it is imperative to remember that a family has to be more than a collection of individuals if they are to act as a coordinated group. As individuals, we each bring something to the table and in families that have a child with a disability, we each may have to bring even more due to added demands on our time, understanding, patience, flexibility, and finances. The ways in which that occurs are not as important as the fact that the partners agree on how that will happen, who takes responsibility for what, and how to make changes as they become necessary.

In general, it is better when there is some mutual participation in aspects of roles. The involvement of both parents often enriches the outcome, but external factors can either help or add fuel to the fire. This is especially true when it comes to dealing with school personnel, who may have personal biases about what roles parents should play based upon their own background, values, and culture. For example: One mother had advocated strongly for her child over the course of many years. She came to every school meeting, brought advocates, convinced a private neuropsychologist to present to the child's IEP (Individualized Educational Program) team but was never quite satisfied with the outcomes from the meetings. Promised plans were never implemented, and the father—who was always too busy at work to come—never participated.

When push came to shove one year, the father showed up at an IEP meeting. Even though he had relegated all responsibility for all school issues to his wife and really had very little knowledge of anything educationally that had transpired, his presence made a difference. The outcomes from that specific meeting were more positive than any meetings before. Although that was truly a positive change, in one sense the mother was furious that her husband received a different reception from school staff because they saw him as sacrificing his work time.

She commented, "It's kind of like when you take your car in to the garage for repairs. The mechanics don't try to rip men off because it's perceived that they all know more about cars, when in actuality, my husband may not know the difference between a battery and a sparkplug."

Renegotiating Roles

It may be easier said than done to agree on who will now be responsible for what. Until you experience the new responsibilities, how could you really know whether it will be too much or whether you will end up resenting issues you haven't even considered yet?

If a parent ends up asking "How did I end up doing this?" and truly is overwhelmed and believes that role division should be different, the couple must communicate. Negotiation with your partner must begin with open discussion about your feelings and an examination of who does what in order to agree on needed adjustments.

> Renegotiating roles requires you to articulate your needs.
> If you don't, little will change.

This section includes examples of what can happen when agreed-upon roles present unanticipated issues and how couples resolved them successfully. For instance: A woman who already had two children and had gone through role transitions common to many of us emphasized the importance of her proactive approach after the birth of her child with severe medical, physical, and cognitive issues. She might not have been as successful without the suggestion of her encouraging social worker, and the flexibility and understanding of her husband:

> **"I** was a professional woman and I liked it, but suddenly I felt I had to be at home and that everything revolved around my daughter. When the other kids got home from school at three in the afternoon, I was cooking, still in my pajamas. I hated it—being at home and dependent."

The social worker suggested she go back to school to retool and be prepared to enter the job market again when she was ready. She returned to school, and her role began shifting again as she took evening classes with less time for home responsibilities. Although she and her husband had always shared responsibilities, he picked up on cooking and other home chores. In order to successfully shift roles, she had to be explicit about her needs.

If your own attempts to negotiate roles are not successful, you may want to seek outside assistance from a social worker, counselor, or someone else who can be more objective about observing the dynamics that may be problematic.

Here is how another wife helped a less receptive husband understand her need for a major role change. This mother decided to stay home and care for their infant son despite her professional background. The first role shift from working at home was challenging because of the changes in her schedule and activities, as well as the exhaustion arising from her sense that her child had an undiagnosed problem. Since she was now home, it became her role to go from specialist to specialist while her husband was at work. As a result, she was the only one who heard the doctors' and other specialists' observations and interpretations, which were at times very technical. She was always the one to "translate" information to her husband. Finally, she decided it was not her role to do this solo. She and her husband had negotiated roles, but crises made them rethink aspects of those shifts.

The next transition occurred when this woman decided to start an at-home business in order to cover the costs of their child's education and therapy services. She built in flex time for transportation and therapy, continued to do laundry and cooking, and began to start a business. In her attempts to shift roles from *fulltime stay-at-home mom* back to *business woman,* she unintentionally retained the "stay-at-home" identification in the eyes of others who saw her at home rather than "in the office." People who viewed her this way (including at times, her own husband), sometimes forgot that she really was working and had professional responsibilities. Consequently, she had to try to deal with phone clients while attending to a screaming child or work on a deadline for a client but have to interrupt for a therapy run. Conflicts occurred because her husband really didn't understand her frustration since he thought of her as being "at home" even though *both* worked.

She had to say to her husband:

> **"T**his would be like you taking our son to work with you and having a conference in one room while trying to help him with his homework in another room, or stopping work in the middle of the day to pick him up, take him to therapy, sit in, and observe while also trying to work on something for a client, go home, cook dinner."
>
> "I had to keep reminding him that I was no longer a stay-at-home mom by joint decision, but I was a business woman and **also** a mom and wife. He eventually began asking if he could help."

Communicating that she needed help and asking him to brainstorm was effective, and didn't involve "demands" made by one person on another. Final solutions also included joining carpools and having her husband transport their child at times.

Open discussion of the frustrations and conflicts about roles surrounding parenting children with disabilities may generate solutions that work for each couple as described above. This is a very complex issue, with the roles we assume resulting from our own backgrounds and assumptions, those we "take on," and our level of readiness to discuss our honest feelings with our spouses.

Role Sharing

In some marriages, all major roles are equally shared. Some couples may find this inefficient; others embrace shared responsibility and genuine equality into the philosophy of their marriage. A good example is found in the words of a father who described a wonderful marriage with his wife, who is now deceased:

"My wife and I met when we were eighteen, freshmen in college, so we basically 'grew up' together. We also spent about ten years together as a couple (five after we got married) before we had kids. All of this meant that we had a lot of time to bond strongly together as a couple and prepare for parenthood. After having two 'typical' children, our daughter was born with multiple disabilities. She has a chromosomal difference that has affected her cognitive and motor development across the board, and also caused hormonal differences and seizures. We have had to see far more than the normal number of doctors and specialists during her now eleven years of life.

"When our daughter was eight, my wife was diagnosed with a rare type of cancer. She died from that two years later after a heroic fight. She was a great mom, and together we made a wonderful team as parents of our three children. Her memory and all that she imparted to the kids lives on in them.

"One of the things that helped us as parents was that we shared the care of the children pretty equally. We were lucky enough to both work part-time, and to be able to juggle our schedules so that one of us could be at home as needed. We also shared everything quite equally, like the housework. I think this helps a couple stay connected and not get resentful. It is hard to work out a balance, but I think balance is what it's all about."

Role Reversal

In a growing number of families, there is a reversal of tradition-al gender-based roles. These involve the male taking on the lead role as primary caregiver or stay-at-home dad. This father is one example of one who does childcare while his wife works:

"I brought home a twenty-three-week-old premature baby on home monitoring and all this other equipment. People thought we were out of our minds. I slept on the floor in her room. My wife worked nights. I was scared to death. Then I had the equipment failure the first night."

He went on to discuss how he enrolled in a transitional care program to learn how to care for his daughter:

"They have a room, usually for mothers. I am one of the only fathers who went down. I learned how to give her medicines and how to do infant CPR."

Many stay-at-home fathers feel comfortable retaining this role, but a number cite one particular problem of isolation during the day. They report that trying to volunteer at school or to join play groups is often been difficult—not because of their unwillingness but be-cause they are frequently viewed as an outsider or stand-in for a mother in these frequently all-female environments.

The Need to Be Creative or "Go with the Flow"

When role division proceeds most smoothly, both husband and wife usually recognize that parenting a child with a disability requires three elements:

1. open communication,
2. mutual decision making, and
3. the flexibility to recognize that roles may need to change over time in a fluid way.

The following statements highlight mothers and fathers who have managed to negotiate livable roles:

"**M**y husband is the go-between and runner to and from the hospital, while still working full-time. I am the caretaker, supporter, and organizer with three young children who all need extra care. We live in the hospital and talk during the two hours that my husband can come to the hospital before taking the children who are not sick back to the Ronald McDonald house for the night. We have found that just being able to rely on one another seems to work the best."

"**I** think it's important for husbands and wives to share equally in all aspects of routine childcare. You don't want one parent to be the expert on what your child eats, how she learns, or how to get her to sleep—it's too limiting for one parent, and your child needs to be flexible enough to do things a variety of people's ways. One of the best routines we got into is to take turns putting our daughters to bed at night and the next night we swap. It keeps us connected with what's going on with both of them."

"**F**ind the things that are most important to your spouse. What roles do each of you think are most important for you to do? Talk these out. Compromise. Don't just assume that these things will work a certain way. Talk them out to make sure you are both on the same page. Men and women think very differently."

Conclusion

This chapter has included some lengthy scenarios that represent both positive and negative examples of role-change issues. We felt it was critical in order to show how changes can occur and we may not even be aware of them until one day we try to reconcile with our dissatisfaction. There is no doubt that *flexibility* and *communication* are essential ingredients in negotiating roles that work for you as a couple. Roles are not static and do change, if only due to our own maturation and life experiences. Parenting children with disabilities introduces additional factors to consider.

Think about your own role and that of your spouse. Consider how you arrived at this role and whether you are satisfied, just content, or unhappy, and discuss your feelings with your partner. Role changes may be difficult, but we have spoken to many partners in longstanding marriages who are successful because they examine and modify their own roles while strengthening their marriages.

Chapter Seven

Stress Management and Coping Strategies
(or Don't Forget to Breathe!)

Fran P. Prezant, M.Ed., CCC-SLP

Anyone who has taken a plane trip with their children has heard the flight attendant's drill about safety precautions and what to do in an emergency. If the overhead masks drop from above, you are directed to put yours on first, then your child's. If our instincts are to save our children, then why are we instructed to do the reverse first? If we can't breathe and subsequently lose consciousness, the chances are much greater that our child will not make it either. We must think about our need to use coping and stress management strategies as breathing so that we and our children will be able to thrive.

[Think about what is in your personal toolbox to build structures, plug leaks, and fix what's breaking.]

Although there are solutions to many of the practical problems we experience in parenting children with disabilities, there will remain stressors and problems that cannot easily be solved with money, babysitters, good teachers, or advocates. At this point, it is the inner resources we have developed that will help. Some of us seem to have a natural arsenal of coping strategies; others seem to have none of these. The good news is, it's never too late to learn to cope better. With some guidance—perhaps working with a counselor, speaking with peers, or reading a constructive guide—you can develop and implement strategies that will assist you.

> Historic myths about parents who have children with disabilities can be damaging to a couple's attempts to cope. Do not listen to them.

Historically, couples who had a child with a disability were automatically considered to be dysfunctional because of the increased stress and the assumption that reactions to stress are always negative. We now know this is not true. Most of the families we spoke with discussed the birth and raising of a child with a disability as a major and ongoing source of stress, but not one they couldn't cope with. We all know families that are dysfunctional. Having a child with a disability isn't the only ticket to join the club. We also know that stress can have positive results in terms of focus, perspective, changed courses of action, career choices, and relocations. For example, one mother of a child who has had sixty-four surgical procedures in less than four years believes that the incredible stress she and her husband experienced actually made them more functional, although it does not appear that way on the surface. For one thing, she says, she and her husband "don't worry about the piddly things that most people worry about."

Like this woman, we need to examine what we can change, recognize what we can't, and work through it in our own way. We probably can't change the fact that our child has a disability, or that our own lives have been altered. Our internal resources, the ways in which we view life circumstances, our perspective on the world around us, and our ability to be proactive, are critical in managing stress and coping. Many parents we interviewed shared their insights and experiences on these issues. In this chapter, we will address ways that strengthen us while coping and adapting.

[Respect your limits.]

Physiologically, our survival mechanisms are not only activated in the face of a direct threat but even when we *anticipate* a threat. This issue is expanded on in Robert M. Sapolsky's book, *Why Zebras Don't Get Ulcers,* with a discussion of the need for coping and management skills. The author describes the ability of the lion or zebra to adapt to the stress of being attacked or the need to hunt for food, both activities necessary to assure survival. Humans, on the other hand, switch on their survival system to deal with psychological threats such as constant angst and worry, which explains why society has such a high prevalence of stress-related disorders.

Threats are ever present in life. In addition to sharing the same worries as other parents, parents of children with disabilities also worry about other problems that further mobilize our "emergency" response systems. These may involve battles over services, problems with teachers, conflicts with insurance companies, or offensive encounters with the general public.

We don't often think about the serious physical havoc we put our systems through by just worrying, being angry, and feeling stressed out, but these psychological reactions are ongoing and chronic for many of us and may activate physiological systems that are not designed to be switched on all the time. This, in turn, can affect our own immune systems through overuse.

[Find your oxygen mask.]

In Chapter 1, we discussed the importance of saving a corner of life for yourself. Although the corner may be small, it is necessary in order to help you sustain yourself and manage stress. This functions as an oxygen mask. It may take the form of protecting time to see a friend once a week, take a daily walk, attend a weekly religious service, or have an hour of downtime to "do nothing constructive" after the children are in bed.

[Use differences to complement rather than contribute to conflict.]

It should be noted that in the context of successful marriages, individual coping is important but should serve to strengthen, rather than weaken the marriage. One parent we surveyed talked about differences between her coping style and her husband's and how that was initially a source of conflict for them. However, they were able to reinterpret these differences and observe that while one of them tended to cope by "making things happen," the partner coped by "allowing things to happen" (she was the go-getter, he was the nurturer). Both were important.

Don't Get Overwhelmed

[Take one day at a time.]

This approach is the backbone of coping with many problems that threaten to be overwhelming. For example, it is at the heart of recovery programs for people who are in recovery for substance abuse. The prospect of never having a drink or drug again is overwhelming, but handling a day at a time (and letting the days add up) is doable. The same is true when it comes to handling the stress of having a child with a disability—especially if it is severe. Facing the future is overwhelming; facing today is manageable (in combination with other coping strategies). A father of twins with severe disabilities shared that he simply reminds himself: "If I can just get through today, tomorrow will be better."

This is not to say that you should stop planning for the future, but breaking the problem down into manageable chunks does help many people cope. Another mother who responded to our survey echoed the same thought:

"I would like to give couples with children with disabilities the following advice. Take every day one day at a time. The only way my husband and I get through our busy days and weeks is by dissecting each day and looking at that day and that day only."

[Remember how to eat an elephant (one bite at a time).]

Create small goals first and handle what would have been an overwhelming task in manageable bits and pieces. Not only is this less overwhelming, but the bits and pieces add up to form sizeable inroads into managing problems.

"In order to survive, I've had to put things in a format that I could process. It always got me from the first day to the second day to the third day. My wife's biting off the big piece, looking at the end while I am taking little bites."

"Sometimes things get overwhelming. Sometimes I cry simply because there is too much to do or remember. But I find myself to be a better parent if I do not get caught up in how much there is to do but rather look at how much I have accomplished today."

[Put it on paper.]

When you are looking ahead at an overwhelming week, you can make it more manageable by writing down what really has to be done in that time. Write a task list, look at your calendar, designate times, and relook at your week. It may not be so unmanageable after all.

Some of us live by sticky notes, lined pads, and calendars on which we write, addend, and rewrite our "to do" lists in order to help manage our time and stress. Crumpling up and throwing the list out at the end of the day also gives you a sense of closure (even if you have to move half of the things to the next day's list!).

[In a pinch, most of us are stronger than we think and can muster up resources we didn't even know that we had.]

We have all heard of feats of stunning strength performed by people in crises, like the adrenaline surge that allows a person to lift a car to save someone pinned beneath. It is important to remember that we do have hidden reserves of emotional and mental energy that can get us through a crisis. We become who we think we are. So, remember to focus on your strength. It will help you accomplish a task that could feel daunting.

> Change your priorities to suit your changing life.
> Radical change is required during a crisis.

You will be surprised at how powerful you can be if you focus on yourself as being strong and combine it with strict prioritizing. When my own child was diagnosed with a life-threatening disorder that required six months of hospitalization, visiting nurses, treatments, and homebound school when possible, life looked pretty bleak. Mentally and emotionally saturated, I had difficulty thinking of everyday activities in the same context anymore. Although some of the activities were necessary in day-to-day life, I reprioritized many in my mind and shifted them to a lower position on the list of *"must do today."* This allowed me to remain resilient and deal with what I could, as well as navigate around what I couldn't change. Perhaps it was my own defense system that activated the autopilot switch. Housekeeping, phone chats, shopping, and cooking fell to the wayside and were replaced by driving to the hospital, lengthy times in treatment procedures, worrying about outcomes and futures, meeting with doctors, dealing with insurers, and remembering another child in the family who needed to continue her life. Sterilizing the phone receiver at home to keep germs from my child's weakened immune system and learning to give injections replaced ironing and cooking gourmet meals (I wasn't too upset about giving up the ironing!).

When I look back, I don't know quite how I, and we, as a couple got through it all but we did. I do remember that one of us was strong when the other was more emotionally susceptible and vice versa. We counterbalanced each other without it being a conscious plan. I did only what was deemed "newly necessary" under the changed terms of our lives. I remember finding internal strength I didn't know I had, and at some level must have recognized that although some things cannot be transformed, we needed to work with the things we could change.

Remember:

☑ It is okay to reprioritize what is important.

☑ You can't do everything. Get rid of some of the things on your "to do" list. And don't feel guilty about it.

☑ If you can, try to balance each other out in terms of taking turns, capitalizing on your individual strengths, etc.

☑ Don't underestimate your own internal resources.

Another example of a necessary and essential shift of priorities can be found in the experiences of one mother of two children who had major medical issues. She said that despite the numerous problems she and her husband experienced, to her surprise, her marriage became stronger. She described strategies they use to address the stress associated with surgeries and life-threatening procedures by categorizing life into two modes: *normal mode* and *crisis mode*. In crisis mode, she said, "we close down to get through and keep our selves sane." For this couple, crisis mode includes:

- role shifts,
- putting all nonessential demands on hold, and
- relying on each other.

Handling the Stress of Unpredictability

"Man plans and God laughs."

This rough translation of an old Yiddish expression resonates with many people. Most people struggle to some extent with the notion that life is sometimes beyond their control. We know it intellectually, but it is hard to accept emotionally. Many of us believe that if we do the right things and plan carefully for the future, it should unfold in a relatively predictable and safe manner. One of the stressful aspects of having children with disabilities is that we are repeatedly faced with unpredictability of events that occur beyond our immediate and total control. But that doesn't mean we have no ability to exert any control in our lives.

Being able to increase your sense of predictability and control can buffer stress. An example can be found in how one mother successfully increased her child's use of predictability to increase control:

"When my daughter was young and had to go to the doctor for regular blood tests, we always went through the same routine in the waiting room. She would ask me how much it was going to hurt. When I responded with 'just a little,' that wasn't sufficient. She would then say, 'show me' and extend her arm in front of me. She wanted me to pinch her to simulate the pain she would experience during the actual test. Once I pinched her, she had an idea about what to expect and could plug that pain sensation into a mental hierarchy of no pain vs. excruciating pain. The fact that she was able to anticipate what, how long, and how much it hurt, helped her to understand it might hurt a bit, wouldn't last long, and would be over very quickly. We must've gone through that routine twenty times before she stopped asking me."

This child above was not able to alter the stressful event or prevent it from happening, but her mother's strategy resulted in an increased ability to predict. She was able to increase her sense of control by asking the doctor to let her know when the test would begin so she could be ready. The process became almost insignificant once she felt she could exert some control.

Most people don't predict having a child with a disability. The immediate response to finding out you have one may therefore be a feeling of helplessness because it wasn't in your plan. Strategies and actions that follow will determine whether you will remain helpless or whether you will proactively and successfully cope with the situation in a way that is productive for you, your spouse, and your child.

[Rather than be paralyzed by unpredictability, get the information you need to enhance your sense of control.]

Let's use the prenatal diagnosis of Down syndrome (during pregnancy) as an example. A couple undergoes routine amniocentesis and finds their baby will be born with this disorder. The diagnosis may initially present overwhelming stress and emotional paralysis. Most people could never have predicted this would happen and feel life is out of control.

When you can predict, you may better prepare yourself for what is coming, make decisions about actions that will be important, or have time to investigate and gather information you may need. For example, many organizations disseminate valuable information regarding Down syndrome. Parents of children with Down syndrome are willing to talk to prospective parents. Educational and medical specialists could be consulted about the ramifications for your child before he or she is born. And there is legislation that guarantees your infant with disabilities the right to early intervention services if needed, as mentioned before. Have you changed the fact that you are carrying a baby with Down syndrome? No. Have you been given the opportunity to become educated, to talk to other families, and to think about early intervention services? Yes. And those actions increase the control that you can have and should emphasize the impact of your involvement in controlling what you are able to.

[
Foster a sense of control by taking charge.
Hold the reins and don't drop them.
]

Even when you feel like everything is out of your control, your choices will make a difference. Although you have no control over some things that happen, you may still be the one to make decisions and choices that may affect what happens next. In that sense, you can exert a controlling factor. Actions that foster and encourage a sense of control may include:

- ☑ becoming aware and assertive,
- ☑ joining groups,
- ☑ talking to friends,
- ☑ becoming advocates for others,
- ☑ reading current information on issues that affect you.

[Remembering that you have some control can foster successful coping.]

People with low estimations of their ability to cope and control outcomes tend to give up easily and are prone to depression. Sometimes friends and family are enormously helpful, but in other situations, family and friends can damage your perception of control when they are overprotective and restrictive. They may try to dictate what you should do and how you should think without understanding your feelings. In doing so, they may not be fostering a sense of control but instead, reinforcing your sense of helplessness or incompetence. It is important to think of yourself as capable of making decisions that will work for your family.

Using a Structure for Problem Solving

Applying problem-solving strategies to real-life situations provides a framework for articulating what the issues are and addressing them in an organized way. This helps when you are feeling overwhelmed and at a loss of direction. Basic steps include:

1. **Identify the issue.** Attempting to break down the problems may assist in identifying and describing what they are and how they interact with each other. Solving one problem may have a domino effect in which solutions to one may ameliorate others as well.
2. **Brainstorm solutions.** This step requires suggesting any and all possible solutions to the problem without making judgments about why one is better than the other.
3. **Select appropriate solutions.** Evaluate each brainstormed solution to determine which might work better and which should be eliminated for other reasons. By editing the original list, you might end up with a few good alternatives to try.
4. **Take action.** Decide on one or two selected actions. Determining criteria for deciding whether or not a particular action is successful will result in a solution or elimination of specific actions.

For example: The mother of a young adult son with significant learning disabilities feels that her life is totally based on her son's pressing needs. She is so overwhelmed that her relationships with others, her job performance, and her personal and professional interests have suffered. Her son graduated from high school, but was unsuccessful in several postsecondary programs. His employment history was poor and he spent many days sleeping until 2 or 3 in the afternoon, and then was bored. He was financially and emotionally dependent on his parents but resented not being treated as a responsible adult. He did not drive and was depressed.

This parent's marriage was affected by disagreements over what her child could or should do. In counseling, we used problem solving to identify the son's unemployment as a major source of stress for the mother, and to identify it as an immediate and solvable problem. After we brainstormed about how to help the young man take ownership and locate a job, we identified places that might need hire him, training programs, and beneficial organizations. Some of the options were eliminated for practical reasons, but the mother and son agreed on several. Using the above steps, the son was able to locate a job and his mother's stress level became more manageable. In addition, once on the job, his mood improved and he developed more of a social network. Life became a little less complicated for his mother through the use of effective problem-solving strategies.

As illustrated, effective problem-solving techniques lead to better coping, even if they don't immediately solve all of the problems, because:

☑ Issues have been teased out and articulated.

☑ Actions are focused.

☑ Specific outcomes have been delineated.

☑ There is increased control in altering events or life conditions.

Coping as a Multi-step Process

In a collection of parent essays, *You Will Dream New Dreams*, a mother wrote:

"**W**e have been told by many friends that they could never cope with having a child like Nikki. This comment baffled us because we wondered what they would do instead of coping if they were in our shoes."

People who make comments like this probably would cope with the same issues if they had to, but it is true that some people just don't cope as well as others. Most would agree that coping is a multi-step process that begins with:

1. appraising an event that occurs as a threat or non-threat in our lives,
2. deciding on resources we have and need,
3. taking action by utilizing coping strategies that can be both cognitive- and action-focused or behavioral in nature.

According to J.D. Brown, in *Cognitive Coping, Families and Disability,* edited by Ann Turnbull et al., having a "positive attitude toward the self, a belief in one's ability to master environmental events, and the conviction that the future will be bright and rosy can reduce stress." He goes on to explain that having such positive feelings can cause people to:

- ☑ view events as *challenges* rather than *threats*,
- ☑ come up with proactive ways to change stressful situations,
- ☑ reinterpret stressful events, and
- ☑ experience less emotional stress.

But what if you doubt yourself, and are fearful of the future? First, you need to build up your sense of self-efficacy. Self-efficacy means you are aware of your power to act in a way that will affect the future. The first step builds on advice we gave earlier about tackling small bits of a problem. It is essential that you start making deliberate mental notes about what you have accomplished. This helps you establish a link between your efforts and results. Make sure you give yourself plenty of credit. Stop looking at what you have not yet tackled and keep your eyes on the mounting accumulation of smaller bits and pieces. In this manner, let your sense of yourself become more positive. Secondly, stay in the here and now, and remind yourself that your feelings about the future are just that—feelings—not facts. The future may be brighter than you predict, but even if it isn't, this view will help you cope more effectively. Because you can't always predict the future, you might as well see it in more positive terms.

[You will function better if you use strategies that help you achieve or retain a sense of hope.]

Dr. Robert Brooks, a nationally known psychologist and public speaker, has spent many years studying people living under stressful circumstances. He tries to understand how two people exposed to similar stressful situations could have such different outcomes—some thriving and some failing. His explanations focus on "resilience" or the ability to withstand, bounce back, and succeed. He found that resilient individuals worked to retain hope about the future and made a practice of finding something positive to look forward to. Hopefulness may be a tool that has helped anchor marriages despite circumstances that would overwhelm many.

[Don't forget the power of illusion.]

Well-known disability advocates Ann and Rud Turnbull advise that *illusions* we have about ourselves and our capabilities, whether they are realistic or not, may actually promote effective coping strategies. An example of how this works was provided by a mother:

"At first I thought I couldn't cope with finding out my child had a life-threatening disability from which he might not recover. My spouse took the news badly. Specialists and other families who had children with issues suddenly surrounded us. I found myself playing mind games with my own head. I was convincing myself that I was stronger than I thought. Making myself believe that I could do what I feared was a strategy that worked."

She convinced herself through *illusions* and *hope* that she was strong, and she reinforced this by repeatedly telling herself she could cope with the situation doing whatever it took. And she did.

Interpreting Events, Reframing, and Assigning Meaning

[We have a choice in how we look at situations. Exercise that choice.]

When parents unexpectedly have children with disabilities, they must determine how to view this in the context of their lives.

Does this pose a threat with negative consequences? Or does it challenge them to reconceptualize what having a child with a disability means? For example, are there possible benefits?

One parent recalled the importance of perspective in reframing a situation. By putting a different spin on it, she was able to cope more effectively.

    "This was the most terrible experience of our lives. I remember thinking this couldn't be real or that a testing error had occurred, wondering how this could be and what had I done wrong. I wondered if this was a punishment. Then I thought about all the things we had complained about and how trivial they were. We should be happy that we got a diagnosis in time to do something about it. We were probably more fortunate than other families and maybe something good would come out of it. At least I would be much more appreciative of what I had. We would get through it."

Parents who say that their relationships have improved, or they have become more sensitized to the needs of others, or their perspective on life has changed, are parents who are able to interpret having a child with a disability as an event that can have positive consequences. For example, one family we have worked with has an adult child with Down syndrome. All of the other six children established successful careers in human service professions. The parents view this as a result of the positive experiences with disability in the family. The family members felt their lives were enriched, as were the lives of others through the services that these siblings provided in their roles as teachers, therapists, etc. However, this positive outcome was not within sight initially.

When the father first heard his son's diagnosis at birth (several decades ago), he became physically ill, and viewed the news as a threat to his security and family's future. With his wife's support and after a period of intense grief, he reinterpreted the event and the importance of his role. The parents gradually came to realize that their son's needs were a challenge they could face and an experience that would bring significant insight to their own lives. Assigning meaning appears to be a gradual process that is refined as parents move through different stages of their own lives as well as that of their child.

One way we mentally frame our situation is by choosing what comparisons we make in life. A coping strategy that parents frequently use is comparing their situation to that of someone else who appears to have even more to deal with. And there always does seem to be someone else who has more on their plate. "My child may have a disability, but at least has an intact family," *or* "My child will need assistance in school but at least he can get to school," *or* "I don't know how I am going to be able to handle this, but if the parent of this baby in the neonatal intensive care unit can, then I certainly can." This downward comparison reminds us that things may not be as bad as they initially seem.

Adjusting Expectations

[
Our emotional reactions change when we adjust
our expectations through acceptance.
]

Nancy Freebury, who wrote the book, *Blossom,* based on her journey as the parent of a child with a neurological disability, advises the practice of *acceptance* as a powerful coping strategy. In our personal interview with her, she discussed the gradual change in her expectations through acceptance, that her son would not fit a mold or someone else's definition of who he should be. She noted that the mistake is to believe that everyone fits a mold. It took intense therapy and one-to-one teaching to get him to read (but he can), or to write (but he can), or to accomplish many skills that his peers have mastered. Once she accepted him for who he is and changed her expectations, she was better able to cope. She wrote:

"Acceptance allows you not only to live with the struggle but to grow from it. It shifts your focus from what is not working to what is working. It doesn't mean you give up on your problem areas. You just don't dwell on them. You recognize the challenges, but you celebrate the gifts so much more deeply."

One couple said that once they understood what their child's problem was, they both "adjusted their expectations"—not lowering them but "finding new levels of patience" in situations that demanded them to. They recognized that love, prayer, and even knowledge doesn't fix everything—some things can't be controlled—but that they *could* control their own reactions once they changed their expectations.

A parent who contributed to the book, *You Will Dream New Dreams,* also discussed adjustment of expectations as a positive move:

"**Y**et we were stuck. Stuck in the despair we experienced when Nikki seemed beyond our reach. Stuck in the fear we would spend the rest of our lives taking care of her. Most importantly, stuck in an unknown territory where our attitudes and beliefs hadn't adapted to the landscape. . . . We realized that we could become more connected to and effective with Nikki. . . if we were able to replace our fear and anxiety with happiness and peace of mind by letting go of any expectations we had for her. We were excited to discover that this new perspective opened the door for us simply to enjoy Nikki . . . as she was, to encourage any efforts to do something new without worrying about whether or not these efforts would succeed."

Prayer and Spirituality as Coping Tools

Prayer and religious practice are intensely personal and based on individual belief systems, regardless of affiliation or non-affiliation with a particular religious group or philosophy. We had not intended to cover this issue, but many of the parents we spoke to identified spirituality as a critical aspect of their coping repertoire. For example, the mother of a child with a developmental disability shared this thought:

"**S**pirituality is very important to me. If my husband and I did not have a spiritual foundation, I know that we would not still be married. I can say that with positive affirmation. The stresses and strains on our marital relationship would have been enough. We always say that would have been enough to knock any couple. We constantly tell ourselves that if we did not have our belief that our daughter was meant to be our child and we were meant to be good parents and we were meant to handle this together, then we wouldn't still be together."

Many of the parents we spoke to relied heavily on religious faith and prayers to cope and keep their marriage strong.

"I'm very verbal about my beliefs and how important they are to me. What if I couldn't have gotten down on my knees when my husband left the house in the morning? If I wasn't able to come into that room and literally kneel down on the floor on my hands and knees and sob and pray to God not for it to get all better and go away, but for the strength? Please give me the strength today, tomorrow, to do whatever it takes."

Another parent viewed her marriage and parenting through the lens of devotion to God:

"I would have to say that our faith is the greatest source of support/resource in our marriage. We take our marriage vows seriously and are bound together by our love for each other and for God. We know that any problem can be overcome through prayer. It's not always easy."

Many families talked with us about the importance of their faith and beliefs, whether as part of an organized religion or as part of an individual sense of spirituality. One reason may be that religious belief provides us with attribution. We can look at a situation beyond our control and attribute its existence to powers beyond our knowledge or understanding. Using that approach, we may also reason that we are not alone; something else may exert a controlling force or give us the strength to make the right decisions and take the right actions. If that powerful entity is good, we should trust it, and assume there is a purpose.

A couple who experienced a traumatic birth resulting in a child who had a serious and life-threatening disability shared that perhaps they were not religious in outward practice but they were, in fact, a very religious family in terms of their belief system. They described their "absolute faith that God loves us and cares about what happens to us." They are careful to separate *religious belief* as a coping and stress management tool from *religious institutions* and congregations that may or may not be sensitive to the needs of families who have a child with a disability that they want to include.

Clearly, parents differ tremendously in the importance they place on spiritually-based belief systems, ranging from having no belief in a deity or powers beyond us, to the ultimate belief that we were chosen to be parents of children with disabilities. Parents voiced this range clearly in our interviews. Contrast the first two parent quotes here with the last two for an idea of the range of responses parents conveyed to us through interviews and surveys:

> "Appreciate the gift that God has given you in this child. I thank God for him every day. He makes the everyday normal successes any parent would take for granted a real success. He sees the simple things as the neatest and greatest experiences. He makes me love him for the small things."

> "The one thing you need to know about parents with children with disabilities is God gave those parents special children for a reason. When I was in my darkest moment after I found out about our son's diagnosis, a young girl who works with me told me, 'God only gives special children to special people who can love them. He chose you to have them because he knew you would love them and take care of them.'"

and

" **I**f one more person tells me how lucky I am because I was special and that is why I was chosen to have this special child, I will strangle them."

" **I**'ve learned to chuckle when people tell us what a blessing my child is. Or how we've been chosen by God for this special task in life. If it's all such a blessing, why isn't everyone praying for a child with a disability? I realize they mean well but it sometimes sounds so absurd." (excerpted from **From the Heart**; see References)

Some parents have mixed feelings on the issue of prayer and religion. They may have been brought up to believe, but through their experience, question the existence of anything. They are not willing to give up on prayer or deny a possible source of help and coping but they feel let down. Some continue to make attempts to believe, but wrestle with this.

" **I**f God was so powerful, how could he let this happen and why should I keep praying for help if this is what happened? My mother always is sure to remind me to go to services but I feel that I have lost the faith that was instilled in me at a young age. I do find comfort, however, being in a house of worship, hearing songs and prayers, and being reminded of my youth in that environment. Perhaps that isn't really religion or belief in prayer, but a comfort that may be more associated with meditation or safety."

Religious participation and prayer is not the right recipe for all parents of children with disabilities, but for many parents we spoke to, it provides a powerful support. The value of this as a coping tool depends on your religious mindset and the importance of religion in your lives. This relative importance can change, with some parents becoming less religious and others becoming even stronger advocates of faith-based explanations and solutions as they experience parenting. It is clear though, that for some people, religious belief or a sense of spirituality is essential in their coping strategies.

Using Humor

The ability to laugh and find humor in situations has long been identified as a stress buster. Norman Cousins, nationally known writer and former editor of the *Saturday Evening Review*, wrote on this topic over twenty-five years ago in reference to the value of optimism, hope, and laughter in fighting off the effects of illness. In *Anatomy of an Illness*, Cousins recounts how his daily doses of laughter and watching Marx Brothers movies helped him recover from a debilitating illness. Medical researchers have studied laughter as the trigger for chemical reactions that release endorphins, which make us feel good and decrease the release of stress-producing hormones.

Laughing comes easier for some of us than for others. This probably has much to do with the genetics that contribute to our own personality characteristics and the experiences that have shaped us to this point. We can probably all think of a friend, coworker, or family member who is always laughing or telling funny stories, even when things are not good.

[Finding the funny side of things is a skill that should be nurtured.]

In a response on the issue of coping, one parent sums it up well: "It helps to be able to look at the world 23 degrees off center. The way I look at it, it's better to crack up with laughter than to crack up with stress. And quite honestly, there have been times when a good laugh was the only thing that has gotten us through the demands of parenting a child with a disability."

One parent who participated in this book explained in detail the value of laughter and the need to laugh often at the course of events and the roadblocks constantly being thrown in her path. Every time she encounters another obstacle related to her child with a disability, she gets to a manageable stage where she can react as if the whole thing is a test, or a joke with a comment like "wait till you hear this one" or "you'll never believe what happened this time!" When she has an experience or observation that only another friend could appreciate, she calls them to share it. Her email messages are usually embedded with humor about real life stories that could be the subject of ridiculous soap operas.

Another parent who responded to our survey had this to say about humor:

"**M**y son has recently gone through puberty. He needed to share the joy of manhood (erections) with anyone who would look. He wanted to touch every woman's breasts he saw. He loved everyone female. It changed us by giving us a better sense of humor."

> Think about the things that make you laugh now and do more of them.

What tickles your fancy? Are you the type of person who laughs when you see a baby? Or are you more the type that thinks it's hysterical when someone falls on the ice? Do you like to tell funny stories? Are you a *Saturday Night Live* fan or a secret admirer of *Stupid Pet Tricks*? Do you love stand-up comedy shows or secretly long to take a chance at the mike on amateur night? Surrounding yourself with people who can make you laugh rather than sad sacks always guarantees more joy.

Writing, Poetry, and the Arts

> How many times have you said "I could write a book"?

Many parents of children with disabilities keep journals to keep track of what has transpired, to vent on paper. One parent we interviewed went beyond that, hoping to provide a resource for other parents who might just be entering the realm that she had been in for awhile. With feedback from friends, she published her journal as a book to be used in raising funds for her son's school. Using this outlet, she recognized her writing as a learning experience, part of a growth process, and her own personal therapeutic tool.

Another parent with excellent writing skills used personal experiences and reflections to create an information packet and materials for parents of newborns with disabilities. An attempt to write a grant successfully supported the development and printing of the material and her area hospital is now distributing the written materials to parents when a child's disability is diagnosed at birth.

One parent of an adult son with mental illness began writing poetry to capture her emotions permanently. She has shared some of the work with her son as a method of letting him know how she feels. She says, "I write poetry because it helps me understand and cope with my feelings." A parent of three children with fragile X syndrome created works that can be found in Appendix 2. Other parents have illustrated or written children's books that document feelings and expressions and also increase awareness.

Based on recommendations from her husband and her counselor to locate new friends and explore interests, one parent found singing to be a wonderful way not only to bond with other people outside the issue of disability and expand her independence, but to be "the singer" as opposed to "the mother of the child with a disability." Her artistry created an opportunity to release steam through an activity she enjoyed and also provided entertainment to others. The opportunity to participate in an interest and develop a skill unrelated to mothering and appreciated by others became a creative way to cope. It not only provided an excellent outlet, but confirmed her ongoing "personhood" in her own right and helped to validate her independence as an individual.

Exercise

Exercise has been widely proven to be beneficial for health. Other than improving cardiovascular functioning and keeping you fit in general, physical activity has also been identified as a way to reduce the effects of depression. A number of people I know have made time in their daily routines for exercise because it makes them feel physically better and mentally more alert.

Exercise has assisted many parents of children with disabilities in managing stress. For example: A parent we interviewed who had been a runner told us that she stopped daily exercise after the birth of her child with a neurological disorder. He was so demanding of her time that she could barely find the time to sleep, and, when she did, she found that she couldn't rest. With everything else that had to be given up in order to care for this child, she felt that her exercise was the most logical activity to curtail since it was something that she did for enjoyment and it didn't benefit anyone else. Over time, this mother became exhausted, depressed, and isolated. But with her change in exercise patterns, she also became sick more frequently. Then, her husband began coming home once in a while at lunch time so she could run around the neighborhood, and she noticed a difference. She joined a health club with childcare and went two mornings a week. Her gradual resumption of a daily exercise regimen may have saved their marriage. Although she was running for forty-five minutes several times a week—time that could have been devoted to childcare— she felt more relaxed and able to deal with the issues at hand.

Introspection: Relaxation, Meditation

Planning to occasionally remove yourself mentally (and physically) from the situation is necessary and reinvigorating and serves as an excellent way of coping. There are various ways to do this. One strategy (used by many of the parents of children with disabilities I know) is to physically get away, either with other friends or alone.

Another parent advised:

"Do everything to get some time for yourself. I didn't for awhile in the beginning and I became burnt out and depressed. It can seem impossible to arrange it but it is so important. I spoke to a therapist about it and she advised starting with little steps in getting time. Can you get twenty minutes to yourself? Well, separate yourself and consciously focus only on yourself and what you want to do for yourself for those twenty minutes. Something that makes you happy."

Other parents have found that relaxation exercises or meditation are effective in altering consciousness, getting in touch with yourself, putting aside baggage that weighs you down or finding new ways to look at life circumstances. Relaxation and meditation have been discussed as forms of achieving "mindfulness," slowing down, and finding true meaning. The success (or at least popularity) of these strategies can be attested to by observing the number of courses and best-selling books devoted to these practices that assist in coping. The practice of yoga, in fact, has shown so much promise in the area of stress reduction that it is being successfully used at New York University Medical Center in studies as an alternative method of decreasing seizure activity with people who have epilepsy.

Helping Others: Volunteerism

66 **W**hen my child was young, there were no advocates to help or guide us through this maze. Even if my life isn't perfect and I feel like I could've done a lot more to assist my own child and strengthen my relationship with my husband, I have all this experience and knowledge that I can pass on that would benefit others. Volunteering to support other parents helps on multiple levels and is a productive outlet for me."

The parent above, as well as other parents we interviewed, found that helping other parents through advocacy, starting groups, teaching, etc. not only increased their own ability to cope but also allowed them to give something back to the community. Some parents rationalize that they knew something good would come out of their own trials and tribulations, and maybe this is it.

Conclusion

The information in this chapter highlights some of the coping strategies that individual parents of children with disabilities have found helpful. Although there is not one coping strategy that works best for everyone, there are strategies that work for individuals to reduce the affects of stress and help us adjust, adapt, manage, and become stronger. Coping strategies can include outlets and hobbies such as skydiving, yoga, or simply sitting in a dark room by yourself. Coping can entail pondering the events you didn't expect and trying to revise the meaning in the context of your life. Stress, if left unchecked, can become a controlling factor in your life and must be monitored at various levels. Chapter 9 provides guidance on where to go for help if your stress seems unmanageable.

Chapter Eight

Heartfelt Conflicts:
Opposing Views on Protection, Expectations, and Helping Your Child

Laura E. Marshak, Ph.D.

Some of the most divisive issues in marriages pertain to parental conflicts about reasonable expectations, discipline, and protection from risks. These often become long-running, very emotional disputes. One partner may see another as too strict and expecting too much, or conversely, as being overprotective or enabling. Consider such scenarios:

"Our son cannot feed himself at home but he can at school. Does mom baby him? Yes. Is it her prerogative? My spouse and I sometimes struggle with this issue, sometimes argue about it, and sometimes it is just the way that it is."

"I guess I had more of a motherly caring style. My husband had more of a disciplinary style. This is where we had our disagreements. I would get really angry at home. I found my husband to be very insulting of me as a mother. I would say, 'You make it sound as if I'm not

doing a good job but I am doing my best. It is not as if
these children with disabilities come into the world with
manuals. It is trial and error.'"

“**W**hen our daughter was depressed and hospitalized,
my husband commented that she would just
'have to pull herself out of it.' In the last few years, he
has become much more sensitive to her needs and is more
patient with her, but in the past, these types of issues
caused much stress between us. We are both on extreme
ends of the spectrum—he thinks she should 'sink or swim,'
and I am enabling."

These conflicts are heightened because both the child's wellbeing and aspects of the family atmosphere are involved in major
ways. For example, a partner may assert that not only doesn't a child
have appropriate limits set on anger outbursts but that the family
is at the mercy of the child's temper outbursts. At a minimum, this
spouse may be upset that her partner is not implementing a behavioral treatment program; in extreme circumstances, she may believe
that her spouse is contributing to their grown child's continued dependence on drugs or alcohol. These issues tend to be an ongoing
daily source of disagreement, and therefore have the potential to affect the quality of marital life.

In this chapter, we will start with strategies for handling disagreements over consistency and protectiveness. We will then focus
on how to differentiate between helping and enabling. This portion
will be most relevant to parents of older children or adult offspring
who have particular disabilities such as psychiatric disorders, ADD/
ADHD, or substance abuse disorders.

Consistency

Often one parent works on a daily basis to establish and maintain a structure for their child only to find that the spouse disregards
part of these routines. The parent who strives to maintain consistency often is upset when the child's program is "undermined." The

other partner may feel as if her opinion is not valued and that she is being treated like a childcare employee rather than a parent. There is plenty to argue about.

There is no doubt that consistency is beneficial and particularly important for children who have autism spectrum disorders and other developmental disabilities. Consistency facilitates skill acquisition and often assists self-control. On the other hand, lack of consistency between husbands and wives is the norm. It is one thing to strive to be a consistent team; it is another to let lack of consistency become a source of ongoing marital conflict. With this in mind, consider the following the next time you and your spouse clash over consistency:

☑ Ask yourself if the problem is likely to change no matter how many times you argue about it.

☑ Question whether the benefits to your child are worth the price paid in ongoing marital conflict.

☑ Pick your battles and strive for consistency on the priority issues.

If you prize joint involvement with your child's care, you both need to tolerate the fact that your partner won't do things with your child your way. In the best of all worlds, you would not need to choose between consistency and partner involvement. But realistically, this often is not the case. Co-parenting must be prioritized more highly than consistency and control.

Under some circumstances, having different ways of doing things can be an advantage. Such benefits are well-illustrated by one parent who provided advice on accepting differences in childrearing and discipline. This mother has three children with fragile X syndrome who require a great deal of repeated instruction in order to learn basic skills. Therefore, she could make an argument for why it is imperative that she and her husband do things the same way. She doesn't and her viewpoint is refreshing:

❝I actually value his different childrearing habits. As much as children need consistency, I think they also need to experience two different ways of doing things. Otherwise, they have only one way of seeing the world. If my husband handles them a different way, it teaches them that different people will treat them different ways and that they need to interact differently with different people. As an illustration, there was a picnic one time and the kids got into a condiment fight where they were squirting ketchup and mustard at one another. Well, the men (there were only guys there) stripped all the kids and hosed them down! What mothers would have done that?! I don't think any. But the kids were fine and had a great time. Guys think of a different way of doing things."

Conflicts over Protectiveness

The desire to protect a child is a core aspect of parenting, almost instinctive, yet so is the desire to see that child be able to make his or her way in the world as well as possible. Consequently, many couples have heated conflicts over how much to protect their children—especially those who are relatively more vulnerable. These conflicts might center around perceived risks such as might be encountered in an inclusive classroom or more independent activities. The perceived risks may be physical or emotional (such as possible embarrassment of the child).

Speaking very generally, how you handle this type of problem determines whether or not your efforts are helpful or simply make matters worse.

> Make sure you don't form an alliance with your child against the other parent.

It is absolutely necessary to speak up on behalf of your child if you disagree with how your partner is treating her. But it creates problems if your child is aware that you are doing this, especially if you do so on a regular basis. (As discussed later, the one exception is with any kind of abuse.) Without realizing it, you may be making the matter worse for everyone by repeatedly intervening. This is illustrated in the following reflections of a mother who experienced prolonged conflict over protectiveness. She fought with her husband for much of her son's childhood and adolescence. Her hindsight is very helpful.

"**M**y husband and son are opposites and never really found common ground. My husband would want him to do many things he wouldn't want to. That caused a lot of tension in the house. As the rescuer, I would jump in and say something like, 'Why does he have to go out and play ball?' My husband would say, 'There is nothing wrong with a father wanting to play ball with his son.' I would say, 'But he has trouble playing ball.' He would say, 'We'll teach him.' I would say, 'Okay, but it's not fun for him.'

"The more professionals explained my son's problem to me, the more reasons I had to 'protect' him. I try to get out of the way now. . . literally. I go upstairs and I remove myself. I used to put myself in a position to hear better. My husband would go into the room with my son and close the door. And I had my ear on the door to hear what they were saying. Looking back on it, I think a lot of the villain that my son sees in his father was activated by me, because I was clearly on my son's side. Then he would get hysterical and I would calm him back down."

Another parent, the mother of a child with an anxiety disorder and autistic traits, similarly cautions about intervening between a spouse and child:

"**S**ometimes my husband gets very upset with our son's behavior and I find myself wanting to intervene, but every time I have, it hasn't helped anyone. I can't solve their problems relating to each other."

Two heads genuinely are better than one when determining how protective to be, as is illustrated by one parent:

"**M**y relationship with my son is tight and I still feel like I have to protect him. Because my husband is so strong in his convictions about the things my son has to do (even though I didn't think he should or could), I think my son developed a lot more independent skills. For example, when he was nine, we decided that he had to go to private school, but the only way he could get there was by taking the train from Philadelphia to the suburbs. To me it wasn't even a possibility. My husband would say, 'This is what he needs. Why do you think he's not capable of doing it?' If it was my decision, he would not have gone there. I was scared to death and afraid he would get off at the wrong stop. My husband said, 'I'll just go and show him a few times and when he is ready he'll go by himself.'

"There was a van that would be at the train station but I always feared that it would not be there. Within a week our son was very comfortable with the trip and I was a nervous wreck. I was the one who drove him to the train station every day and watched him get on the train. It was a safe area (but no area is really safe). My husband would say, 'What do you mean it's not safe? Are you going to smother him?' We fought a lot over those issues. Now, I can look back and say, 'He was right!' Absolutely."

There are some useful questions to think about when "debating" issues of protectiveness with a partner:

- ☑ What is the worst thing that could happen to our child if we let her do this?
- ☑ What is the probability that this dreaded event would happen? (It is often useful to identify probabilities in percentages such as 5 percent, 25 percent, etc.)
- ☑ What skills would the child need to learn before the more protective spouse would feel comfortable letting her do it?
- ☑ What is the worst thing that could happen if we *don't* let him do this?
- ☑ Would you rather be safe than sorry or accept a degree of risk in the interests of inclusion and quality of life? (The latter has been termed "the dignity of risk".)
- ☑ Is your child in a position to offer her opinion?

If Abuse Is Involved

Up to this point, I have repeatedly emphasized that parents should never form alliances with their children against the other parent. However, the major exception is when there is any form of abuse.

[When there is abuse—emotional, physical, and/or sexual—
you absolutely must intervene.]

It is well documented that children with disabilities are the victims of far more abuse within the family than are other children. Under no circumstances can you tolerate any form of abuse of your child. There is no acceptable form of abuse, no matter how trying your child is. If your child is being abused, it is essential to protect her emotionally and physically. Do not rationalize abuse in the name of "discipline." Discipline teaches, does not humiliate, and does not cause physical pain, bruising, or fear. Emotional abuse involves ridicule, humiliation, and degradation.

If any form of abuse exists, your alliance *must* be with the child and not your spouse. If you think someone else is abusing your child but your spouse doesn't agree that it's abuse, you still need to follow up with your instinct that abuse may be occurring. The guidelines discussed throughout this book about prioritizing your marriage simply do not hold true in this type of circumstance. Protecting your child is the priority. Abuse is an important reason to end a marriage if it is the only way to protect a child

Enabling vs. Helping

Enabling is a process of shielding a person from the consequences of his or her behavior. Normally, this is problematic because, typically, people need to experience such consequences in order to stop self-destructive behaviors. However, these general statements do not entirely apply when someone has a psychiatric disorder, a neurobehavioral disorder, or some other disorders such as a severe attention deficit disorder. Under some circumstances, self-destructive behavior or an inability to control behavior may be more powerful than the aversive consequences.

Some of the most difficult decisions couples face together are those that pertain to whether or not they are enabling or helping adolescent and adult children who have psychiatric disorders. Mental health disabilities that have both a biological basis and many behavioral manifestations are a particular challenge to come to agreement on. It is important for couples to accept that they are attempting to make decisions under extremely difficult circumstances. We will explore some of the complicating variables and then highlight useful principles to follow under these circumstances.

[It is often unusually difficult to determine what behaviors
are within a young adult child's control.]

For example, if an adult child fails to follow-through on responsibilities, it can be related to:

- the disorder itself as seen in depression, schizophrenia, head-injury, etc.;
- side effects of medication;
- substance use driven, in part, by a desire to self-medicate; and
- lack of maturity or (garden variety) laziness.

To identify the best way to handle such problematic behavior, parents must determining what factors are contributing to the problem. Additional factors, however, make this process even more difficult. Even when parents have accepted their child's diagnosis, psychiatric or neurobiological disorders often don't feel as real to us even though they have physical bases. As much as we recognize these are real disorders that sheer will power cannot cure, it is harder to hold onto this. One mother spoke about her difficulty with her adult daughter's bipolar illness:

"It has been difficult to not get angry at my daughter for her craziness. It is easy to excuse our younger daughter because she has a physical reason for her problems. You can see the eye turning, the uneven gait, the problems swallowing, and we know that she didn't talk until she was three years old. But the older daughter, I ask, 'Why can't you be straight? Why can't you be honest? Why can't you tell the truth?' And as much as I would say to myself, 'It must be difficult for her to be her,' it is still very hard for me not to get angry with her."

There is no doubt that psychiatrists and psychotropic medications are often an essential part of treatment; however, there is more subjectivity in mental health treatment than in many other medical specialties. Most mental health professionals acknowledge that some decisions are judgment calls with a degree of subjectivity. Similarly, there are times in which it is very difficult to tell whether emotional and behavioral problems stem from the worsening of a disorder or medication, or whether the child is acting out and the behavior is under her control.

I have known this professionally for years. As a mother, I have experienced a great deal of useful professional help as well as substantial mistakes made by these same people. For example, my husband and I can now look back and see that some of our child's behavioral disturbances were indeed side effects of medications, although treating professionals assured us that they were unrelated. On the other hand, professional advice has often been invaluable. This means that life is not as simple as just relying on a professional point of view.

Couples can sometimes rely on each other to serve as a good sounding board to determine what is actually within a child's control. For example:

"**M**y husband will remind me, and I will remind him, 'She's not doing it on purpose . . .' or, 'You know, I think she did this one on purpose.'"

[The conventional wisdom about "tough love" and enabling is much more complicated when dealing with children who have psychiatric disorders and substance abuse problems.]

Many parents of grown children with psychiatric disorders struggle with decisions such as whether to aid a child financially or to let a child keep living at home. Husbands and wives typically disagree with each other in the process of sorting out what is helpful and what is enabling. For instance, the mother of an adult daughter with a psychiatric disorder made the following comments:

"If my husband and I have disagreements, it is in that area. He gives her money—not to go out and buy frivolous things but she spends the money that she does have frivolously. And then he gives her the money she needs for necessities. I'm not talking about five and ten dollars here and there. I'm talking about hundreds and thousands of dollars. And this makes me angry. I think that he is too much of an enabler. I need our daughter to hit bottom and get on with it. He's still saving her. I think he sees this as his loving responsibility as a father."

As a child gets older, the stakes may get very high when it comes to making a distinction between helping and enabling him. As mentioned above, enabling is usually problematic because most people need to experience the consequences of their behavior in order to stop self-destructive behaviors. But if someone has a psychiatric disorder, self-destructive behavior or an inability to control behavior may be more powerful than the aversive consequences. On the other hand, expectations that are too low are as problematic as ones that are too high. So it is difficult, but necessary, to find the right place on the continuum between expecting too much or too little.

"My husband and I periodically take opposing positions only to find them switching over time. I think this may have to do with the fact that (in all honesty), neither one of us is deeply confident that anything is right. We both struggle with wanting to do the best thing for our son. We worry that we are too permissive. We worry that we have not acknowledged the full impact of his disorder and that we are expecting better behavior than he can manage. So we switch back and forth and argue both sides, depending on the moment because neither option seems acceptable. Am I angry at my husband while it is occurring? You bet. It is like a teeter-totter. His leaning toward one side upsets me but I recognize in calm moments that I may want him as a counterbalance on some level."

More Serious Conflicts Over Enabling

Several parents we met were faced with the hardest decision of no longer letting a child live at home. These situations involved adult children with major psychiatric disorders that were compounded by substance abuse. Substance abuse problems are common because they are often due to misguided attempts to self-medicate.

Conflicts over these kinds of decisions can be very divisive in a marriage. In addition, credible opinions from friends, family, and mental health professionals vary greatly. There are generally strong and compelling arguments for the divergent paths of tough love and for unfailing support. So in the end, you and your partner need to reach a working consensus.

I have known many couples who have faced such serious problems where there is no single clear course of action. Inevitably, emotions and dangers run high. My rule of thumb is to proceed as if you were both lost in the jungle and needed to find your way out together. Under such circumstances and to avoid perishing you would:

- work together;
- examine and talk about the potential of different paths;
- not be sensitive or defensive about *whose* ideas are acted upon (or not);
- eventually try one path *together* knowing the outcome is not guaranteed.

The same general orientation applies to such high stakes parenting. The following contribution from a parent illustrates one path that eventually paid off.

"Our son, who was an extremely loving, family-oriented child, developed a strange viral illness that looked like meningitis. A definitive diagnosis was never confirmed; however, within a very short period of time, he became severely depressed and oppositional. He believed that parental influence and control was totally unnecessary and a violation of his rights. His personality was almost unrecognizable, and frequently his behavior was extremely difficult to manage.

"My husband and I had a very different perspective on the situation. I believed that much of the negative behavior had a profound biological basis, whereas my husband believed that his behavior was primarily a reflection of the challenges of youth. My husband tried to force our son to obey the minimum house rules and meet the demanding schedule imposed by high school, while I was far more lenient and interested in his biological and emotional recovery. My husband demanded that our son attend school on time, while I was more willing for him to sleep in and recover. Was my husband unfair, or was I enabling?

"The differing performance expectations resulted in highly stressed family dynamics until we developed a common approach. Never relinquishing our commitment to nurture our son and support him through the illness, we finally agreed to offer him several positive options. One of those options was to complete his senior year in high school abroad. This is the option he chose. During this period, we were intimately involved in his life. With frequent visits and almost daily telephone calls, we maintained our optimism and faith that he would successfully work through his challenge and return to the family. We constantly demonstrated our faith in him and his ability to achieve his dreams. It worked."

This couple could not have predicted with certainty whether this unwavering nurturing approach would work. It was a judgment call that the husband eventually supported despite reservations. In essence, they picked one path out of the jungle, although with unavoidable doubts and fears. Sometimes the path needs to be a form of "tough love" such as requiring substance abuse treatment as a prerequisite to living at home. This involves a calculated risk. Sometimes it works when nothing else will and prevents terrible harm to the child. Sometimes it fails and places the child in danger, out of the home and without a "safety net." It is a heartrending gamble. Some very involved parents who had supported their children for years spoke of considering removing their child from the home. This was considered as a last resort after years of trying other routes.

Following is an illustration provided by the mother of a son with a severe psychiatric disorder that would have very much disrupted his functioning even if it was not compounded by many years of substance abuse.

"**M**y husband used to say, 'Why should he be home? Why should he be comfortable? He is not going to want to change anything if he is home in his bed and comfortable.' I saw his point but it is very hard to see your kid in a shelter. Intellectually you can say, yes, that's probably something we should do. But how do you get your kid in a car and drive him to a shelter? He's not going to jump in a car and want to do that. But I know my son has to take the consequences."

Such critical decisions need to be made as a team with a willingness to shoulder any risks together for choosing any particular path.

Bear in mind the following:

- There is more than one justifiable way to approach a child's disorder.
- If you and your spouse disagree, recognize that the other point of view may be very legitimate.
- The verdict truly is out when it comes to how to manage some disorders—especially those that disrupt behavior.
- Have empathy for your partner, even if you vehemently disagree, because these matters strike very close to the heart (our basic concepts of what it means to be a good mother or father).

Getting Outside Help

Virtually all of the parents quoted in this chapter also spoke of the benefits of having a professional involved when facing difficult decisions about enablement versus protection/support. For example:

"**T**he therapist helped us see how we were both enabling. We had to recognize that we enabled but we could call each other on it and in a very non-threatening way at this point. Counseling helped us to

get on the same page, even if it was just temporarily. She
helped us come up with a plan that we could both agree
on. We would talk about what could happen. She would say,
'What would you do if your son did this?' 'What would you
do if the school told you this....?' 'What are your options?'
'What are you going to do if...?' So it did help. It also
helped show us not to overreact and not to immediately
always come up with the worst case scenario. That takes a
while to get to that point because you get into such a mode
of negative thinking."

Support groups for families of people with mental illnesses can be
very important if they give you access to others struggling with similar dilemmas:

"Going to support groups helps me see what other
people are doing. You see other people survive
locking the doors and not letting your kid in the house.
We never got to that point."

One national organization that provides valuable assistance in
the form of support groups, family training, and relevant literature
is NAMI, the National Alliance for the Mentally Ill. You can visit
their website at www.nami.org or contact them by phone: 703-524-
7600 (main number) or 800-950-6262 (HelpLine). If substance abuse
is a problem, AL-ANON can also be invaluable in helping families
learn to handle some of the heartfelt conflicts discussed in this chapter. You can contact them at 888-4AL-ANON (888-425-2666) or online at www.al-anon.alateen.org.

Conclusion

I believe that if there was ever a need for *teamwork,* it is when
faced with such kinds of upheaval and conflicts described by parents
who are faced with these very difficult issues. This teamwork (which
is useful under other circumstances as well) includes:

☑ Allowing disagreement without blame and accusations;

☑ Remembering you are on the same side in life, even if you are on different sides of the argument;

☑ Enhancing connectedness no matter what else is going on. This may mean going out together for a bit even if life remains chaotic. Doing something underscores that the two of you need to have a life together no matter what else is happening.

Lastly, let me emphasize that when the stakes are high, you have to agree at least on a relatively short-term plan of action. This must be done because you need to live together with the consequences and because whatever path you choose is likely to be more effective if you are pursuing it as a couple. This holds true whether you choose to practice a "tough love" approach or more of a sustained traditional, nurturing one.

Chapter Nine

Supports Outside of
Your Family

Fran P. Prezant, M.Ed., CCC-SLP

[You can get by with a little help from your friends....]

Most of us have a support network of some type that consists of friends, family, and outside groups. Parents' needs fundamentally change, however, when a child with a disability enters the family constellation. As one father put it: "The support from outside usually doesn't increase as much as the demands and the responsibility have increased."

Finding adequate supports outside of the family may be a critical aspect of sustaining your marriage. Without these, a couple is stretched too thin; anxieties increase, resentments mount, and the pressure brought into the marriage can crowd out positive aspects of life together. Positive external supports help reduce stress and provide tools, information, and opportunities to build camaraderie with others. They also give rise to new ideas about how to manage the present and plan the future. The presence of social supports is one of the most powerful factors in buffering stress. Indeed, just having someone to talk to can be a lifesaver, according to one parent.

Although getting support from your spouse is important, the needs for support often exceed the couple's capacity within their relationship alone. Many parents don't avail themselves of supports that are available and often tough it out alone due to a lack of awareness of existing resources.

In addition to lack of awareness, several emotional obstacles hamper accessing necessary support. One of the most common obstacles mentioned elsewhere in this book is difficulty acknowledging the need for help. Asking for help implies that there is a problem and many people have difficulty admitting this. "Sometimes you don't want to admit you belong to the group, but you need help." This is what one couple said about their creation of a group to assist other families. In retrospect, they acknowledged that their own difficulty admitting the need for support was the impetus for creating a parent group. This brings to mind the old Groucho Marx quip about not wanting to belong to a group that would have him as a member.

Another significant barrier is the belief that asking for help means you are "incapable." Many of us are uncomfortable asking for help for this reason. Professionals in the field who have children with disabilities may also feel this way and be more comfortable in the role of help "provider." Men may be more susceptible to this line of thinking because societal gender-based rules have taught us to believe that they should be the protectors and problem solvers. Sometimes fathers benefit from the role models of other fathers who do acknowledge the need for help. Attending at least one session of a support group where other fathers are present can be one way to diminish this initial reluctance.

Based on our work with hundreds of families, this chapter addresses common supports that parents find helpful as well as discussion about how to mobilize resources that may be overlooked or underused.

Parent Training and Support Groups

People often overlook the value of support groups because they assume these groups are just a bunch of people talking about their problems. This can seem like a depressing waste of time. What you may not realize is that a good support group is quite different from this notion. Many provide useful information, training, mentoring, or just a forum to share feelings with other parents of children with disabilities. If you can't convince your spouse to go, try this option by yourself. It has helped so many other parents find support, solve problems, and pool their strength :

"The most helpful source of support is the parent group I have been involved in since our daughter was six months old. To hear other parents' concerns and how they deal with issues helps me to cope with issues we are confronted with daily."

"Since my spouse isn't interested in learning about autism, I have found talking to other parents of disabled children helpful...this has helped me and my marriage greatly."

Groups vary in quality and purpose, so finding an appropriate one may take some trial and error. Don't give up if the first one you try doesn't seem to be a good fit. There are many ways to find a good group. Some of these include:

☑ Ask your pediatrician, early intervention specialist, other healthcare providers, or your child's teacher or PTA networks.

☑ Disability organizations frequently maintain local listings and contacts.

☑ Websites or Internet searches may provide good leads.

☑ Look at brochures you have picked up.

☑ Talk to members of a religious congregation or other groups you already belong to.

☑ Let friends and neighbors know you are looking for a good group. Even if they do not have a child with a disability, they probably know someone who does.

Frequently, informal conversations yield the best information. When you locate a group, call a group member or leader to find out the purpose and activities of the group. Ask if you can come to one of the sessions to observe a session.

[If you build it, they will come. I know.]

If a support group doesn't exist in your area and you think one might be beneficial, then chances are there are other parents who could benefit as well. You can begin your own, but this does require some commitment and innovation on your part.

- ☑ Locate a few parents who are interested and agree on the purpose and planned structure for a group. Divide up the work involved in getting up and running.
- ☑ Look at the resources you already have. If one person works in a school, grocery store, Social Security office, Chamber of Commerce, local newspaper, etc., then you may already be a step toward mobilizing those resources.
- ☑ Identify a physical space for an initial meeting. A public space like a school, library meeting room, religious organization, or community clinic is usually available at no charge if you approach the administration in the right way.
- ☑ Plan a first meeting and advertise through flyers, newspapers, local radio, and by informing professionals who come in contact with parents. Let parents know that this is a new group, and they can be instrumental in the formation.
- ☑ Plan an icebreaker event and be sure there are refreshments available. Getting people there for the first time is only the beginning. The meeting must be one that makes people see its potential value and makes them want to come back. You don't want a free-for-all in which nobody does anything except complain, but do want to run a session that identifies issues and a plan for how to address them.
- ☑ You might want to have a questionnaire to get identifying information on attendees and a prioritized list of issues and proposed actions.
- ☑ Planning an engaging agenda that interests people in attending and gaining some benefit from an initial meeting may be the best way to increase the likelihood that people will return for a second session.

Good examples of session agendas can be found in a great guide for parents, *How to Get Services by Being Assertive,* by Charlotte De

Jardins. The book's suggestion for one group meeting begins with discussing the issue that many parents are not assertive enough. The suggested focus for a group meeting addressing this is for the group to delineate all the ways in which a parent group can make you more assertive. They can include but are not limited to:

☑ Learning about your rights under IDEA;
☑ Assisting in preparation for IEP meetings;
☑ Negotiating with bureaucracies and negotiating complaints;
☑ Having parents rehearse their presentations at school meetings.

Parents are encouraged to add more items to the list followed by discussions about how the group could assist by sharing information, bringing in speakers, etc. Each one of these topics could end up as a full session workshop. If the group takes off and looks like it will continue, it will be necessary to locate some financial support or in-kind supports that will pay for advertising, refreshments, and printed information.

Parent-to-Parent Groups

These are a unique type of parent support program that originated in the 1970s with one family in Omaha and has spread nationwide. The model is based on matching a trained veteran parent (called a Pilot parent) with a parent who is seeking support and guidance. Pilot parents attend monthly meetings to refine their skills and agree to volunteer their support for at least one year during which they may be matched with parents in their area. Parents are matched by a host of factors, including disability, family size, family issues, etc. An excellent resource for these programs, *The Parent to Parent Handbook (2001),* provides a wealth of information about how to start such a group. Currently most states have a statewide parent-to-parent organization as well as regional chapters.

Parent Training and Information Groups

These may differ from support groups in that they focus more formally on providing information and training and less on emotional sharing. However, parents often meet and provide this for each other in informal ways. Sessions for parents may include information about special education, legislation, parent rights, resources, etc. A combination of professional and parent staff may also steer the group direction as opposed to one or the other. Some of these programs are administered through federal/funding with regional branches (Parent Training and Information Centers) in each state. Others are coordinated through disability-specific organizations (Epilepsy Foundation, The ARC) or university grant funded projects.

One such project, The Parent Information Project, was a program I initiated in 1990 in Indiana, Pennsylvania, with ten parents who found themselves at the university speech and hearing clinic waiting room on a weekly basis discussing ways to help their children while they passed time waiting for them to come out of therapy sessions. It was apparent that this informal network had great potential as a budding support tool for the parents and also for a much larger potential parent population in the area who needed resources. The development of this project and its format might be useful to readers as an illustration of how a small program can grow and develop into a multifaceted, widely used resource.

With meeting space donated by the university's Special Education Department, the project expanded to serve over 1200 families and provided external support in ways unimagined. Many parents who were supported learned to be confident about their knowledge, and this strengthened their role in educational meetings about their children *and* discussions with their spouse. What was initiated as a method to provide basic information and connections for parents grew exponentially to encompass a variety of support options. They included:

- Workshops featuring guest speakers
- Informal chat groups for parents to share experiences and helpful management strategies
- Matching of mentor parents to parents whose children were newly identified
- Direct/indirect advocacy—project staff (two professionals who were also parents of children with disabilities) met with parents individually to review reports from schools, individualized education programs, and give advice
- Lending library
- Parent newsletter

- Speaking opportunities for parents (some parents shared their insights and experiences in order to train better prepared professionals by speaking to university classes; several attended state and national conferences and were presenters or panelists)

The critical factor in the success of this program was its flexibility and concern about identifying the support needs of parents and responding to them in a meaningful way. The program was created by parents' suggestions based on their own support needs. In this manner, The Parent Information Project remained truly parent driven.

Internet Support

The Internet has virtually reduced the size of the world by enabling us to obtain information and communicate with people we don't even know. And in many ways, it has increased communication for both people with disabilities and their families. The Internet age has spawned the birth of numerous online groups such as Family Village, Schwab.org, LDonline, and many disability-specific groups which provide information, link to resources, list events, describe laws and rights, and host chat rooms where parents can communicate with each other at all hours of the day or night. The wonderful aspect of communicating with someone you don't know over the Internet is that you are anonymous, and, as numerous parents have discovered, you can assume more freedom in sharing feelings and insights that you might be hesitant about sharing with someone you knew. Conversely, you may find unexpected support by "chatting" with someone who shares information openly because they too are anonymous.

According to one mother:

66 The first place I found support was through an Internet group. That was my lifeline and I used to be online till two, three, four in the morning. There was one mom whose kid was born a week apart from mine, and our diagnoses were happening at the same time. To this day, I've never met this woman. We would be a great reunion

on a talk show because we shared this experience so intimately at night. She was my 'husband' and I was hers.

"I remember finishing a conversation with her and going in to talk with my husband who was working. I was mad that he was working because he had something else to do and I only had this. That was my first support with another parent—even though she couldn't really tell me how to handle things because we were both in the same place."

The same woman tells of meeting another parent online who helped her immensely over weeks of online conversations. Unbeknownst to her, he was a social worker who lived in the very next town:

"I was suicidal. I was very open. I needed that one place to let it all out. I was talking about things that must've made it seem like I was in terrible trouble, and the parent who was also a social worker got on and asked pointed questions that helped me a lot."

Some parents begin their own organizations or support systems through online sites such as KidPower Family Support at: www.kid-power.org.

Counseling

Self-help goes a long way but sometimes couples need direct, professional intervention.

A skilled therapist can serve as a unique resource either for an individual or a couple. Whereas some people welcome counseling, many have misconceptions that prevent them from using this source of help. One of the most common mistaken beliefs is that needing the services of a therapist equates with personal failing, and that if the couple tried harder, counseling would not be necessary. Another misconception is that counselors mostly listen and the same benefits can be gotten from talking to friends or family members.

People's expectations for counseling are often too low. They may not understand the benefits that can be reasonably expected and what qualities to expect from a therapist. We will begin with the question of what therapy can offer, especially if your problems are based on circumstances such as a child with significant problems. Part of the value of counseling is found in the fact that it is unlike all other relationships you may have in life.

A good therapist does not simply commiserate with you. The therapeutic process should produce far more than this. Therapists should initially strive to understand your world through your eyes, yet add new perspectives that enable you to manage life differently. Research on the effectiveness of psychotherapy indicates that improvement should be apparent within several weeks or months. By improvement, I am referring to some relief of distress, a sense that problems may be less overwhelming, and some changes in problem solving or emotional control. Something different should be in place as a result of good therapy.

People who "can't tell" over the course of several months whether therapy is working are typically either in need of different services, meeting with the wrong therapist, or, perhaps, reluctant to implement therapeutic suggestions. A good therapist needs to do far more than merely reflect back your own thoughts. However, the sharing of new ideas and perspective needs to be done in a manner that is not dogmatic and in a spirit of collaborating and consulting with you in order to find solutions and ideas that work for you. Amongst many functions, therapists can listen to your deepest fears and "confessions," sit with you in joy and sorrow, and help you set goals, recover from "setbacks," and find a place to begin when feeling overwhelmed.

Let me add that a good counselor does not need to have experienced the same problems as you in order to be helpful. An excellent therapist may or may not have children with disabilities or illness; the critical factor is whether he or she can listen and understand what it is like for you without preconceived notions. In other words, they "get it." Whereas some therapists with similar life experience may have good insight, they also may be sometimes mistakenly assume your situation is like theirs.

Qualities to look for in a therapist include:
- the ability to understand and empathize,
- the ability to be open to questions,
- a general lack of defensiveness, and

- the ability to respectfully express opinions that differ from your own.

It is also important that the therapist be able to provide ideas for you to employ between sessions as part of managing your life or marriage more effectively.

Regarding marital therapists, it is important the therapist helps you both eventually move beyond blame into mutual changes through creativity and active involvement. The quality of therapeutic input should ring true on a gut level even if you don't necessarily want to hear what has been expressed. For example, the therapist might raise the possibility that you have a role in creating a problem when you had previously thought it was entirely your spouse's fault. Good therapists can help get the message across in a way that enables you to change because they do not rob you of your dignity.

Therapists' credentials provide an indication of how much formal training they have. Licenses similarly provide some information. However, years of formal training do not always translate into being effective helpers. For example, a talented social worker may provide more help than some clinical psychologists. Talented, good, mediocre, and poor therapists can be found in all of the helping disciplines.

If you are in therapy and question its effectiveness, by all means, discuss your concerns with the therapist. It is reasonable to expect him or her to be able to discuss them in a productive manner and determine if something needs to change so that you can work together more productively. Good therapists may be perceptive, but they are not mind readers. Naturally, there are times it is reasonable to conclude that you are simply working with the wrong therapist and seeking another may result in vastly different results.

Therapeutic Marital Support

One couple that we interviewed for this book referred to the positive impact of marital counseling by noting that they periodically see a therapist in order to "shake up the snow globe." This is a fitting metaphor for the therapeutic process because it keys into one of the main benefits of marital therapy; that is, a skillful therapist can help couples see new perspectives and question assumptions that have held some dysfunctional patterns or emotions in place. It can often help people get "unstuck." One of the goals of therapy is often to enable individuals or couples to manage their problems without the therapist's help in the future.

One of the many benefits of marital counseling is that it provides a safe setting to discuss difficult things. The presence of a good therapist often provides a way to limit extreme reactions so that both partners can have the emotional space to express themselves completely and to listen thoughtfully to each other. It is not unusual for a partner's words to be understood in new ways when a therapist mediates the process. The therapist may say something to your spouse that you have said a million times and suddenly your spouse will think it is a great point (as if he or she had never heard it before). A counselor is often able to present new points of view to both partners in a way that they can hear them without being defensive and mobilize both to try some new things. The counselor should feel like a helpful collaborator for *both* spouses.

Sessions may include a venting of emotion and a rehashing of problems but, for the most part, need to extend far beyond these. It is best when the therapist helps each partner identify what new behaviors they can try out in between sessions. The main exception is when there has been an affair. In this case, many more sessions are generally spent on emotional venting and this catharsis is often necessary for a long time before a couple moves on. On the topic of affairs, marital therapy is often very helpful to the healing process; however, it is futile if the affair is ongoing during therapy. See Chapter 10 for more discussion about affairs.

With the exception of healing an affair, it is reasonable to expect that some progress should be apparent after about five sessions. Progress may include a somewhat better understanding of each other, less hostility, new ways of communicating, or even an improved desire to work on the marriage together.

It is almost typical that if I advise a wife that she suggest marital counseling to her husband, she replies, "I'll *ask*, but I don't think he'll go." Sometimes it is the reverse, yet men are generally hesitant about counseling. My experience has consistently been that husbands tend to agree with much more readiness than anticipated— often at the first request. Although it is not always this simple, in my twenty years of experience, the vast majority of spouses have agreed to come for counseling if the request is stated in a manner that does not put them on the defensive.

If you are trying to get your spouse to go with you to counseling, it is useful to emphasize that although you are initiating the request, you feel it would help *both* of you. For example: "I think we need someone to help both of us sort out these problems. I believe that neither of us feels this marriage is working as well as we had hoped." The art is in dispelling the notion that going to marital counseling will be a lot like going to the principal's office as a child. If you are sincere in expressing the desire to have someone help the two of you move forward in your relationship, you have a strong chance that your spouse will agree. It sometimes helps to ask a reluctant spouse to agree to come to *one* session and see how he feels about it.

It may also be useful to know that even if the two of you have tried marital counseling before, this does not mean that it cannot be done again with better results. A great deal depends on finding the right therapist. Word of mouth from friends is one good method. In any case, a talented therapist can make a monumental difference.

We asked the father of twins born with severe multiple disabilities what he thought was the most important advice to give a couple in a similar situation. Understanding the magnitude of the issues many couples face, he stated that counseling is critical "from day one." Another parent with similar sentiments wrote: "A personal counselor, helping the whole family unit, has been invaluable in sustaining our marriage."

Although most couples use marital counseling on a short-term basis, some use it as an ongoing resource. The mother of a child with an autism spectrum disorder wrote that she and her husband have undergone therapeutic counseling constantly for eleven years, which has helped their family tremendously.

Friends and Family

All too often, parents assume total responsibility for their child while neglecting friends and family, ultimately resulting in social isolation and loss of interaction. Some parents become isolated because of life experiences that shift their perspectives. One parent talked about friends drifting away because they "no longer knew how to relate to us," even though they had been friends for years. Isolation from family is also an issue for couples whose relatives have excluded the child from family events, causing tension rather than support.

One danger of social isolation is the obvious absence of supports and lack of contact with people and situations beyond your own. That contact may be critical as a lens with which to view the world outside of your own issues, a way to balance perspective. Another danger in social isolation for couples is that members of the couple may disagree about whether they should withdraw from groups and contact with family. Without any outside friendship or family supports, your views and reactions to each other may become restricted and strained. Good social supports from friends and family should be recognized as a normalizing force for parents as individuals as well as for couples.

I am a big believer in energy audits. With our homes, it is practical to look at where we have "leaks" that cause energy to be wasted. In our close relationships with family and friends, it is similarly important to maximize our sources of energy.

Friendships

[Not all friendships are equally supportive.]

Friendships naturally go through phases during which time the proportions of giving and receiving support fluctuate. But overall, there should be a good reciprocal balance. Some friends, without making judgments or giving advice, provide valuable support by reflecting back your own thoughts that help you evaluate your circumstances or situation. Some friends, especially those who also have children with disabilities, can be safe places in the harbor because they probably would not be shocked by your feelings and reactions, and they may be the only people who have been able to identify with your experiences through their own. They may also share the strange sense of humor that many of us develop as a coping strategy. One mother said she had a pact with two other friends that should something happen to her, the friends would intervene to advocate for her child since no one else (including her husband) understood the educational and social issues as intimately.

This is not to say that parents of children with disabilities should only seek out other parents in similar circumstances as friends. Disability is only one component of life.

Friends can provide support in multiple ways, with concrete assistance and on a more emotional level that doesn't always directly involve discussing disability issues. Friendships based on personal interests and hobbies can benefit you by getting you involved in other activities and helping you be a well-rounded person.

Some friendships may change over time and take on different dimensions. Once supportive, friendships can take a different direction and become detrimental and counterproductive.

[
It is important to assess, over time, whether a friendship is adding to your life or taking a negative toll on it.
]

One parent shared with us that her long-term friends repeatedly offered her unsolicited advice. Although her friends intended to be helpful, their companionship left her feeling that she wasn't good enough. She also became tired of discussing disability issues all the time. She distanced herself to change those relationships and made concerted efforts to find new friends who didn't know her through the lens of her child's disability. She has located new friends who support her in different ways, by sharing interests and recognizing her strengths as a person without ever discussing disability. She also compartmentalizes whom she talks to about her children and just doesn't share as much anymore.

[
Some friends may contribute to marital adjustment while some may undermine it.
]

Friends can influence our views of our own marriages significantly. Sometimes if your friend is unhappy in his or her marriage, this spills over into your relationship. For instance, your friend may press you to agree about how rotten marriage is. On the other hand, friends who are healthier for your marriage can commiserate with your marital discontent without making matters worse by increasing your negative feelings toward your spouse.

> **"I**think a healthy friendship is one in which our friend can support us while we vent but does not add fuel to the fire. My best friends listen to me when I speak of my disappointments with my husband, yet they gently point out his good qualities so I don't lose perspective."

Friendships between males and females seem to differ in nature and the specific type of supports they may provide. In general, men's discussions revolve less around personal issues while women's discussions cover everything from in-laws to parenting to family arguments and issues. And invariably, if you get two women together who both have kids with disabilities, it's an immediate icebreaker if they don't know each other, and an ongoing topic of conversation if they are already friends.

This doesn't necessarily mean that men don't share the same concerns as their wives, but they may express them differently or may not be comfortable verbalizing them to male friends. Men handle their relationships differently and may find support simply through sharing activities rather than conversations. It is important for women to recognize this is an equally important and valid source of social support, even if it appears less valuable to them than their own preferred style of interacting.

Parents and Extended Family

[Sometimes we find help where we least expect it.]

As a parent, you expect that as you move toward middle age, you may be assuming more responsibility in caring for your own aging parents. You may anticipate becoming a member of the "sandwich generation," caring for your children and parents at the same time. You rarely consider how important or necessary good support from your own parents might be, in ways that maintain your marriage as you parent children with disabilities. We have no difficulty thinking of our aging parents as needing help, but often hesitate to ask for their help. This is the reaction of a couple who were fortunate to have unexpected help from aging parents:

"**W**e moved from another state to be close to our octogenarian parents thinking they might need our help. Ironically, with the sudden onset of our son's life-threatening disability, it was our parents who helped us by being available, running errands, cooking, cleaning, and providing child care for months on end—which kept us from losing our jobs. The way they jumped in helped to save our sanity. If we hadn't moved back, those supports would've been absent and eight hours away. Serendipitously, their involvement allowed us some semblance of a family life, but also gave them an important sense of purpose at a time when many elderly couples are feeling irrelevant and undervalued in our society."

[Sometimes we need to ask in order to get.]

Major obstacles to receiving enough support from your family may be in avoiding discussion of your child's disability and also not explicitly asking for help.

Some parents we interviewed feel that they don't get family support even though they do ask for it. Actually, many participants in our book spoke of problems stemming from a failure of family members to understand their child's disability. This seems most common when the child's disability is not visible. A lack of understanding, often combined with denial, can result in minimizing both the child's needs as well as those of the parents. This is exemplified in comments such as "he'll grow out of it" even when faced with diagnoses such as autism spectrum disorder:

"**S**ome family members still don't get who our son is. They buy him baseball gloves, bats, ball when all he wants to do is stand and watch trains. He can no more catch a ball than he can catch the moon. But they feel that buying him 'normal' things will make him 'normal.' They are always saying how he is getting better and he just has a cold or something."

Some relatives feel that such comments help, while some of them actually believe that the child will just grow out of it. Sometimes it helps to explain what the facts are, that their concern is appreciated but that their support in understanding and being realistic will actually help the child advance. For example, explain that Johnny's hearing will not improve, *no* he doesn't have a cold or wax in his ears, and that his language has been affected because he can't hear. Also explain that Johnny can be very productive and happy, is still very smart, but in order to plan for a positive future, he may need a different way to learn.

Sometimes children are treated as if they are simply unruly, disrespectful, or stupid by extended family. In these cases, visits with family can be dreaded. Equally upsetting are situations in which the child is excluded from family events.

And then there are relatives who feel they are the experts:

"**E**veryone in our families feels free to give us advice, but no one really knows what we go through day in and day out. My in-laws insist we visit them and they refuse to visit us. They do not understand why a strict schedule has to be followed in my house. 'The kids can go without a schedule for a day,' my mother-in-law would say, but she does not have to live in my house the rest of the day after this sacred schedule is broken."

It makes sense to try a variety of ways to educate these family members about your child's disorder. Strategies you can try:
- Watch a video about the disorder with them.
- Ask them to accompany you to a conference or parent group to hear what other parents have to say.
- Take them to a school meeting to hear about the educational issues discussed.

Although obviously not all family members will help, efforts to get them on the same page in terms of understanding the issues is important and worth the initial investment of energy.

[You may need to do an "energy audit" on how you spend
your energies with family members.]

There are indeed circumstances that may require you to think about spending less time with your parents and other family members. As uncomfortable as this is to think about, you may find that less time with family enables you to feel better. Practically speaking, it may be too much to expect of yourself to watch your child be excluded or to have another lecture about how the problem is with your parenting skills.

Religious Institutions

Although the issue of religion was already addressed in Chapter 7, in this chapter we are discussing people *and organizations* associated with religious institutions. Parents have discussed the value of support from "church families" who bring "prayers, meals, and listening ears." One parent said that her parish priest could not have been more welcoming. Another said "the church has been our only salvation and the only reason I am still married to this person."

For many, the church, synagogue, temple or other religious organization represents a type of family and many such organizations are very supportive of family unity and stability. If both spouses are in agreement, having a sense of belonging to a congregation or being supported by a religious leader may actually strengthen and validate a couple's responses to their child and to each other.

[Teach your leaders. They can learn from you too.]

Another wonderful resource for those seeking more support in religious institutions is the Religion and Disability Program at National Organization on Disability in Washington, DC. This organization works with congregations and ministerial professionals all over the country to sensitize religious leaders and congregants to these issues both in terms of having a welcoming community spiritually for everyone, and having physical access for people with disabilities to attend services, school, programs, etc. *That All May Worship* is an excellent publication available through their office and is an informative guide for religious leaders and institutional staff about including everyone.

Negotiating the Maze of Services

In seeking out sources of support for your family and child, be sure to explore overlooked services that may be valuable supports.

Two parents emphasize the need to be persistent in locating the help you need:

> **"I** didn't know what I needed to know (said one parent of a medically fragile child who didn't even know what to ask). I needed to be taught and asked personnel in the hospital to describe everything they were doing. It's important to talk, ask questions, and keep asking for help. Don't stop until you have the answers."

> **"A** sk doctors, nurses, social workers and everyone if there are services available or resources to tap into. It almost seems that you have to trudge through a muddy maze to find all the resources available to you. If you don't like your doctor or therapist, find another one."

Hospital Social Workers

One mother remembers that the person who helped the most before her baby with a congenital disability ever left the hospital was a social worker in the neonatal intensive care unit. She was reassured at a time when she was still in shock from finding out that both of her twins had profound disabilities. This social worker helped to involve her, helped her to gain perspective, and reminded her to nurture her marriage. Once her children became a little older, this mother provided the same support for other parents in the

NICU and worked with the hospital to try to assure that such supports could be available.

Social workers can be invaluable sources of support to families, particularly soon after the birth of a child with a major disability. In a world of sometimes sterile institutional care, these are special people who become involved in the fiber of the family and can use their knowledge and insight to strengthen relationships, find solutions to issues like therapy needs, or information on how to navigate the healthcare bureaucracy without destroying your credit rating, emptying your bank account, or having to remortgage your home to pay medical and treatment bills.

In some hospitals and clinics, the role of the social worker is to support the family by *answering* questions and providing morale support and also by *asking* questions of the medical specialist for them, perhaps questions they have not even discussed. The reasoning behind this is that this may be a traumatic time when your child is being diagnosed with a life-threatening disorder. You are overwhelmed, overloaded, and not processing well enough to ask the questions you would have thought of if the context of the meeting were different. Therefore, he poses questions aloud, and the doctor responds with options and answers.

Because of the social worker's questions, one family sought consultation and treatment from a fertility specialist for their adolescent son who was about to receive medical treatment that would most definitely affect his developing system. That visit may have changed his future, and the parents were so focused on other aspects of treatment that they would never have asked the question.

How do you locate these services in hospitals or other service provider organizations where you may see numerous specialists and medical staff without any regularity? Ideally, procedures are designed to be family centered, and social workers, nursing staff, and physicians are patient friendly. If this is not the case, ask to speak with the social worker or identify a staff member to ally yourself with. This person can be invaluable to you. Sometimes pediatric units have parent volunteers who are very helpful for parents new to the process. Speak with the physician often so he knows who you are and the nature of your child's issues. Hospitals also have patient advocates who are there to work with families and assure that the patient is getting the best possible service.

Wrap-around

Mental health, mental retardation, and other state-supported community centers (often funded by Office of Mental Retardation/ Developmental Disabilities funds or Vocational/Educational Services) provide other types of support. An example of these services are wraparound services or therapeutic staff support that are usually earmarked for children with multiple and/or severe levels of disability. *Wrap-around* signifies just that. In the past, children who received numerous services delivered by different professionals may have had very fragmented services. "Wrap-around" addresses the need for coordination in service provision.

> " The best outside support my husband and I have received is from wrap-around services. These are individuals who come to the house twenty hours a week for one of our sons with autism and twelve hours a week for the other son. They do the kids' therapies and spend one-on-one time with each of the boys. The wrap-around services make it possible for my husband and me to spend extra time with our other two children, clean the house, and spend some time simply sitting and talking to each other. Through wraparound services, a behavior specialist comes to the house and helps us learn to discipline the children. My husband and I seem to let out a lot of frustration with her. She always comes back the next visit with solutions to the problems. We have a case manager and advocate who visit the children in school and report back to us about how the kids are doing. The advocate also reports to the boys' doctor."

Information on wrap-around services may be provided by your community mental health counseling center, child social service clinic, or the ARC. As illustrated above, many children who receive these services receive behavior support.

Respite Care

Respite services through your Department of Social Services can help you find some time together without the children. As discussed by parents who participated in the book, this time together can lead to an increase in communication.

What is respite care? It is short-term temporary care for children or adults with disabilities or chronic conditions. Some people think of respite as babysitting or child care services, but frequently this service may be provided overnight or for several days. Frequently it is provided by individuals with expertise in a specific disability or health condition. Most importantly, these care providers support families while preventing overload, burnout, or abuse. The availability of respite care may mean the difference between whether a family can care for their child in their own home or must send him to a residential placement.

How do you find respite services, who provides them, and how are they funded? Various types of agencies provide respite and many meet licensing standards, meaning that their workers have some type of credential. They track and do follow-up on families served and may perform periodic inspections. Some respite services are publicly funded, while some charge based on your ability to pay. National nonprofit organizations frequently are a source of respite care (ARC, UCP, Easter Seals). So too are local grass roots groups or religious groups. Community mental health or guidance centers often provide such help. The National Locator Service, although not a complete directory, can help you locate services in your local area (www.respitelocator.org).

If your family is currently working with a social worker or counselor, try asking him or her for information or referrals or contact national organizations. Each state has a Developmental Disabilities Council, which may be a source of assistance and they may have a Respite Coalition as well. Respite Coalitions promote respite in policy and programs at national, state, and local levels. To find out more go to www.Archrespite.org.

A common misperception is that respite is like charity—for the poor and truly needy—and therefore, maybe you can't access it. Although sometimes income is a consideration, often it is not. Clearly, parents can be needy for reasons other than financial. Respite services may be just what you need.

Conclusion

Outside sources of support are extremely important in providing tools, clarifying our needs, and identifying and accessing resources. These supports strengthen us and may help to make us more informed, but do not replace responsible parenting and decision making. As this parent indicated:

> "It helps to have a good circle of friends, lover, siblings, parents, but ultimately you need information and to make decisions, and the conclusions you come to may be different than those of another parent. You don't lose who you are because you have become the parent of a child with a disability. You're still the same person but you have to learn another set of skills."

Do not underestimate the value of outside supports. Many of those supports can end up being critical to your sense of wellbeing and control. Although you and your spouse may not find the same resources helpful, proactive exploration of what is available will provide direction and options that will assist you.

Chapter Ten

Serious Marital Troubles

Laura E. Marshak, Ph.D.

If problems in your marriage have reached a point where you question the value of your relationship, this chapter is for you. It covers factors that color people's perception of the viability of their marriages and discusses several problems that, if unchecked, will deeply erode the foundation of a marriage. Serious marital troubles we refer to include sustained resentment, detachment, and affairs.

We will begin with the comments and advice of a woman whose marriage ended in divorce:

"Our first and only child was unexpectedly born in 1995 with Down syndrome. What had previously been a good marriage became full of problems of acceptance, coping, and adapting to our new roles as parents. The time that I had previously spent indulgently on my husband was consumed with caring for our son. This ultimately was a real marriage buster. My once attentive husband took up two new loves—music and motorcycles—which led him to spend more time away from home. It took me a year of grieving and guilt—including severe depression and getting into therapy—before I could accept Down syndrome in my son."

It is clear that many marriages that end in divorce do so for matters unrelated to having children with disabilities. It is not clear that this woman's marriage would have survived under other circumstances, but it is clear that several of the seeds for its demise were disability related. These included her overwhelming grief, her husband's and her failure to stay connected as a couple as each attempted to cope, and problems readjusting marital roles to meet new demands.

The wife offers three pieces of advice based on hindsight and an understanding that marital problems are often contributed to when *both* partners overlook aspects of the marriage:

- Talk. Talk. Talk. Your child is "perfect" as is. Don't get stuck in a blame game to deal with the guilt of having an unexpected child.
- Don't exclude your partner from sharing caretaking. This is his (or her) child and responsibility too.
- Don't retreat from home to avoid adjusting.

Look at Your Marriage More Clearly

It is important to look at your marriage as objectively as possible if you are experiencing significant disappointment with it. Although being disheartened about your marriage does not always lead to divorce, at a minimum it usually results in a marriage in which one or both partners is no longer trying to make a marriage.

[Remember that love often develops from struggles that are resolved over time.]

Many people are disappointed that the period of enchantment so characteristic of the beginning of romantic relationships is typically followed by a period of disenchantment. If you don't understand that such a period is inevitable, you may become unduly negative about the future of your marriage. In reality, various combinations of acceptance, problem solving, and commitment can enable a couple to navigate this period and other rocky periods that may follow. Typically, by working through periods of disenchantment, you reach maturation as a couple and more sustained periods of contentment.

One parent we interviewed for this book was very articulate about what she saw as the essence of marital life:

66 **Y**ou have to realize that marriage is a struggle. And it doesn't matter what the issue is—every marriage has a struggle. (You just don't realize that the people next door have theirs.) On the other hand, if you are not married, you also struggle. Relationships are a struggle. Life is a struggle."

While you are in the midst of working through problems in a marriage, it is sometimes hard to recognize that you may be on the road to a different yet more mature marriage. This is not to say that all rocky periods are on the path to maturity; this would be falsely optimistic. Let me add that sometimes we do marry the "wrong person" or a person for the "wrong reasons." *Some* of these marriages do work out well nonetheless; of course, this is not true for all of them.

Time is essential when evaluating your marriage. This is particularly true when disability enters the picture because of the initial upheaval that may be caused. This reminds me of the upheaval when a house undergoes major renovations—it is an awful mess for a while before it becomes a very nice home.

Personal Factors

Early life experiences with love may distort your view. If you did not receive sufficient love in childhood, this can make it harder for you to accurately appraise your marriage. First, some people continue to feel unloved even though they are involved with a loving spouse. They are often skeptical of expressions of affection, questioning whether the partner truly means to be loving. Furthermore, people who did not receive adequate love in childhood are particularly prone to feeling rejected by relatively minor events.

Just as some fail to recognize the extent of love they actually receive from a spouse, others may accept poor treatment because their childhood experiences did not provide them with an ability to differentiate between love and abuse and/or neglect. These are only some of the ways that emotional wounds from childhood may affect your ability to objectively evaluate your marriage.

Note, however, that a skillful therapist can be a valuable partner in disentangling the past from the present.

Midlife and Other Crises

Adult developmental crises may greatly distort how we look at our marriages. Most people have heard of midlife crises. They involve a preoccupation with time marching by, an awareness of mortality, and a fear that you are not living the life you want. Other life events can also jolt people into this frame of mind. It can be the sudden awareness that we have lost our youth (and freedom), signified by the birth of children. These feelings may be heightened if the child born has a disability because the future may appear to be a road full of unremitting obligations and responsibilities. Flaws in a marital partner are magnified and seen as limiting potential happiness in life. In other words, you may feel trapped in life with your partner.

The death of your own parents may also result in a period of marital problems. Some people feel "liberated" from desires to please their parents and may question the value of hanging in there with a difficult home situation. Having a parent die, especially if it is the remaining parent, also often triggers a fleeing into what *feels* like life-affirming activities. Often there are increases in affairs at these times.

Depression

Depression is an additional personal factor to be aware of if you are trying to decide whether your marriage is viable. Depression often makes situations look more hopeless than they are. One woman, now happily married, commented on the irrationality of her thought processes during a life-threatening bout of depression triggered by the birth of twins with severe disabilities and the upheaval that followed.

"My husband and I were just living parallel lives during the time I was depressed. So I had that urge to leave. I actually vacillated about taking the kids. I was going to split with them at one point. But I was also planning my suicide. I had that worked out. I have always been very detail oriented regardless of what my plans were. I was vacillating between the two courses of action, and suicide was winning for a long time. That is when I went into therapy and I actually ended up on medication— just for a year and I started to feel better. Eventually, a really good social worker helped us both pull through."

Cognitive Style

Your own way of thinking, or cognitive style, may lead you to lose objectivity. More specifically, all people have selective attention because it is not humanly possible to pay attention to all that occurs in our lives. What you habitually tend to pay attention to colors your view and has implications for your marriage. Watch out for the common problem of focusing on the deficits and overlooking the strengths of your marriage. For example, I spoke with a woman who used the fact that her husband ignored her twenty-pound weight loss as evidence of his lack of love for her. As the conversation continued she was able to recall that he never commented on an approximately sixty-pound weight gain either. She realized then that it was not disregard—rather, that he loved her at all sizes. It is important to look at both deficits and assets in order to objectively evaluate a marriage's potential.

The common practice of seeing some things as "symbolic" causes a similar loss of perspective in looking at your marriage as a whole. When we selectively elevate behavior and label it as "symbolic" we are saying this reflects the *true nature* of things. More often than not, this sweeping judgment skews the bigger picture. For example, one woman described seeing her husband step over a puddle on the kitchen floor and spoke at length about how this symbolized his true belief that all the housework should fall on her. While making this single event symbolic, she was effectively discounting all the times that he did indeed help. Another example would be a husband who felt that his wife's failure to remember their anniversary with a card was symbolic of her not valuing the marriage.

Additional Considerations

Here are three other factors that may contribute to serious marital difficulties:

1. If a child has a genetic disorder, one or both spouses may also have symptoms of the disorder.

For example, mothers of children with fragile X syndrome are "carriers" and may themselves have some fragile X traits. Children with AD/HD frequently have one or more parents who also have AD/HD, and learning disabilities and autism spectrum disorders sometimes "run in the family."

> **"It** is useful to consider a spouse's intentions rather than simply judging specific behaviors. Disappointments and hurts that were not intended are a different matter than those that were intentional. This is particularly relevant when your spouse has a disorder that disrupts his or her functioning. If you look closely, your partner may have some of the same traits as your children who may have full-blown disorders."

2. Having a child with a disability my reduce tolerance for your spouse's shortcomings.

For instance, one woman said: "I have a special-needs son—I can't also have a special-needs husband." This point of view is commonly seen in marriages where there is a child with special needs. This woman's viewpoint resonates with the subconscious belief that somehow in the cosmic scheme of things we *should* have fewer difficulties with our spouse to compensate us for all the extra work and possible problems. There is no "special-needs dispensation," however.

3. Your view of your marriage is very likely distorted if you are having an affair.

Objective evaluation of the potential of your marriage is nearly impossible while you are having an affair. Feelings of infatuation greatly affect judgment. Furthermore, feelings of guilt often lead people to rationalize their involvement in an extramarital relationship. This is typically done by focusing on your partner's "flaws." Not only is this an excuse, but you may also end up distorting your perceptions of your partner at a time when it is critically important to keep him or her in realistic perspective.

What Is a "Good Enough" Marriage?

Judith Viorst is one of several experts who have written of unrealistic expectations we bring to a marriage based on unfulfilled needs of the past; often these are childhood needs:

> "Whether consciously or unconsciously, we always ask more of a marriage than marriage can give us. We idealize the person we marry; no matter how certain we are that we're seeing clearly. We bring our secret hopes to the married state."

The concept of being "a good enough" parent is fairly well known and based on the recognition that one does not have to be a perfect parent in order to provide a child what he or she needs. The same holds true for marriages. Excellent marriages are not perfect at all. Rather, they are characterized by merits and some disappointments; however, disappointments are kept in perspective and don't overshadow the positives. It is not unusual for excellent marriages to be made with partners who have flaws and deficits.

One mother of a child with Down syndrome offered the following advice on determining whether your marriage can be successful:

> "If you can answer "yes" to these two questions, then your marriage has a fighting chance: 1) Does he love me? And 2) Does he love and accept our child? If you have love, you can work on accepting the differences in dealing with your child's disability."

This does not mean that you should regard everything that troubles you about your spouse simply as a flaw. You need to sort out for yourself what is the bottom line in a marriage that can't be crossed. It is necessary to separate the large, critical (bottom line) issues from those that are less important.

Dealing with Deficits

For those whose marriages are within reach of being "good enough," a common need is to learn to love and accept. Given that deficits are inevitable in "good enough" marriages, we need to return to the principle of changing what can be changed and accepting what can't *within limits*. Not everything should be accepted. Abusive behaviors, active addiction, and repeated infidelity are a few problems that absolutely preclude a workable marriage. If you are dealing with any of these issues, we suggest you turn to Chapter 12.

In the introductory chapter, we wrote of the importance of working as a team. Teams take for granted that members have their strengths and weaknesses and make necessary accommodations for this. Spouses can be likened to copilots of the family plane. Taking this analogy a step further, if you were flying together in a plane that needed skill to maneuver safely, you wouldn't spend much time criticizing the copilot for inadequacies. Rather, the focus would be on pitching in and assisting the copilot to do his or her best.

Very often, I see people for therapy who are upset about their partner's shortcomings and express resignation that they are simply part of their partner's personality—*"That's just the way he is."* This brings us to the complicated issue of what is fair or practical to expect a partner to change. My own belief is that you need to limit requested changes to the behaviors that are most important in making the difference between a reasonably good marriage and one that is not. This is not to say, over time, you can't simultaneously improve how you function together as a couple.

A woman who initially assumed her marriage was untenable spoke of growing beyond this point. She spoke of a lesson she had to be "taught" by a psychologist who helped her with this growth.

> "Instead of giving up on my spouse, why not train him to be supportive? This last lesson was pivotal in my understanding of my marriage. I began to train my husband to be helpful instead of stewing about his lack of support, and it has made a world of difference in our marriage."

By "training," this woman is referring to the practice of being clear and specific about asking for what she needs, and being positive about recognizing progress even if the progress is not absolute. In her case, she found it advantageous to spell out which specific behaviors she needed from her husband rather than continue to engage in discussions about his not being "helpful."

When working with couples, I sometimes use the analogy of the "new growth" of behavior change being like tender young plants. For a small new plant to survive, we need to see that its environment is tended to, the soil is tilled, and that it receives nourishment. Similarly, a spouse's new growth needs to be protected and nurtured within a marital environment. This means you must take care to support, rather than inadvertently undermine, change. Points to bear in mind about encouraging changes in behavior:

- Behavior change will be undermined if you ask for, but don't recognize and reinforce, your partner's attempts at behavior change.
- Remember that success breeds success. If you fail to reinforce changes because you are upset about other behaviors, your partner may decide it is hopeless to try to please you.

Living in Limbo

Some of you will find that problems are bad enough that it is unclear whether or not your marriage is workable. The wisest course of action is to work really hard on your part of the marriage *and* your own life while the verdict is out. What gives you strength to hang in there and do your part while in limbo and trying to control your frustration with slowness of change? How do you not criticize, nag, fight, and worry?

- Remember that you need to do your part well for a limited period of time—not forever.
- Don't hover over your marriage. As hard as it is, get into the habit of seeing your marriage as only one of several important parts of life.
- Develop other aspects of life such as new friendships or hobbies, or involve yourself in education or career activities.
- Recognize your need for refueling so that you can continue to work on the behaviors you need to give the marriage the best chance to succeed. This can take many forms such as going for a walk, getting an absorbing book, finding the time for coffee with a friend, etc.
- Bear in mind that all your efforts to manage your life well will be fruitful regardless of the ultimate outcome of the marriage. Ultimately, you are taking the high road for yourself.

Problems That Erode the Foundation of a Marriage

Detachment

We spoke of the importance of connectedness in previous chapters. The reverse, detachment, underlies many of the most serious problems that can beset a marriage. With detachment, we withdraw our feelings and stop investing in the marriage. Not surprisingly, it withers. Energy that had once been invested in the marriage goes elsewhere. It may go into the children, addictions, affairs, work, or other separate pursuits. The diminishment of talking is an important warning sign. Arguing at least still means that you are connected. Silence is worse.

Detachment is sometimes caused by a spouse feeling overwhelmed. It may also be fueled by a need to maintain denial over the seriousness of a child's problems:

"For the first four years, my husband refused to believe our son has autism. This year, he finally admitted it, but he doesn't want to talk about it."

When someone is overwhelmed, it is necessary to make things as manageable as possible so they don't simply flee in mind, body, or spirit. You may have already tried to lighten the load, but it is helpful to manage your own distress and stretch as much as possible to make the home livable. I say this with awareness that it would be easy to misinterpret my intent here. I am not suggesting that your spouse's needs are more important ultimately than your own. I also hesitate to sound as if I don't understand that you are not already overwhelmed yourself at times. But, in the shorter run, this is necessary advice. I am not saying that all the pressure should be on you—rather, if your spouse is in danger of fleeing, the priority is to get her back into the home and marriage. Over the longer haul, a better balance needs to be restored. This is a temporary strategy.

One father emphasized that there is a critical point in terms of being detached from each other:

" There is sort of a gravitational pull and at some point you spin out of the reach of that gravitational pull and . . . you know what? You are in outer space and you are out of the relationship. And you never can connect again. You can't. You are past that point."

How do you reconnect if things have gotten to the point that you rarely talk? As mentioned before, behavioral patterns in marriages become reciprocal to some extent. My advice is to change your part of the disconnection. This means swallowing your own hurt and anger and repeatedly initiating contact. Sometimes getting physically closer promotes conversation even in more estranged couples. So, make opportunities to be side by side. For example, join your partner while she weeds the flower bed, suggest you drive out with her while she drives to pick up someone at the airport, or sit down with your partner as she is eating breakfast alone. It may be sitting on the patio and asking your partner to join you. An attempt to reconnect starts with the decision that you will try regardless of whether your partner is ready to or not. It may require a thick skin at first because a pattern of rejection may have been established.

Sometimes detachment is due to significant untreated emotional problems. Then the solutions are beyond the scope of the marriage itself and additional assistance is necessary. For example, severe depression or substance abuse can be so powerful an influence that the other partner simply cannot make the marriage work.

Resentment

[Sustained feelings of strong resentment are dangerous to a marriage.]

There are probably few marriages without some resentment. However, if these feelings are allowed to proliferate, they are destructive. Earlier in the book, I used the metaphor of a garden to describe marriage. Resentment and the ill will that is generally an element of resentment can be likened to weeds or plants that are so invasive they crowd out the others and keep them from thriving.

Excerpts from a description one woman provided of her marriage illustrate how common resentments, held by both husband and wife, emerge:

"He resented the time I spent trying to find ways for our child to communicate and to obtain the best educational setting for him. Meanwhile, I have grown to be very resentful of his extracurricular activities. I cannot 'take a vacation day or days' during the school week without having to pull together respite care, transportation, and a variety of other supports. My competition is the mistress of the great outdoors. I resent the way he uses his vacation time."

If you have mounting resentment, there are only two choices:
1. Continue to try to fix the problem in a variety of ways (see Chapter 4).
2. If this doesn't work (and you want to sustain your marriage), you need to find a way to live with your resentment as a perpetual problem.

One of the worst choices is to remain resentful and upset on an ongoing basis. Then you have neither much of a marriage nor a life on your own. Relegating a conflict to the role of a perpetual problem involves a change of perspective. Sometimes this has to do with making sure you don't get "self-righteous" and trying to find some merit in your spouse's viewpoint. My experience over the years as a psychologist and marital therapist has impressed me with the fact that there is usually another quite compelling side of "the story" of marital conflict.

If the problem is not going to change, you may need to change how you look at it—*for your own sake.* Dwelling on resentment makes us relive that very incident(s) that angered or hurt us in the first place.

Sometimes when resenting a spouse's perceived shortcomings, it is useful and humbling to ask yourself, "What is it like to be married to me?" Chances are you have your own shortcomings in the marriage that also need to be accepted. This is sometimes useful as a way not to ignite the embers of your smoldering resentment by adding the fuel of self-righteousness. I have found it helpful to understand that all people are flawed and naturally bring this into the marriage.

Resentment is one of those "it's not fair" problems. We need to find ways to accept that we can't necessarily fix the problem that is causing the resentment and make other aspects of life more pleasant. You may need to do it creatively and in ways that do not revolve around your partner. Sometimes I have asked myself if I can still have a good life if a problem does not change. Generally it is "yes" unless I get stuck on thinking my spouse *must* be how I would want him to be if he came custom ordered. People tolerate disappointments and a sense of injustice better when other aspects of life are better. There are times to de-invest energy in some problems and build up new sources of pleasure in terms of activities and friends.

Forgiveness

Forgiveness is a necessary element in marriage. There is the type of casual forgiveness that we need sometimes to practice daily when we let go of smaller disappointments and grievances. Without this, we create conflict and haul around grudges. Then there are larger difficult aspects of forgiveness.

It is important to understand what constitutes forgiveness of these large hurts. Contrary to common belief, it does not require you to relinquish all negative feelings stemming from your partner's "wrongdoing." It also does not mean that all hurt and anger are resolved. Rather, it means that you essentially release your partner from your desire for retribution. In addition, you permit positive feelings toward your partner to exist side by side with more negative feelings.

[Forgiveness does not require us to ever accept the behavior that caused us harm; rather, we are simply enabling our partner to dig his or her way out of the hole.]

Dictionary definitions of forgiveness include phrases such as "to grant freedom" and "cease to demand penalty." As hard as forgiveness can be, lack of forgiveness is a state that is barely compatible with marriage. Forgiveness enables our partner to be accepted as an equal partner in the marriage. Without forgiveness, she remains in a "one-down" position, which eventually becomes unlivable.

Sometimes one partner appears to be perpetually in "debt" to the other with no conceivable "final payment" in sight. This brings to mind bankruptcy laws which enable people to get a "fresh start." If there is no way out of a "marital debt," the temptation is to simply eventually leave. The loss of any hope in the marriage is often its demise. Forgiveness involves relegating an event or series of events to the past. This enables us to move forward, although this does not imply that we are forgetting the past. Rather, it means that new life can be lived in this marriage; new experiences and new feelings are able to develop.

I certainly am not advocating forgiveness under all circumstances. Some people put undue pressure on themselves to be a "forgiving person." The conditions may not be in place for forgiveness to be reasonable. The following three factors facilitate forgiveness.

1. Apologize.

If you are the one to cause hurt, bear in mind that a sincere apology often works far better than explaining "why" you did it. This is a simple but underused skill.

"My husband does not like to apologize. But when he does, there is nothing that melts my anger like a simple, 'I'm sorry—I will try not to do it again.' End of story. Resentment that I thought I could not get rid of without a huge effort no longer seems to be much of a problem. I wish he would remember how well it works."

2. Allow your spouse to make amends.

It is optimal if forgiveness is a shared process involving a flow between you and your partner. The hurt individual is better able to move toward forgiveness if she is able to spell out the impact of the hurtful behavior while her partner hears her out without resorting to explanation or defense. The pain and hurt has to be acknowledged. You also need to begin to think about what you need from your partner to help achieve a state of forgiveness. This may include what can be done to make amends or how to begin to repair the relationship. Often this involves an act that is also symbolic in the sense that it is the reverse of what caused the hurt in the first place. Naturally, spontaneous demonstrations of goodwill can hasten the process, but if they are not forthcoming, my advice is to ask for what will help you forgive.

3. Do not keep bringing up the past if your spouse sincerely tries to change.

It would not be reasonable to expect yourself to forgive serious problem behavior that continues unabated. So, rectifying the initial problem is a precondition. If genuine behavior change is sustained over a significant period of time, it is reasonable to expect your spouse to stop bringing up the past.

In sessions with couples, I sometimes speak of drawing a "line in the sand" to demarcate the past. The phrase "that was then and this is now" is useful to remind people to focus on the present. One very important exception is bringing up matters related to an affair. Because the effects linger or resurface for years, this demarcation between past and present is not feasible. However, this does not mean that forgiveness and a fresh start can't take place—simply, that the process is different.

Affairs

Statistics vary somewhat regarding the frequency of affairs. Estimates are that lack of fidelity affects between a third to more than half of all marriages. There are no studies as to whether these figures are any different for couples who have a child with a disability. However, one of the dynamics of an affair is that it enables one to transcend the generally unavoidable strains of daily marital and family life. There is no reason to think this is lessened in marriages of parents of children with disabilities. In addition, one of the most common explanations for an affair is the expressed desire to have someone who pays attention, listens, is not critical, and understands. These factors, rather than sex, are what more often initially propel individuals into affairs.

"Affair" is a term used broadly and includes romantic intimate relationships as well as relationships that have not been consummated. What is the harm if it is not sexual? Actually, it has been said that mutual affairs of the heart that are not sexual are often the most damaging to a marriage. They still cause energies that would be put into one's marriage to be drawn off and feelings of betrayed intimacy. Furthermore, feelings of infatuation may last longer than in other kinds of relationships because they are not challenged by the realities of daily life.

> **"I** don't smoke, I don't drink. My addiction is to him."

This comment, made by a mother in a rather tongue-in-cheek manner, holds much truth and illustrates some of the problems of even nonsexual affairs. Although not true addictions, they bear some similarities in terms of how they function. Like addictions, they have the illusion of removing us from the problems of daily life (for a period of time). In addition, we tend to deny the impact of the activity as less harmful than it is and assume more control over stopping it—*"when we want to."* Like addictions, they often consume energy that needs to be directed elsewhere.

> **"C**ould I ever have been married to him? I would probably say 'no,' although there is part of me that feels our souls are married. I really believe I have been carrying on two marriages. The difference is that I don't sleep with him. There have been three people in this marriage for the last twenty years."

Part of what is addictive is often the other person's view of you; you are seen in the most flattering light. Two women recall comments about themselves that were endearing:

"You are iridescent."

"You are an angel."

As a result, much of the addiction is to a view of yourself supplied by the other, often on an ongoing basis. Furthermore, the new love often insists that you are the love of her life and she would commit to you if only you were free. Clearly, this is powerfully uplifting in terms of a view of yourself—in the short run.

The opportunity for intimate exchanges and having someone who listens, provides support, and reveals himself or herself is every bit as powerful in terms of drawing people into affairs.

"I have this emotional attachment. We can talk about anything and everything. He confides in me—he didn't go to his mother; he didn't go to his brother—he came to me. He trusts me. He respects my opinion. He has a high regard for who I am."

There are times in life when people are clearly more vulnerable to having an affair. Loss and stress are some of many triggers. It is common to seek out a friendly confidant during these times and not at all unusual for the confidant to eventually become a lover.

"Our son was sleeping an average of three hours a night. I was at my wit's end. But because my husband wasn't here to experience it, he did not understand how desperate I was. When I tried to talk about it, he shut me down. I was very alone, exhausted, desperate, and not thinking well. At the same time, our son with a disability was not sleeping, was abused in a classroom situation, and I was fighting with our school district—heading into a lawsuit—all by myself. This led me to seek companionship and a listening ear outside of our marriage and eventually to an affair. This is something my husband still feels is all my problem and he had no part in. (It's true he didn't participate in the affair, but....) While I will never be sure, I have to wonder if I would not have felt that intense despair that led to the affair if our son was not disabled. At least I would have been sleeping."

Many affairs have their roots in "friendships." Although I do believe that some relationships between men and women are truly platonic, many that are described as friendships have an undercurrent that is perceivable long before matters get out of hand. People seem to have a hard time being honest with themselves about the undercurrent of some of these friendships and they protest that their spouse is jealous for no reason. They use this to justify not keeping the partner apprised of ongoing contacts. Although it can be hard to be honest with yourself about these kinds of friendships, it is essential. If you don't want your partner to know about a relationship, it is probably not as platonic as it may seem. Secrecy is a red flag.

Problems in a marriage cannot be worked through while one partner is having an affair. However, many marriages can recover from an affair when it is terminated. I have known some to become better than "new." This is because the affair is often a catalyst to address problems in the marriage that have sometimes been longstanding and not well addressed. However, this is only possible after an affair has ended, and requires considerable dedication and work.

In fact, one of the best marriages that I know is one that recovered from an affair. The recovery included about two years of marital counseling. It began with uncertainty regarding whether the wife wanted or could commit to stay in the marriage after feeling devastated by her husband's affair. Some of their comments and a candid discussion of their marriage are found in the following chapter.

It is not possible to do justice to this topic in the confines of this chapter. Making a marriage work after an affair is not for the fainthearted. It requires honesty, a lack of defensiveness, a strong commitment to change, and a desire to learn how your partner feels even if what you hear is very upsetting. It also requires fortitude and patience. For example, if you have been unfaithful, you may experience your partner's wrath at you at unpredictable times, over and over. You may feel discouraged that it will never end; it does.

Lasting change in a marriage in which there has been an affair requires an understanding of what led up to the affair and what will minimize the likelihood of it happening again.

The resource list in the back of this book includes useful texts on coping with the impact of an affair on a marriage.

Concluding Thoughts

Let me close this chapter by sharing the poignant thoughts of one woman we interviewed. She sheds additional light on how to think about what constitutes a "good enough" marriage:

"I would have been a lot angrier ten years ago. I was also a lot less aware of the positive things. Now our children are older and I am not in the midst of things. I can now see his relationship with me and the positives and why I married him. I used to not remember. It was too hard to see.

"I guess I feel lucky that I was able to get to the point where I can look back. I sometimes think that if I was a stronger personality, I probably would have divorced him. But now I can see that he's a great person to grow old with. The kids won't be there. He's still fun. He still has all the positive traits that I went into the marriage with. It's lucky. I don't think everybody keeps their positive traits. I see a lot of men his age who are a lot more sedentary. And now he's calming down. I am just getting to the point where I can live with him.

"It became clearer as I got older. About a month ago, I had surgery. And it was really a minor thing in life, but it made me look at him a little bit differently. Not differently, but with an awareness that was, maybe, sharpened for a minute. He was always very squeamish, but if the kids got sick, he would gag and clean it up. I couldn't stand it and I would let him do it. I'd say, 'how can you do it?' He'd say, 'the kid is sick—you have to clean it up.'

"So, I had this surgery on my head—right on the top. They give me directions on how to clean it. It was really deep and if I didn't clean it, I could have a really big problem. I went home with my directions on how to clean it and with my peroxide and Q-tips and all my gear. I looked into the mirror, but I couldn't see the top of my head. And I was really upset—how was I going to take care of this thing? And my husband came in and said, "Let me help you.' I said, 'You don't want to look at this thing—it's really disgusting and you're going to gag.' He said, 'do you need help or don't you?' And he did help me.

"As I matter of fact, I went back to have the stitches out and the nurse said, 'This looks great! I was a little concerned that you wouldn't be able to see it.' I said, 'I couldn't. My husband did it.' The nurse said, 'I really am so impressed.'

"At this point it is pretty well healed, but my husband said, 'I'll miss doing it for you. I like taking care of you.'

"You think about it. You're going to get older, and the kids won't be around...."

Chapter Eleven

A Marriage Transformed

Laura E. Marshak, Ph.D.

This chapter centers on the words of a couple I have had the pleasure of knowing well for many years. They speak candidly of how their marriage deteriorated to the point that an affair occurred. More importantly, they speak of rebuilding their marriage into one that exceeded all expectations. The marriage remained vibrant and carried them through the husband's battle with brain cancer.

The Husband's Perspective

"I wasn't focused on my marriage. I was focused on me. We had just lost a business and were very deeply in debt. I opted to start another business on a shoestring. At the same time, my wife and I agreed it would be best for her to be a stay-at-home mom since our children were ages four, two, and six months. I started my company in a 10 x 10 office and spent six full days in the office each week trying to get it started. At this point, we were on two completely different paths. My wife focused on our children and I focused on our business. For me, it was a struggle to keep us out of personal bankruptcy. For her, it was a struggle to care for the young children. Our two youngest children encountered health issues that required even more attention. So my wife became even more committed to them.

"My business was starting to really take off, so I spent even more time in the office. One summer (about six years ago), I began a relationship with another woman. I felt as though I was starving for attention and I wasn't getting it from my wife. It seemed as though we were just living together, without really knowing one another the way we used to. My outside relationship ended after seven months when both of our spouses discovered the relationship.

"My wife and I agreed to see a counselor versus choosing to divorce. Through our therapy, we rediscovered our love for one another and learned that we both require attention. We were both very lonely and needed each other. In therapy, we learned about each other's needs and desires, and we learned about ourselves. We soon realized that we had to make our marriage our number one priority; the kids, the business, and other things had to be lower priorities.

"We were committed to saving not only our marriage, but more importantly, the friendship that allowed us to fall in love in the first place. We were once again able to communicate our deepest thoughts and fears, and were able to recommit to one another. About a year later, we celebrated our ten-year anniversary with a very special trip to Aruba—just the two of us. I put the business behind me so I could focus on her. She put the kids and other responsibilities behind her and focused on me. The combination saved our marriage.

"Today, our marriage is stronger than ever; we know and respect each other's needs. We communicate about everything. We learned how to keep our marriage our top priority and how to deal with outside influences. We are more in love today than ever before."

The Wife's Perspective

"My husband had left a really good job to pursue a career in his family's business, where I had also worked. As the business expanded into three stores, my husband and I were faced with more responsibilities. He was basically running the business along with his parents and his two brothers. We took a drastic pay cut in order for my husband to work with his family, which was his dream. As I look back, it was at this point—after about nine years of marriage—that we began to drift. As you graduate from college and become a married couple there are dreams and expectations: a house, children, and so on. We were both set and knew what we wanted in our lives but I feel that we were too focused and began to lose our friendship. We had a daughter in these years. Three years later, our second daughter was born. As we were preparing to leave the hospital, our daughter had a life-threatening condition and was rushed to the children's hospital in NICU.

"My husband and I spent the next six weeks in the hospital with her. Our lives were not normal. It was touch and go with our daughter. At the same time, the economy was declining and the family business was suffering. We were both going through some changes and not **really** communicating. My husband was always the strong one and calmed my fears as well as trying to help his family through a crisis.

"After two surgeries, we brought our daughter home from the hospital. Our lives were in disarray, but we plugged along and just kept on going. I was laid off work and went on unemployment and focused on our children. Seven months later, I became unexpectedly pregnant with our third child. We were very concerned, as we had not planned to have another child. Some medical questions rose as to the health of this child. I became consumed by health issues of our children and felt that my role was to be a devoted mother. As unemployment compensation was ending, I began a new job to help make ends meet.

"Our son was born healthy. I continued to work, take care of three small children, as well as two elderly grandparents. We were blessed with a wonderful life and family . . . so I thought. Two years later, my grandmother died unexpectedly. Meanwhile, my grandfather had cancer, and it was a very sad and troubling time as my mom, sisters, and I took care of him until his death three months later. I had just resigned from my job to take care of him when he passed away. The family business went into bankruptcy and our new home was pledged as collateral. I had cosigned a loan to help my husband's parents and was now faced with the possibility of losing our home. At the same time, my husband used the little money we had saved and started his own company. He worked day and night to get the business up and running. We were on two separate tracks. He was working constantly (even on weekends) and I did most everything else to keep the family running. I felt that by giving my husband the time needed to establish a business that I was helping, but we were drifting apart.

"Later that year, our son, age two, was hospitalized for a week and was diagnosed with juvenile diabetes. We felt that we could cope with this challenge, but our lives changed drastically. I became overwhelmed with the care that was required for my son as well as our other two small children. Our son's blood sugars were very inconsistent and I don't think that I slept for the first three months after the diagnosis.

"These events preceded the worst of my nightmares. One evening, I received a phone call from our babysitter and my friend. She told me that she and my husband had been seeing each other for the past six months. I was stunned and devastated. I remained calm and asked her many questions. My husband was working late and I confronted him when he came home. I was so lost. I asked him three times if it was true and he denied it.

"I left and went for a long ride, not knowing where to turn. This was, by far, the most horrid time in my life. How could I have been so blind and trusting of him? I felt as if I had taken on so much so that he could start the business and travel and so on. As I came to my senses I realized that divorce was not the answer, although I felt like kicking him out. I didn't want to be taken advantage of, yet I knew that I loved him. When I came home late that night, he apologized. What really hurt me was the loss of trust. As we talked, he told me that he didn't want to be with this other person. We then went to a psychologist for counseling.

"That was the beginning of our rebuilding our marriage. I can't say that it was easy, but looking back, it was essential. We both learned more about each other's personalities, likes, and dislikes. We learned how to be friends again. I don't think that anyone can prepare you for marriage, life, or children, and all of the responsibilities. As we learned to communicate more effectively, we learned how to accept our differences and build our marriage on our strengths. We had lost our friendship, the most important thing that had brought us together. As life's challenges faced us, we had dealt with them, yet we had drifted onto two separate paths. With counseling, we learned to get reacquainted with one another. As one matures, one changes. No one stays the same as the day they were married.

"Divorce is such an easy way out of a marriage in today's society. I feel that people don't try hard enough to make a marriage work. Both my husband and I felt that divorce was not an answer. When my father had passed away when I was young, I saw how sad it was for my mother and for us as a family. My mom didn't even date until I was twenty-four. She dedicated her life to us. I think in some ways I had learned to do the same, yet forgot that I had a partner to share things with. I had to learn to share the diabetes responsibility, which was probably one of the best things to come out of the affair. My husband and I began taking turns getting up in the middle of the night to test our son.

"We learned to listen to one another, not just hear. My husband cut back his hours at the office and we were able to have quality family time as well as date time. Once a week, we would go out by ourselves just to talk. If that wasn't feasible, we would have a date in our home after the children were asleep. I would try to surprise my husband for lunch or meet him at the office after work. We were finally able to laugh and be childlike again. If we were having a bad day, we would tell each other. This eliminated the questioning of ourselves. If there is no communication, it is easy to assume that someone is mad at you. It's by communicating that you can share your thoughts with your partner.

"We would take time to e-mail our thoughts if days got too hectic. I would talk to my husband on the phone when the children were occupied so that I could really give him my undivided attention. We would leave each other notes. We made our time fun. We spent time relearning each other's likes and dislikes. I made more time to go on trips with my husband, as well as attend business functions. One time I blindfolded him and drove an hour for a weekend away. We also stressed that we each needed some personal time.

"A few years ago on my birthday, it was very chaotic getting the children ready for school, picking up from kindergarten, running to the doctors, attending a function at school in the evening. My husband surprised me with a birthday cake in between functions. I was totally exhausted by the time we got home, which was around 9:00. My husband had managed to get a sitter for the kids so he could take me out to dinner. I would have rather stayed home, yet I knew that he loved to celebrate birthdays, so I went. We passed the restaurant and went to a local hotel. Well, boy, was I surprised! All I could think about was that I had not yet checked homework or made any lunches, had left the sitter no instructions for diabetes care, and had commitments early the next day. How could I possibly stay overnight?

"My husband became disappointed as I became unglued. Then I began to use what we had learned over the years from our psychologist. I first apologized, but my husband was already hurt. We then discussed what I was feeling as well as what he was feeling. As the night progressed, we were able to make the most of our time together and we compromised and had fun. It was the most wonderful gift that I had ever gotten.

"About a month after this, my husband was diagnosed with a rare, malignant brain tumor. With surgery, chemotherapy, and radiation he is doing well and is in remission. I feel that everything happens for a reason and everything that we had learned about each other since the affair played a big part in his recovery. I had learned so much about my husband, which may not have been possible without the help of our psychologist. Time heals all wounds and with hope, much work, perseverance, and determination, a couple can get through any crisis.

"We have learned to have fun and to enjoy each other again. On an anniversary trip to Aruba, I realized that I had finally come to grips with the affair. I had purchased a new wedding ring for my husband (he would never give up his original) and secretly hid it in a muffin. Meanwhile, my husband had a beautiful watch hidden under the bed that he slyly pulled out. We renewed our marriage on that trip, and today, we are best friends."

Commentary

It should be clear that a marriage based in friendship can still succumb to near destruction when couples go too far in following their separate paths without paying enough attention to each other or the marriage. When it came to rebuilding their marriage, our profiled couple made their marriage a priority. This enabled both to find ways to cut back on what were previously seen as indispensable activities in the business and the home. Communication was the backbone and provided the way to share loving feelings as well as cope with distressing ones such as those engendered by memories of the affair. Forgiveness was made possible by both of them. She repeatedly spoke with honesty about her feelings and the hurt she experienced. He listened at each opportunity, no matter how many times he had heard it before.

Both husband and wife were expressive of their needs and reactions. He did not become alienated by the fact that it took her a long time to trust him again even though he acted in a trustworthy manner. He accepted her requests for reassurance or checking for evidence of a continued affair as part of the recovery process. The ability to articulate needs and be receptive to what their partner had to say was central. They made a commitment to express their needs honestly and to listen deeply even if they did not like what they were hearing.

In addition, they both worked on personal issues that may have affected their roles in marriage. This included the way that the wife had rather automatically patterned her role within their marriage after her own mother's, even though this didn't fit her own circumstances.

During the time that it took them to heal from the affair, they put many loving compromises into place and their roles became less rigid. Their daily lives became more intertwined in the best sense of compromise and commitment.

Chapter Twelve

Divorce Considerations

Laura E. Marshak, Ph.D.

We feel strongly about saving marriages if at all possible and reasonable. But this feat is not always possible. The prospect of divorce is the elephant in the room when people think about marital problems. This chapter is intended to provide food for thought and keen insight from people who divorced for a variety of reasons including infidelities and emotional estrangement. Comments from women who have established new romantic relationships or marriages, and those who have altered their priorities to establish a satisfying life without much dating, may add to your own point of view. Despite the variety of situations and reasons for divorce, our interviews uncovered a clear commonality: everyone who did ultimately divorce went through a tortured period of deciding whether to continue with a semblance of a marriage or to divorce.

I am very conservative about choosing divorce, but do believe there are circumstances where it is the better option. If you are considering divorce, it is imperative that you make your decision with thoroughness and care so that you can best face the future without regrets.

Following is a list of questions you need to answer for yourself honestly during a period of careful deliberation. Most likely, there are also other questions specific to your situation that must be answered as well. Although presented in the form of a list, by no means is this a checklist to quickly proceed through. You must explore these questions in conjunction with the material presented in the preceding chapter on handling serious marital problems.

☑ Are your expectations for marriage realistic?

☑ Have you balanced both the problems as well as the merits of your marriage?

☑ Have you nondefensively examined your role in sustaining marital problems?

☑ Have you taken steps to change your role in the ongoing problems in your marriage?

☑ Have you gone to marital counseling?

☑ Are you making this decision while you are not involved in an affair or romantic relationship?

☑ Have you made this decision over a relatively lengthy period of time?

☑ Did you set a clear and reasonable bottom line? Has it been crossed? Has this happened more than once?

☑ Is there physical abuse or repeated emotional abuse?

Potential Impact of Divorce on Children

For many couples the overriding concerns focus, not surprisingly, on the potential impact of a divorce on the wellbeing of their children. Determining the potential impact of divorce on children is not as simple as is often implied in the popular media. Divorce does pose the risk of harm to children *but* children are also harmed by living in a home where there is constant fighting, hostility, or a number of other serious problems. The negative effects of divorce often need to be balanced against the negative effects of staying in a toxic home environment (that has defied improvement, despite prolonged and comprehensive efforts).

"Being divorced is probably the hardest thing you ever have to go through. It is pure emotional hell between the games you play with your ex and the guilt people give to you. People would say to me, 'You gotta

think of the kids.' And I would say, 'I am thinking of the
kids. If I can't be happy in my marriage, then I can't be
a good person and I can't be a good mom.' Now that I am
remarried and have a wonderful relationship, I am happy
and I can be a good parent to the kids."

Even if psychological studies had been able to reach a general conclusion on the impact of divorce on children, this would not necessarily apply to you or your children in particular. There are predictable risks and protective factors that can also alter the outcome for your children. It is in your best interests to be familiar with these risks.

The best resource I have found regarding the impacts of divorce on children is the book, *For Better or for Worse: Divorce Reconsidered,* by E. Mavis Hetherington and John Kelly. This book reports the outcome of the most extensive study of the post-divorce experiences of thousands of families and children. Many of the children were followed by the researchers from preschool through their own decisions to marry. Comparisons were made between children from divorced and nondivorced families. One of the important findings is that 80 percent of the children from divorced homes adapt well overall. Of course, this is not to minimize the 20 percent who end up very troubled. However, this research does not address whether children with disabilities cope any differently with divorce than do other children.

According to the study, some harm could be avoided if divorced parents exercised control and shielded their children from some of the harmful effects of divorce. This body of research identified two particular hazards that could be avoided with diligent self-control and some insight:

1. exposure to conflict between you and your ex; and
2. having children emotionally "parent" you.

Although this chapter is not a primer on managing divorce, we do wish to point out that care and self-control in a few key areas can have an important impact on minimizing harm. This is important to factor in when you think about the potential effect of divorce on your children.

[
Your children are less likely to be harmed by divorce if you do not expose
them to hostile feelings toward your ex-spouse.
]

It is sad and ironic that couples often divorce to spare the children from a home filled with conflict but then expose the children to additional animosity. Although most parents know this is harmful, a sizeable number give in to the temptation to fight within earshot of their children anyway. Hetherington and Kelly found that as long as six years after divorce, almost a quarter of divorced parents were still exposing their children to verbal attacks on the other parent, heated arguments, and other manifestations of their disdain for each other. So if you are strongly motivated to protect your children from the negative effects of divorce, you need a firm ongoing commitment not to do these things even if your spouse does. It is hard but it is possible.

> The risk of harm decreases if your children do not feel pressure to take care of you.

By nature, children worry about their parents and it is easy for them to slip into this pattern. Although we all want our children to be caring individuals, there is a hazard in letting them feel responsible for a parent's emotional wellbeing. This interferes with their own development. For example, some adolescents and young adults refrain from going out with their peers on weekends because they wonder who will keep their parent company. Others are apprehensive about moving away from home because their parent will be lonely. Some of these children become very codependent and consistently feel that they must make sure everyone around them is happy before they can address their own needs. With these dangers in mind it is necessary to:

- ☑ Provide reassurance that you are fine.
- ☑ Do not appear visibly upset in front of the children.
- ☑ Refrain from confiding your feelings about the divorce or your ex-spouse to them.
- ☑ Find other sources of support.
- ☑ Encourage your children to go out with their friends.
- ☑ Establish as much normality as possible.

There are special considerations related to divorcing when you have a child with a disability. Problems children routinely experience may be exacerbated. There are some good resources available for children in general. One outstanding book is *Helping Your Kids Cope with Divorce the Sandcastles Way* by M. Gary Neuman. This book identifies useful strategies for developmental ages ranging from infancy through adolescence. For this reason, parents of children with disabilities will find many useful strategies for helping children cope with divorce even if the book is geared for more typical children.

Personal Concerns

A secondary concern for most people we interviewed centered on their own wellbeing and security. Many questioned whether they could raise children with disabilities without a spouse. "For a long time prior to the divorce, I wondered, can I handle these two by myself?... but then I realized I already was." When discussing the relatively higher rate of divorce amongst parents of children with disabilities, one mother made an interesting observation. She suggested that parenting makes the mother stronger and better able to live independently if necessary. This would hold true for fathers under similar situations.

Other parents we spoke with struggled with the question of whether to stay in a marriage only for the sake of their children and questioned where the quality of their own life should fit into the decision-making equation. I personally believe that *all* lives matter and that it is too much to ask a man or woman to entirely sacrifice the prospect of a loving relationship. So I do believe our own quality of life has to be one of the factors to consider. Parents of children with particularly high needs for order and consistency (such as with autism spectrum disorders) sometimes expressed the opinion that they did not have the same option to end a marriage as other parents did. However, we do know of several divorced parents of such children who were indeed able to establish healthy childrearing environments. It is harder, but not impossible, and may be a reasonable option if there is no prospect of repairing your marriage.

A mother of a child with Down syndrome advises fellow parents to think carefully of the additional cost of raising a child with a disability before they agree to a divorce settlement. She noted that there were no special provisions in the law in her state that differentiate the financial needs of children with disabilities from others. Most strikingly, child support ends at age eighteen even though expenses of children with disabilities often don't. She noted that reliable childcare, which was necessary in order for her to go to work, cost about $10,000 last year. And there was a three-year wait for respite care. The cost of summer camps is often draining or prohibitive for many families. She advised that parents (especially primary caregivers) embarking on the divorce process seriously consider taking out a loan, if necessary, to hire a really good attorney, especially if the child is relatively young. It would be advisable to seek a lawyer who has experience in handling divorces involving children with disabilities because of the complexities introduced by virtue of disability-related needs. For example, provisions for health insurance might be important to include in a divorce settlement. If children have been receiving health insurance through their father's or mother's job, there may be problems getting new insurance for the child with a disability due to a preexisting condition.

Doing It Right: An Excellent Example

We want to share the experiences of a woman interviewed for this book who showed impressive coping skills in handling the long process that culminated in a divorce. She illustrated excellence and integrity throughout the process, including these important phases:

- persistent effort to save her marriage, including seeking professional intervention;
- clarity and comprehensive deliberation regarding the alternative of a divorce;
- finding the strength to implement her plan without jeopardizing her children.

Her story begins with the further deterioration of a shaky marriage after the birth of her son with Down syndrome. This is also an example of how serious preexisting problems became exacerbated with the birth of a child with a disability. Although this example is from a particular woman's point of view, it is not meant to contribute to gender stereotypes. Husbands and fathers are equally capable of handling the end of a marriage with the same integrity.

Persistence in Trying to Fix a Fractured Marriage

      "I'll never forget my husband saying in the delivery room, 'Oh great, we have another son. There will be bunk beds and football teams and baseball teams.' When we found out our son had Down syndrome, he didn't even cry. He didn't turn to me for any kind of consolation. It was as if it was okay. He never really got involved. He didn't ask questions. I think at that point he had made a decision that he was going out searching for something else. His way of coping with it was to run. We had a wall in the back of our house that needed repairing from the day we moved in. When our son was born, I remember watching him work on the wall. I was crying about having this son who's not perfect. I remember looking at my husband and saying, 'Oh my God, look at how well he is doing.' He was out building this wall, the radio was blaring; he was singing and building a wall like you've never seen. Now that I look back, I was the one who was dealing with it. I was mourning and he was building a wall literally and emotionally because he couldn't deal with it.

"Even before our son was born, our marriage wasn't real good. It wasn't strong. Once our son was born, my husband continued to go out a lot. He belonged to two softball teams and I felt trapped in my home with two little kids. And that's when I think the trouble started. I am not sure when he found his girlfriend, but I think it was shortly after our second son was born. He never really involved himself. I used to go out to ceramics class for my sanity once a week. He would say, 'Do I have to baby-sit the kids tonight?' And I would say, 'These are your kids; you don't **baby-sit** your kids.'

"For the next five years, I tried everything I could to make our family perfect. I was raised with very high moral standards and a good work ethic. All I ever wanted was a husband, two kids, a cat, and a dog, a white picket fence, and a station wagon in the driveway. So I decided at that point I was going to do anything and everything that I could do to make this marriage work. I went to many counselors. One said, 'Let him do what he needs to do and be there for him.' It didn't work. I went to another counselor who said, 'Force yourself upon him, and let him know you are there emotionally as well as physically.' I did that too. I tried so many counselors. I wanted to make this marriage work.

"I had been furloughed from my job and we decided to move to a small town hours away where he had been transferred. I sold my house. I said, are you sure you want to do this? Two days after we moved to the town for a fresh start he said, **'I miss my girlfriend.'**"

Careful Deliberation

"My sister used to say, 'Why is she staying with him? She has a college education; she is a smart woman. Why would she stay with this man? She can make it on her own.' This was true. When I look back, I did everything. I cut the grass, washed and maintained the car, and paid the bills. I did the laundry all on my own. And the nights that I was home alone with the kids, he wasn't there anyway. What was he contributing to this family? Very little.

"I was beside myself . . . what was I going to do? My oldest son was starting to treat me like my husband was. I did not want my boys to ever treat a woman like they saw their father treating me. That was what really pushed me over the edge. I went to a priest and said, 'Here is what's on my plate. My mother has just been diagnosed with cancer, my husband is cheating on me, and I have a handicapped son.' The priest said, 'You cannot control the fact that your son has Down syndrome, you cannot control that your mom has cancer . . . but you can leave your husband.' So a priest told me to leave him! I left. I'm not real religious but I do have a strong foundation in Christianity. And I thought, I can't leave him because I said 'I do' for better and for worse. When a priest gave me permission I was out of there.

"I didn't do any kind of artificial means of dealing with things. I didn't drink. I didn't do any of that. I didn't want to mask my feelings—I think that is just so crucial. Time is important to look inside of yourself. I knew that to give my children the best, I needed the best for myself. I needed to get to a point where I would be okay, and then they would be okay."

Remaining Strong Despite Mammoth Obstacles

"I moved at the end of January. I had two crying kids because they missed Daddy. I had a crying father because his wife was dying. I was going through a divorce. I had no job or money. My sister-in-law right down the street was having a baby. I was the person, believe it or not, keeping everything together. No alimony, none, even though I was unemployed. I was expected to get a job comparable to the one I left. My mother died on a Tuesday. My moving van had already gone back. Saturday, I took the two kids with two suitcases in my car. I had twenty dollars in my pocket and I had no place to live. My great aunt said, 'Come live with us.' We went to church Sunday morning and my great aunt said we needed to go to the grocery store to get some food. We came out of the store and I put my key in the car; half of my key got stuck in the ignition. I had to get my car towed. I cried.

"And my aunt said, 'You just hit the bottom. From here on in life will be better.' (My aunt is eighty-three and to this day, says to me, 'If it wasn't for you, your kids wouldn't be who they are.')"

Prioritizing and Enjoying Her Children

"When I left, I decided that I needed time for me. I'm not desperate. I'm not old. My kids are most important. My focus needed to be on getting us back on track. I didn't even want to date. I just didn't want to do it (although I did eventually end up in a long-term relationship). I used to plan my Friday nights just for me and my kids.

"One day my son said, 'Mom, I love you in my heart. And when you die I'm going to miss you. But when you die I'm going to Disney World.' I'm thinking, 'Oh shit—how am I going to afford this one?' I don't know if it was an angel, God, or my mother. I went down to AAA and said, 'I need to get to Disney World.' We were in Disney World for his birthday. And I paid on it all year. I just made payments.

"When my son with Down syndrome was born, I pitied myself. **What did I do so bad in my life to deserve this? Look**

**at all those people who have normal, healthy kids. Look
at that teenage girl that I know doesn't know crap about
being pregnant and motherhood; why isn't it her instead of
me?** And I was feeling very sorry for myself. I now look at
pregnant teenagers and others and say, 'Thank God he is
mine and not yours. He's my favorite person in the world.' If
you would say, do you want to spend time with this person,
this person, or this person... I would pick my son definitely."

Romantic Life after Divorce

Fear of dating again is one consideration for many people who con-
template divorce. After divorce, self-esteem may be at a low ebb. Many
worry about who will want them with children, much less children with
disabilities. One woman, a mother of three children (two of whom have
severe disabilities) shared these thoughts along with the good advice
she had received. At the time of our interview, she was engaged.

"I have had quite a few men shy away from me as soon
as they learned about my kids. You know what my
best friend told me? She said, 'This is the best screening
process. There are other women who meet men and there is
not a challenge there so they don't see what they are made
of. If they pass the kid test, then they are a special person.
If they can't, then they don't have what it takes.'"

She proceeded to discuss a series of bad dates that lasted until
she met her fiancé. She noted how on their second or third date, he
was part of a scene at her daughter's group home that involved the
police, ambulances, and a 302 (involuntary) mental health commitment. As deeply committed as she is to this relationship, she notes:

"He has known from day one that my kids come first.
And then he comes next. But it is not obvious. I
try to meet a balance."

This is an excellent example of how priorities need to be established
after divorce.

Chapter Thirteen

Remarriage:
The Need to Do It Differently

Laura E. Marshak, Ph.D.

When there are children involved, the path to a successful re-marriage is very different than the path taken in a first marriage. Most successful remarriages and stepfamilies do not ultimately replicate the nature and structure of traditional families and need to be different. These differences include expectations regarding child-parent relationships, roles, harmony, and overall family structure. If everyone in the family accepts the need for these differences, your chances for success are increased.

Some difficulties in remarriage stem from the lack of realistic images of what stepfamilies are often like. Few people experience step-families like those portrayed in television sitcoms. In fact, most experts have observed that it typically takes between five to seven years for a stepfamily to coalesce to the point that it feels comfortable. How long it takes depends, in part, on the ages of the children. For example, a three-year-old would generally have an easier time getting used to new siblings and a new parent than a twelve-year-old would. If you can re-member that things are not going to happen over night, you have a better chance of persevering with the difficulties you will encounter on the road to developing and sustaining a rewarding family and marital life.

Many books and articles write of "blended" families. The Stepfamily Association of America has stated that this term conjures up an unrealistic picture of what occurs when members of two families combine following a remarriage. The idea of blending into a new family obscures the strength and importance of ties children often have to another stepfamily or single parent outside of this new family. The idea of blending into a new whole implies that differences somehow melt away and individual ingredients are not recognizable. A better cooking analogy, according to The Stepfamily Association, is that the members of the two families are "folded in" or gently combined. This distinction matters when trying to understand the pressure on children (and their natural resistance) to simply "blending" into a new family.

The Children's Experience

Why does it take so long for adjustment to occur? The answer can partly be found in the emotional tasks facing many of the family members and most especially the children. Many of the typical adjustment issues will be intensified for children who have disorders that impair their comprehension or emotional control. This is all the more reason that parents of children with special needs must carefully and respectfully help them adjust to the magnitude of the emotional tasks they may face.

[Be sensitive to the losses children have when they enter a new family.]

Some say that for children, adjusting to a stepfamily is even more difficult than the transition resulting from the initial divorce. Whereas adults can see the potential that a new family and relationships can bring, children are more acutely aware of the losses involved along the way.

One of the most emotional losses is of the dream that their parents will reunite. Children often cling to these dreams quietly despite all evidence that a reunification between parents is not realistic. Another deeply experienced loss is of a somewhat exclusive relationship with a mother or father. This is especially the case when the parent and child have formed a particularly close relationship following a divorce—when they have formed a team of just the "two of us." Perhaps the parent had been turning to him often for companionship and a sense of emotional closeness that has been lost with the spouse. Now, however, the child finds that the new spouse is replacing him in ways that are ultimately healthy but make him feel excluded or displaced.

Children also feel displacement and loss if they now have new siblings. The "baby" of the family may find that he is no longer the youngest child. It is even tougher to have to adjust to the birth of a new baby to the parent and stepparent. Children with disabilities encounter additional complexities related to new siblings. For example, new siblings may not know how to communicate with them or understand their need for certain routines. Children with some developmental disabilities may be especially prone to jealousy when they see "their" parent treating the new sibling like their own child.

In addition, children may also lose their residence or "turf" if they need to move to a home with new siblings. A child accustomed to his or her own room may now be sharing and feel there is nothing in his life that is untouched. A move may also require a change in schools, neighborhood, and even friends. Children with disorders such as autism spectrum disorders may have an exceptionally difficult time with such changes.

Adolescents sometimes lose freedom and autonomy because there is now a new authority figure. Some may have been accustomed to filling the role of the man or woman of the house and may resent the loss of this role to someone who feels like a virtual stranger. Adolescent daughters and sons may experience anxiety about boundaries. That is, sexually developed children may feel uncomfortable or unsafe living with an unrelated adult of the opposite sex.

Children often express their loss through anger and acting out, so it is not surprising that the first years after a parent's remarriage are tumultuous. If you have a child with communication difficulties, you can expect even more "behavior" problems as he attempts to use behavior to communicate his frustration with the changes.

[Realistic expectations will go a long way in helping a couple achieve a good and satisfying marriage and family life.]

Some of these realistic expectations may be hard to initially accept. Experts often remind new stepparents that stepchildren may or may not form loving bonds with them. They also warn couples that love for stepchildren is not instant or guaranteed. It is one thing to love your own children no matter what; it is another matter to feel love for a child simply because you love his or her parent. Certainly there are some exceptions. But the expectation that this *must* occur is not realistic.

If this sounds as if I am pessimistic about the potential of remarriage and stepfamilies, I am not. Stepfamilies can be wonderful, but are different from the family you initially had or tried to have in your previous marriage. I have seen some tremendous stepfamilies with and without children with disabilities. I do know they need to be developed with extra patience, flexibility, and with a close marital bond. Overall, the rate of success in remarriages is 40 percent. For any individual, the odds are improved with a wise choice of partners, a mature approach to handling interpersonal conflicts, and a perspective on what it takes to make a stepfamily work.

Building a New Family Structure

The ways you structure the roles and boundaries in your new family need to vary according to desires, needs, and the realities you face such as the children's ages and personalities. There are many workable approaches to building the structure that guides aspects of family functioning. But there is far less latitude in laying the foundation for this family structure—your marriage. Your marriage needs to be solid and well maintained in order to provide a means to protect it and persevere with the difficulties that typically are encountered in stepfamily family life.

If They Can Do It...

I met a remarkable couple while working on this book and want to share with you their strategies for making their marriage work. They also serve as great role models for couples trying to sustain a remarriage despite unremitting major stress. The wife has two young children with severe developmental disabilities, ages five and nine. Both had serious cognitive and communication disorders and the daughter was prone to violent behavior. Her mother described her as functioning on a level equivalent to a two-year-old. The couple had just returned from their honeymoon; this was her second marriage and his first. They had lived together for a year so they would better know what they were getting into. The husband, said, "I figured if I could live with her for a year and be happy I could spend the rest of my life with her. And I was—I was happy as a lark."

He made the following comments when asked about his experience with children who have disabilities and his initial reactions to his wife's children:

> **"I** didn't know anyone who had special-needs kids. When I was in high school, I'd see special-needs kids walking through the hallways and things like that. But I had never really met anyone with special needs at all. At first it took a lot to get used to. It scared me. I ain't going to lie. And there are still times where it does still scare me. Our daughter has a bad problem of wanting to choke her brother. And she is a strong young lady. And it always scares me when I think about what happens when she gets older and I come home and she has my wife down and is choking her....
>
> "Where are we going to be five years from now with the kids? Where are we going to be ten years from now? I mean, I know I want to be with my wife no matter what, but you always have to think about the kids. Are we going to be able to do anything normal as a family with the kids?"

Despite his worries, this couple is sustaining their marriage with affection and respect while handling these problems in a trailer (while saving for a larger home). The key elements they have identified that have helped them stay together—and that are crucial in any remarriage—include:

1. a commitment to stay connected;
2. communication;
3. maintaining romance;
4. and being in it together.

A Commitment to Stay Connected

"One of the key things that I would tell anybody with special-needs children is that you have to set aside being a parent to be a couple also. I don't think a whole lot of people with 'normal' children do that enough. And it is probably one reason that divorce rates are so high. You are so intent on being the parent and supporting these children and doing this and that . . . and you forget to support each other and to be in love and to do fun things together."

This couple practices a commitment to stay connected in a variety of facets of their relationship. The need to stay connected pervades how they handle communication, unavoidable conflicts over childrearing, educational planning, the resolution of anger, and the protection of their romantic life.

Communication

This couple talks about things on an ongoing basis to make such a complicated marriage and family life work. Although they have their arguments and hurt feelings, they are proactive about not staying angry for long. This keeps resentment from building up.

"Even when we argue, my husband makes me sit next to him. Or if I'm in the kitchen and I'm yelling across the room to him, he usually comes to me and closes that gap."

Maintaining Romance

Remarriage is instant parenthood, so finding time for romance is particularly important. In first marriages, a husband and wife have a period to bond romantically and sort out roles without children before becoming parents.

"After the kids go to bed, we usually stay up for another hour or hour and a half. That's usually when I'll have a beer or glass of wine and he will sometimes rub my back. We burn a lot of candles. It just kind of relaxes us.

We've got a double bed. There is just enough room for us. When he (my second husband) moved in, the kids didn't want to sleep in their own beds. We said 'no, this is our room.' The first couple of nights were very rough, because the kids were used to sleeping with an adult. For the first couple of nights, I had to lie in their beds for a few minutes and wait for them to go to sleep. Then I'd go to bed. Now it doesn't bother them at all. Since we have a smaller bed, there isn't room anyway. When we're mad, even when we go to bed . . . he can't sleep on one side of the bed. We're too smashed together."

"Being in It Together"

This couple carved out a realistic role for the husband's genuine involvement in many areas of childcare. This includes advocating for the children to get appropriate services. Rather than have the wife continue to assume all responsibility for educational advocacy, her husband learned about pertinent legislation, how the educational and service systems worked, and the relevant terminology. Although the husband also is substantially involved in discipline, the wife does appropriately pull rank on issues she deems absolutely critical. "Being in it together" does not mean that all parenting must be shared absolutely 50-50.

"My own father was very gruff. We were a military family. And I thought, I am not going to have this again. There are times when my husband knows he has gone above the limits and I let him know. He usually listens. Sometimes I get frustrated that he is not more patient. But then I have to stop and think that he is more patient than any guy I can imagine willingly taking on these kids. The children were born to me. I don't have a choice. He had a choice."

Parental Roles

The biggest conflicts in a stepfamily usually revolve around co-parenting children. This may be why remarriages that include children have a higher rate of failure.

[Discuss and negotiate parental roles rather than assuming there is only one right way.]

There are two main schools of thought on deciding who does what with the children (and a variety of potential modifications of each):

1. Absolute involvement of both parents with all children;
2. True involvement of both parents, but with partners retaining some authority over their own children.

Absolute Involvement

The couple described above mostly uses a model aiming for eventual full involvement by the stepparent in all parts of parenting. The wife recounted the brief discussion that led up to this:

"When we were dating, I think he flat out asked me, 'What do you expect from me?' I told him, 'If you are going to come into this as the parent, then you have the rights that come with this.'"

This was a very reasonable approach for this couple, given their own preferences for this approach, the nature of the very demanding childrearing issues, and the ages of the children. In their case, both parents wanted the stepfather to assume a full-fledged parenting role that included discipline. The children have responded positively to this approach.

[Younger children are often better able to accept a stepparent in an authoritarian position.]

This type of approach requires the original parent to step back and the stepparent to step up in terms of childrearing tasks. The original parent has the difficult task of surrendering control over half of childrearing. This is hard even with the best intentions:

"I've dealt with it since they were babies. And he's still learning the process. I guess the thing that worries me is that he can separate himself. Say it was horrible—he could divorce and he could move on. They are my children and they will be my children whether we are together or not. So I guess in that sense, all the worries do affect me differently."

A few additional considerations:

- ☑ If half of discipline is shared, the stepparent needs to also be as actively involved in all other aspects of childrearing.
- ☑ Fully sharing discipline is rarely successful when a child is approaching adolescence or older.
- ☑ If the child has a disability that results in behavioral problems, the stepparent will need to learn what forms of discipline work and do not work with the child; what kinds of incentives work for encouraging good behavior, etc. He or she may need to take some classes in behavior management, communication, or other techniques to get up to speed.
- ☑ Especially when a child with disabilities needs routine and consistency in order to function on a day-to-day basis, the new parent has to be willing to handle discipline the same way as the original parent does.
- ☑ The new parent also has to understand what is and is not under the child's control—what behaviors are manifestations of the disability and what are not.

True Involvement within Confines

Many experts suggest an alternative to both parents disciplining the children. This alternative structure is based on the recognition that in many circumstances, discipline is better handled by the parent who has raised the child. The stepparent can consult with and support the original parent in discipline, but he or she should focus on building a different sort of relationship with the stepchild or children.

In this model, the stepparent does not impose his or her authority but does seek to gain influence through trust and respect over time. This scaling down of expectations that the stepparent will assume all parental roles works well in many families. This works especially well in families with children who are resistant to change such as children with autism spectrum disorder.

A stepparent does not need to be a disciplinarian in order to have an influence on childrearing or an engaged relationship with the children. This leaves a multitude of roles including sharing activities, providing support, involvement in childcare activities, sharing interests, getting to know the child as an individual, and supporting the spouse in disciplinary decisions. This is very different from simply disengaging from the stepparent role. Stepping back from a disciplinary role does not exclude the possibility of setting some house rules mutually agreed upon by the couple. This is particularly important if a stepparent is alone with the children for long periods of time while the other is at work.

Readers will find books that exemplify both of these models in the resource list.

Avoiding Common Sources of Trouble

There are three common pitfalls to beware of when it comes to stepparenting:
1. overeagerness,
2. family divisions, and
3. competition.

Overeagerness
Some parents are overeager. This may be fueled by a desire to rescue the spouse (usually the wife) from what they perceive as an out-of-control situation or chaotic family environment. The attitude is one of "I will set things right around here." Sometimes they feel driven to compensate for what the child or spouse was missing earlier in life. An overeager parent may not appreciate the "learning curve" that comes with understanding a child's disability and needs.

He or she may then suggest too many changes before truly understanding why the other parent or professionals take the approaches they are using. Overeager parents may also try too hard to get close to the child too quickly. Often, this feels invasive or even disturbing to some children (such as those with autism). It also sets the stepparent up for failure.

The best guideline is to be flexible, available, and engaged yet willing to accept that children may not regard you as you would wish. The longer view of what it takes to grow into a family is important to maintain.

A Divided Home

It is natural for children to be more closely bonded with their biological parent. You need to avoid a house that is divided and is split, however. This can occur even if only one spouse brings a child into the family. It is even more likely when both spouses enter the family with children from prior marriages. So, another important parental and stepparent function is to work on building a sense of family over time. You can help build this sense if the original parent does not generally intervene when the new spouse is interacting with his or her stepchild. If the original parent stays out of the middle of that relationship, the stepparent and child have a better chance to forge one together.

Family identity is also built through shared activities and routines such as encouraging everybody to be home each week on a certain day(s) and time for family meals together. The goal is for an overarching umbrella structure to grow over time over all family members.

One of your challenges will be to support more comfortable connections between the child with a disability and the range of stepsiblings and the stepparent. The parent and the siblings of this child will have much more knowledge about his preferences, idiosyncrasies, and needs, and will need to share this knowledge and help the stepsiblings and stepparent feel more comfortable interacting. It is natural for a sibling to be protective of his sibling with a disability when the stepsiblings move in or to guard her secret knowledge about how to interact with the child. As a parent, you can be a positive influence by encouraging the sibling to share her special knowledge in order to "be a great help" to the rest of the family. Without this type of sharing, the stepsiblings may be reluctant to interact with the child with special needs. They may give him a wide berth, if they've had little experience with disabilities or if the child has a disability that results in unusual or difficult behavior. It is this sharing and teaching that can help the family avoid splitting up into "us" and "you." This requires being willing and able to relinquish the "expert parent" and "expert sibling role."

Competition

Both children and adults are bound to feel ignored or excluded at times during the process of establishing a new stepfamily. This is because of the complexities of relationships. Parents may rightly feel they need to spend some individual time with their child. After all, that child is used to a special relationship with the parent. The stepparent may or may not feel resentful when this occurs. Similarly, in shared custody arrangements, the new spouse may feel ignored when the child comes to stay. Some family occasions may involve extended family, including the ex-spouse. Some spouses take these events in stride; others have much more difficulty. The pitfall to avoid is a situation in which the spouse feels they need to compete for their partner's attention.

The solution is a joint one. No matter how busy life is, there is no genuine reason why there should not be enough love and affection to go around. Spouses who view love as a limited commodity to compete for run the risk of setting up a self-fulfilling prophecy. I have found that adults whose personal needs were not well met by their own parents have a particularly hard time when their spouse attends to his or her children from a previous marriage. In this case, individual therapy may be helpful.

When one parent is spending time with children from a previous marriage, he or she should also be careful not to make the problem worse by being more than casually inconsiderate of his partner's needs. There are many things that can help and some are quite simple. For example, you could tell your spouse, "I know I don't have much time to pay attention to you when Charlie is here for the week. I try my best but feel stretched too thin because I am trying so hard to make him feel welcome here. Could we plan on next Saturday night just for the two of us? I would really love that." Or, you could take the time to tell your partner something nice before you head off for a graduation celebration that includes your ex-spouse. Neither one of these takes much time. However, this way of connecting, when sincerely done, helps your partner remember that he or she is special to you even if your attention is primarily focused on others for awhile.

Competition with your new spouse does not generally seem to be as problematic as competition with your child's other parent. For example, you may be frustrated that your attempts to be supportive and close with a stepchild are taken for granted while the child jumps at the chance to be with the original parent no matter what. If you find yourself dwelling on these matters, recognize that it is both impossible and unnecessary to compete. It can also be helpful to understand that a child with disabilities, especially one with an autism spectrum disorder or mental retardation, may not be able to understand that he is hurting you and that he is probably not knowingly doing this. Often stepparents can come to terms with this on their own. If not, counseling might be needed.

Concluding Thoughts

Given all the caveats mentioned, it is important to bear in mind that many remarriages work very well over time and that the stepparents often come to embrace the children fully. However, accomplishing this takes a thoughtful approach and communication that enhances the likelihood that important needs will be met, feelings respected, and problems managed or resolved.

One woman with two children with severe disabilities and a successful remarriage who exemplified this approach told us:

"My second husband will come up and cuddle with me or want to kiss. Then my son will come up and try to come between us because he wants hugs and kisses too. And my daughter will want kisses from my husband. They just started calling him Daddy."

Chapter Fourteen

Learning from
Long-Term Marriages

Laura E. Marshak, Ph.D.

We hope that you walk away from this book with a better sense of what is possible in marriage and the many ways to achieve a satisfying one. Toward this end, this chapter takes a closer look at four marriages. Each of the four couples have been married for more than twenty years and all have raised children with very severe disability-related problems. Although each couple emphasized a different marital philosophy and took different paths to achieve their goals, they all ended up with successful, fulfilling marriages.

Part of the value of looking at selected aspects of successful marriages is that it can shed light on varied aspects of sustaining a marriage. I have learned even more about marriage from knowing these couples and I am certain they can serve as additional inspiration and sources of additional ideas for you as well.

Fifty-plus Years of a Happy Traditional Marriage

The first couple I would like to highlight, Elaine[1] and William, had raised four children and sustained a happy marriage for fifty-

---

[1] This name, as well as all the other names in this chapter, are pseudonyms.

six years when I interviewed them. I met with them about two years after they lost a daughter, at age forty-three. She was their youngest child and had a form of mental retardation that resulted in diffi-cult-to-control behavior problems that persisted throughout her life, despite excellent help and parenting. It was clear that parenting her was demanding despite her very sweet and loving nature. For ex-ample, even when she was an adult, they still had to get up several times a night to check on her for a variety of reasons. Part of what impressed me initially about this couple was their mutual humor and goodwill. The husband expressed their philosophy:

> "You can grow apart or grow closer depending on whether you work together."

When I took a closer look at how they had implemented this philosophy, two prominent components of their marriage seemed to lead to good daily practice:

☑ demonstrating goodwill and appreciation towards each other;

☑ making sure to enjoy their child and protect themselves from negative feelings.

Goodwill and Appreciation

Daily acts of goodwill and appreciation for the other's work es-tablishes positive rather than negative cycles. This is a key strat-egy Elaine and William used naturally in order to keep resentments from developing. Some of the ways they showed goodwill included:

☑ forgiving the small day-to-day disagreements;

☑ being willing to support and show appreciation for each other's roles.

These enabled them to work well within traditionally structured roles, in which the husband worked outside of the home for five or six days a week, and his wife stayed home taking care of the children.

For Elaine and William, expressing appreciation through words and actions for each other's efforts was a key component. On week-ends, William pitched in without being asked, as a way to express his appreciation for his wife's efforts throughout the week. For example, each Sunday morning he made a big breakfast for everybody and sometimes helped out with the cleaning. Elaine instituted a family routine she called "first and second supper." Noting that the children could not really wait to eat until her husband got home, she would make the children something simple like a grilled cheese sandwich. When her husband got home, everyone would sit down together to a large dinner. Her husband, during our interview, commented on how much he looked forward to this connective routine. From my point of view, the gesture also served many good purposes. It was a show of appreciation, a way to maintain cohesiveness and communication, and an act of prioritizing the marriage. Setting up a positive cycle in this manner makes it easier to work as a team so the effort expended is returned multifold.

Enjoying Life and Having a Positive Perspective

Although they did not speak of the "Serenity Prayer" mentioned previously, this couple illustrated its philosophy in action. More specifically, William spoke of a strategy that combined controlling what could be managed (through good treatment and parenting) and "just kind of giving up" attempts to control his daughter's behaviors that were not going to change. This required them to learn how to set aside occasional embarrassment. Elaine gave this example of enjoying their daughter without worrying excessively about her behavior:

"We would go places with our daughter sometimes and I would say, 'I'm getting embarrassed. She's approaching every stranger like they're her best friend.' And he would say, 'What do you care what people think? She's happy. She's having a good time.' We'd be sitting in a restaurant and at the top of her lungs she would say, 'I JUST CHANGED MY PANTS!' [laughs] Well, this was our daughter. We got our pleasure out of our daughter."

In coping with their daughter's death, William and Elaine acknowledged how much they had valued her as a person and how much they deeply missed her presence. Sharing positive memories of their daughter was central to how they coped with her loss.

"**W**henever she would see a limousine, she would yell: 'LOOK AT THE LIMO!' [They laughed together.] So, whenever we see a limousine we say: 'LOOK AT THE LIMO!' We miss her input. We miss the fun; there was nothing like our daughter. She would come and say 'HI!' like you were the best thing that ever happened in this world."

Part of this couple's approach to life is an implicit decision not to get mired in negative feelings, including resentment and self-pity. Like others I have known, they know that dwelling on the negatives just makes life harder. For example, Elaine shared how she tried to maintain a unique perspective on the situation with her other daughter:

"**M**y daughter accused me of not being realistic about things. I tailor things to what I am comfortable with. If there is a bad situation I cope by altering the situation a little bit. It doesn't seem as bad as it could be. That's my coping strategy. I can cope with something if I can manage it. So if I have a situation that seems hard to manage, I guess I will fudge it a little."

At the time of their older daughter's sudden death she was in residential treatment and close to her family both literally and figuratively. After her death, they were faced with questions regarding whether a treatment error contributed to her death. They initially held different opinions, but the wife came to support her husband's desire not to pursue this issue. He explained:

"**I** think if there was some change in medication, it was purely accidental. We had nothing to gain from asking the staff more questions about what happened. What would it have proven? Why be angry with people who had been so good to her? She loved it there."

William's opinion was influenced by his gratitude to his daughter's group home and a desire not to focus on the negative. Elaine's feelings were influenced by the desire to be a team with her husband and make the kind of compromises characteristic of this loving marriage.

Admirable Teamwork

There is a lot to learn from the second couple Sharon and David. They describe their marriage as "sort of a crisis-management marriage" and acknowledge that they face tremendous stress. They have two children with demanding disorders. The older child, a young adult, struggles with mental health and substance abuse problems. The younger child's disorder is similarly serious, and involves behavioral problems and uncertainty about his future.

Their marital philosophy enables them to sustain a loving, respectful marriage that provides a haven for them. David expressed their commitment to making their marriage work:

"The advice that I'd have for other parents is to have as strong and healthy marriage as possible. Otherwise it just makes the whole situation that much more difficult. In any situation with special-needs children in the house, marital problems just create more problems and controversy in a situation that is already explosive."

It was remarkable the extent to which this couple could practice teamwork under pressure and while experiencing strong emotions.

Factors that enable them to have a thriving marriage are:
- ☑ prioritizing their marriage and taking care of themselves;
- ☑ practicing mutual influence and teamwork;
- ☑ maintaining respect for each other, even in the midst of heated arguments.

Prioritizing Their Marriage

This couple is absolutely dedicated to their children. They provide first-rate parenting but prioritize their marriage above all. This is how the wife explained it:

"The most important thing in my life is my marriage. The children are an added bonus to my marriage. But my marriage is what I want in my life—to be married to a man and be happy. Raising a special-needs child takes so much energy that I think we have to remain as healthy as possible with ourselves and each other."

They take care of their marriage through weekly counseling to help them negotiate the many high stakes situations they find themselves in. They also routinely take time away together, which wasn't easy initially because the children acted out as a way to "punish" them for going. "But we went any way," said Sharon. "No matter what. We need to be alone sometimes. We need to get out of the chaos to see each other and to know that this is not all of who we are."

Teamwork and Mutual Influence

The concept of teamwork and mutual influence pervades everything they do.

Husband:

"It doesn't pay not to approach parenting as a team. Twenty-six years ago we made the decision that no matter what happens to us we're going to get through it. I think that with each situation we have learned how to work through it. And each situation demanded different responses, different reactions, compromising, coming to a new place, moving forward with the decision."

Wife:

"And there are many times when we will have to step aside from the situation and go in a room and talk about it. We're both passionate about the way we approach a problem. When it is completely different, we need to decide how we are going to approach it. It's a matter of teamwork; compromise is another good word. There are times when we must trust the other's opinion and one of us just has to give in."

The concept of mutual influence is also a prominent component in their decision-making. Mutual influence requires each partner to:

- ☑ Be open to their partner's different perspectives and emotions.
- ☑ Refrain from power struggles.
- ☑ Understand that better decisions will arise from the joint process.

Passing the Baton

The second couple's teamwork extends to emotional functioning. They don't expect their partner to be at the same place they are emotionally at any given time. They regard this as creating a balance. When one is feeling an emotional meltdown, he or she steps back while the other takes over. This is passing of the baton as you might see in a relay race. It is accepted as natural, rather than a weakness—that one partner becomes emotionally and physically depleted and needs the other's help.

Respect

Respect was a repeated theme in this couple's dialogue. It is important to note that David and Sharon do argue, but they practice guidelines that enable them to treat each other with proper respect in the process.

"I really respect my husband's viewpoint and who he is as a person. We treat each other very honorably. We don't degrade each other. We don't put each other down. We don't name call. We don't do the things that a lot of couples do when we are angry with each other. Our fights are usually clean-cut fights. They are usually fueled and fiery, but then they are over. We just had a fight the other night. I blew up over the stupidest thing and I blamed him for something that he had absolutely nothing to do with. It has to do with my feeling of powerlessness over my daughter. At first we screamed and then we sat and talked."

The Real Secret to Their Commitment

Husband:

"**W**e both had been through so much together we could have easily walked away, quit, or tried it differently with someone different, but it was never an option."

Wife:

"**Y**ou can tell her why we really stayed together...tell her our real secret."

Husband:

"**W**e've always had an arrangement that whichever one left had to take the kids. That's always been our joke."

Clarity on What Matters Most in Life

The third couple featured here stands out in my mind for the way their value systems sustain their marriage. Allen and Joyce have three children; their middle child has almost no speech, requires ongoing vigilance, and has cognitive disabilities that will make independence as an adult impossible.

The couple's philosophy and strategies for their marriage are based on:

- restructuring their values in a way that differs from general society;
- steadfast commitment to the "greater good" of the family unit.

Although we had shared many conversations, it was not until this interview that I clearly understood the value of the accommodations Joyce has made on a personal level. She has put aside her own needs for professional accomplishment in the interest of other values. As a friend, I used to see some of her compromises as "giving in" or lack of assertiveness. When examined more closely, what appeared to be "giving in" seems more like a reordering of what is meaningful and a prizing of collectivism. By collectivism, I mean viewing the greater good as being what is good for the group (in this case, family). This is seen far more often in other cultures and family structures than in America, where individualism, competition, and perfectionism are prized. For this reason, its value is often overlooked. Some reflections from Joyce follow:

"People who know me well feel like I don't set enough limits with my husband—that I'm not hard enough on him. There's no way I can know if it would have been different without my son. My son is very rigid and he's very fixed and very stubborn. Without my son how would I have played it? I don't know. Would the marriage have lasted? Maybe not. I kind of can't afford to rock the boat in any area of my life. My life is really more about survival and not about the little stuff. It's really about the big stuff and keeping my energy positive and keeping healthy. Without my son, I don't think I would have been like that.

"Keeping peace, keeping routine, keeping stability, becomes so essential in raising a kid with the kind of handicap that he has. Almost everything else seems to pale; it's wonderful and it's limiting. The wonderful thing is, it gives you perspective on life. It's similar to how people felt one hundred years ago when they didn't think about little stuff; they thought about survival. They thought about making it as a family. It's wonderful because it really teaches you a vast appreciation for things. I don't really sweat the stuff that I see other people sweating. Having a child like my son puts it in perspective. It makes you focus on the bigger picture and I think that's an incredible gift. I think that's a gift you usually get with age and I think I have it twenty years before everybody else."

Commitment

Allen, Joyce's husband, shared his thoughts in an individual interview. He identified commitment as the critical component he wanted to emphasize for readers.

"It really does take incredible commitment because there's so much that can go wrong and does go wrong during twenty years of marriage. Most of our friends' parents, even the ones who seemed unhappy, have stayed married. They actually have taught us quite a lesson. It is not that you should not be happy in your marriage, but if that you work harder, maybe you will find the things that will make you happy, or that will make you want to stay together."

Like his wife, he has great commitment to the family as a unit and spoke of the need for vision. This includes envisioning what they want their son's life to be like ten, twenty, and even thirty years in the future. He adds that part of his marital commitment is due to recognition that achieving this vision is difficult enough without thinking about doing it alone, or "in two different ways in two different households." He further illustrated that a long-term commitment provides a way to make difficult periods more tolerable:

"If you are in it for the long term, then if you've had a bad day, week, or month in your marriage (for that matter, if you've had a bad year or two or three), you say, 'Well, this is a small part of the years that we're going to have to put together to get this all done. We can work our way through that because I see where we're going to be at the end.'"

He elaborated when I commented that I was glad to include this advice from a man (because there was less male input in this book):

"Society says we're supposed to be stronger. We're not supposed to give in. When I go out and I play sports, I want to win. And I play as hard as I can. But that's different. The goal there is to win for your team. But the team in marriage is you, and your wife, and your children. That is the team. So, if you're fighting with your spouse over an issue and you're winning, it doesn't mean that the marriage is stronger. It might mean your marriage is weaker. You know, it's a different type of key team concept."

What this interview may not capture entirely, is the enjoyment and satisfaction that this couple has with their family. They engage in many family activities and have successfully raised children who look out for each other. Their son with disabilities is exceptionally well-integrated into the community.

"Rather than think about what we've lost in a sense (although sometimes I do think about that), I think about what we've gained. Having three perfectly normal kids would have been wonderful, but I don't feel bad for us. I feel bad that our son can't talk (for him). I feel bad that he doesn't understand everything (for him). I would love to see him communicate the way everyone else communicates. I would love to hear what's going through his mind, but that's for him, not for us. You know, we live with whatever we live with."

Generosity of Spirit, Mutual Caretaking, and Valuing Life

There are many things I admire and enjoy about this last couple, Ann and John. Wonderful aspects of their marriage are best understood in the context of their family life. Now in their later 50s, their married life and family structure differs a great deal from more ordinary ones. Their daughter had seizures and behavioral problems since childhood, then developed many more difficulties. In adulthood, she struggles with delusional thinking that followed brain surgery. In more recent years, she has developed alcoholism. She now lives with her parents, along with her own two children.

This is a very happy marriage and in more than ten years, I have never heard Ann speak negatively of John, although he certainly is not perfect. Their marriage emphasizes:
- mutual caretaking of each other;
- generosity of spirit with each other;
- valuing life as it is (not as they wished it was);
- dark humor.

John described what it is like to live with their adult daughter and her children:

"Everything got worse and worse as she got older. Now the stakes are higher. Now if we start to discipline her, she gets real angry, starts swearing, and it keeps escalating. She doesn't let go of anything, no matter how small. If something bothers her, she'll keep going back to it. She takes the money she gets and spends it on herself or gambles it. Oh, once in a while she will buy the children clothes and such. It's very seldom that she buys groceries or anything. We support her and her kids. Which is no big deal, but what is really aggravating is that she wastes her own money and then wants to spend our money on gambling or cigarettes; and she has no life."

There is no easy answer to this couple's dilemmas and they have explored so many avenues and services over the years.

Husband:

"You can't throw her out of the house, because you know she has nowhere to go and no matter where she goes, she'll end up in trouble."

Wife:

"And she'll be back."

Husband:

"She'll be back with more problems. And she's got her kids. Last time she bought that mobile home and then she went down that hill in her car with the kids after drinking."

So, for Ann and John, the art becomes living with unending stress and realistic fears and enjoying life as it is. Although it may appear as if their approach to life comes naturally, several attitudes stand out that enable them to accomplish this well.

Mutual Caretaking and Generosity with Each Other

Generosity is one of the first words that comes to mind when thinking of this couple, and it is expressed in many ways. Ann's attitude toward her marriage conveys this:

"You have to like yourself when you come to the marriage. Then you're not so consumed with yourself and you're not always thinking of yourself and what you can get out of the marriage. I think that's what's killing everybody's marriages; they are always thinking, 'What's in it for me? Am I going to get a return on my love instantly? And am I going to get this and that?' I don't think we've thought like that. I think that the more you do for the other, the more you accomplish, the more you feel good about your life."

Part of the generosity has to do with genuinely looking out for each other and recognizing small ways to make each other's life a bit smoother. This couple also has a very nice way of disagreeing with one another and offering their input to each other in a respectful manner. For example, John feels Ann is too attentive to their daughter when she ruminates about her delusions. He notes:

"I worry that it's getting too stressful for my wife. I try and tell her 'Don't get so worked up over it. Our daughter is going to do what she wants to do no matter what we say or do.' We can talk to her for an hour and a half and she'll turn around and do what she's going to do anyways. No matter what you explain to her, she will ask that same question again in fifteen minutes, and fifteen minutes after that, and fifteen minutes after that. It never goes away. So, I'm better at that [not engaging with her on these issues]. But my wife has a tough time doing that because she has a bigger heart than me."

They are both good at enjoying and valuing what they have in life rather than focusing on how atypical their family life turned out to be. John reflected philosophically on the differences between their life and what might have been:

"Really, right now in life, we should be sitting at home by ourselves. Maybe my wife would be reading a book or doing something that she wants to do, and maybe I'd be out there with my car. It probably would be nicer if we had our daughter bringing our grandkids over once and a while—instead of having them in our face every day and needing to entertain them and pay for them. But I think it would be a little boring if we had too many days where we were all by ourselves, without the activity."

Ann added that even if the goal of solving her daughter's problems is not ever fully achieved, she recognizes there is something satisfying about knowing that she will have made her very best effort.

She often simply deals with things rather than spending energy complaining. It is not that she pretends everything is fine. She acknowledges in discussion how hard this all has been and that it wears her down sometimes. However, also is clear about valuing what is important in life. This includes her husband and marriage, her children, her family, and friends. Over the ten years I have known her, I have not heard her speak of any shortcomings of her husband; this seems to be part of her understanding that people don't have to be perfect to be wonderful spouses. As part of this exchange, she accepts that her spouse doesn't talk much at home. She joked that I heard more words from him than she did in their thirty-eight years of marriage. However, they are a great example of how a couple can stay connected thanks in part to learning to read body language and not insisting that everything be put into words.

This couple has learned to value what is good in life. As Ann notes:

"Our needs are so small. We can enjoy going up on the highway and watching the sunset."

And there is always humor to get them through hard times. One laughed while the other said:

"We'll be dying and our daughter will be saying, 'What have you done for me lately?'"

Chapter Fifteen

A Closing Thought

Laura E. Marshak, Ph.D.

One of my favorite reflections on marriage was provided by a mother of three children with significant disabilities. Spending time with her and her husband made it clear that she lives by her marital beliefs:

"I like to use a boat analogy when talking about marriage. The way I see it, you and your spouse start off kind of on these little rafts, drinking pina coladas out in Aruba and Jamaica. You don't realize that you have to get over that horizon eventually. And so you party and party without realizing that you need to build your boat up and go through a couple of storms to make it to the horizon. You have to prepare yourself for the future and start nurturing and caring about the boat.

"The advice I give to couples who sail into a storm and are fighting is: Don't hack at your boat in a storm. If you are in the middle of a crisis, don't take the very support you have and start whacking at it, because that is dumb. You should love, nurture, and care for that other person or you are not going to make it through the storm.

"My husband and I are in a gorgeous boat right now
and I appreciate that. One of us will steer. Me. And he is
the guy back there making sure everybody is comfortable."

This woman's comments are especially compelling for many reasons. First, they reflect the importance of viewing your marriage as larger than the two of you. But her advice not to "hack at your boat in a storm" is an easy refrain to remember because it could not be truer. These straightforward words can guide many of your marital actions and decisions, if taken to heart. We think her advice is a fitting way to close this book.

More Advice from Parents

The outpouring of good advice provided by parents of children with disabilities who participated in this book resulted in an abundance of valuable thoughts.

Recognizing the positives

- "When dealing with the less than positive aspects of parenting a child with disabilities, sit down and make a list of the positives."

- "I know I am a better person now that I have my child and have walked a road filled with grief and joy! I am also a better doctor. Somehow I am able to empathize and support my patients and their families."

- "Our marriage has grown stronger as we have bonded with some very special people (other parents) we never would have met if it were not for our children!"

- "We are both less self-centered now. When you have a child with a disability or even a formerly nondisabled child who gets injured, one's priority cannot be oneself."

- "I think having children in general changes a marriage. However, how you handle the extra stress of a disabled child shows how strong and committed your marriage is. When everything is easy or going smoothly, your marriage isn't tested. Because my husband loves our daughter and is so supportive of her, the positive effect is that it reaffirms to me that I married the right man."

- "It gives you something in common to work on that is not part of what you each brought to the marriage."

Handling emotions

- "Become a **partnership** facing a problem that will last a lifetime. Your child's future depends on it."

- "Try to be open about your feelings and don't hold things back. For every negative thing, try to find the positive in it."

- "In the midst of all of the chaos, try to enjoy each other!!"

- "You are best off if you can get your emotional arms around how your life is turning out, let yourself grieve, and get on with helping your child. Denying the situation only worsens it."

- "We don't let ourselves think about the way things were. We simply focus on the beauty and the brightness in our relationship and in our marriage as it is today."

Being a couple

- "Be as caring and tolerant with one another as you are with your child."

- "Look for **common ground** and use it to your advantage (rather than argue over differences)."

- "We recognize each other's need for space and an opportunity to vent."

- "Relationships are hard work but a good one is worth having and keeping."

- "Hold and care for each other first. And don't lose your connection. Then care for your child or children. That may sound terrible, but we believe that's the answer for us. We come first. And I don't mean material things at all. I mean caring for each other."

- "We get babysitters so we can go out together, including a rare weekend/weeklong vacation. As long as my needs for vacation and time together are met, I can handle the daily care."

- "We always make time to sit and talk with each other. We always make time for each other (even if I'm tired, I find the energy)."

- "I think at some point a couple has to realize that the child with a disability **can't** come first 100 percent of the time. Sometimes the other children must come first and sometimes it needs to be the couple."

- "Communication is the key! Talk about your fears, concerns, excitements, and pleasure."

- "Enforce a 'no talk about kids' rule during some of the alone time."

- "We work as a team, giving each other breaks and realizing that we are in this together and can share in our joys and disappointments."

- "My husband and I have been each other's strength in our times of weakness. We look at our marriage and raising our children as a team project."

- "Having a child with a disability has caused us to work together with a 'tag team' approach. If one of us is getting stressed out when working with our son, the other jumps in and takes over."

Advice designated by survey respondents for husbands:

- "Help your wife with the little things. Actions speak louder than words."

- "You can't fix it. Let your wife talk. She doesn't want the evil Special Ed Director fixed, because it won't happen. She doesn't want the disability fixed, because it can't be done. She just wants your love and support."

- "Ten minutes of 'I care' can take away a whole day's worth of problems."

- "Try to 'see' your wife's stress and help."

- "Listen to your wife's problems. You don't have to have **all** the answers. Help us take mini breaks from the chaos—make a cup of tea for us to drink together; meet us for lunch while kids are in school; take care of the kids while we phone a friend."

- "You must take time to get away with your wife, even if it's just a walk around the block or a visit to the local coffee place. Grocery shopping can be good too! Don't let one spouse (usually the wife) take all the load, even if he/she doesn't complain."

- "Send cards to each other; send flowers."

- "Validate your wife's feelings—just listen sometimes and show empathy. Give her a break from the child or children and let her go do something away from home with you or with friends."

- "Don't assume your wife knows everything because she is the Mom or main caregiver. I get very frustrated when my child is sick or angry and I can't figure out what's wrong. Help your wife...don't walk away and throw your hands up in frustration."

- "Give your wife a hug every once in a while. Let her know she's doing a great job. Do things that she needs or wants without being asked."

Advice designated for wives:

- "Despite the craziness of the day, make time for just the two of you—and don't pick the end of the day when you are ready to drop into bed! Let your husband know he is appreciated and loved. Write him a love letter, make his favorite dessert. I know—am I living in the **real** world? It takes extra effort, but his happiness is worth it! He needs to know he is important to you and that your relationship hasn't been lost is the 'shuffle of life.'"

- "Understand that your husband is probably suffering too, even though men try to hide it."

- "Women need to talk to women in the 'same boat' to blow off frustration or just talk about difficulties of everyday life. That way our husbands get a break from hearing it day in and day out."

- "Understand that men just don't think the same way as women or may not show their emotion the same way we think they should. Your husband is probably not at home dealing with your child all day and may not understand that you need a break."

- "When your husband helps with the childcare, don't criticize him because he's not doing it your exact way. So what if he packs the 'wrong' snack to take along to the park? So what if he dresses your child in an outfit that you wouldn't pick to wear to school? He's not going to keep helping you if you constantly tell him what he's doing wrong."

- "Make sure your husband is NOT in denial about the child's disability. It takes some dads a long time to come around and precious early intervention time is lost. Try marriage counseling."

Coping:

- "In the back of my mind, I always keep the old saying, 'there is someone out there that has it a lot worse.' Everyone has issues in their lives to deal with and how we deal with them will determine our own happiness."

- "Take some time regularly for yourself and get regular exercise—maybe even together."

- "We don't let ourselves think about the way things were. We simply focus on the beauty and the brightness in our lives and in our relationship and in our marriage as it is today."

- "Remember, you wanted that child to **enjoy**—so, do it. Our son is really a treat, even when he's standing in the middle of a store shouting, 'Hello everybody!' We cringe and then have to appreciate his joy."

- "Don't allow your own pride to bring you heartache and shame."

- "Your spouse needs just as much attention as the children. Use respite care and get your needs met. Be selfish. Keep physically fit, take that college course, keep growing as a person, and be committed to each other."

- "When our child is having a good day, we try to live life in the present, enjoy our brief good fortune, and not dwell on any difficulties in the past. We try to make the most out of such days for they are rare, particularly in the early years."

- "My best advice is to make time for each other no matter what and **do not** feel guilty about having time to yourselves."

- "Be open with each other and honest about your feelings. If you need help from others don't be afraid to ask. Keep an open line with your church advisor and pray continually!"

- "Take one day at a time and don't look back or forward."

- "First and foremost, do not blame each other for whatever the problem is. Next, communicate all your feelings, good and bad, to your spouse. We tell each other when we are scared and when we think something's unfair, or we just need to complain about the situation. We also keep the best sense of humor that we can regarding our son."

- "Allow each other the opportunity to use your own coping mechanisms without criticism."

- "Allow your spouse to have some activity that he or she enjoys and balance the schedule to allow each of you weekly time to enjoy these activities."

- "Take each day one day at a time. The only way my husband and I get through our busy days and weeks is by dissecting each day and looking at that day and the day after only. Sometimes I cry just simply because there is too much to do or remember but I find myself to be a better parent if I do not get caught up in how much there is to do but rather look at how much I have accomplished today."

Finding additional support

- "I honestly believe that having someone you can talk to confidentially separately and together is an essential component of survival for families of kids with disabilities. Even if you use it very rarely, it helps to know where you can go for those moments when you're spinning your wheels and cultivating hurt."

- "Find a resource group or play group with children of similar needs. Another parent with similar issues can provide a world of understanding that a spouse may not be able to."

- "ASK for help when you need it: from each other, from your friends, from your family, from professionals. Don't wait for it to be a crisis."

- "Church has been our only salvation and the only reason that I am still married to this person."

- "I am quite sure that the only reason we are still together is because of our faith in God. We could never have done this alone."

- "I would have to say that our faith is the greatest source of support/resource in our marriage. We take our marriage vows seriously and are bound together by love for each other and for God. We know that any problem that surfaces in our marriage can be overcome through prayer. It's not always easy. We are not always happy. There are times we don't like each other, but we always know that we never stop loving each other."

- "Meet other parents of children with similar disabilities. You feel less isolated. You can learn so much from others who have experienced what you're going through."

- "Friends who have children with disabilities are a source of support for us. We find that we aren't so atypical, especially when compared to other families facing the same issues."

Appendix Two

Experiences Transformed into Poetry

Loose ends
By Judith Price

too many loose ends
not tidy enough
frayed edges
unraveling
uncomfortable conversations
in straight back chairs
no amount of rehearsal
or reversal
will make a difference

My children have a syndrome called Fragile X
By Dian Bolling

My children have a syndrome called Fragile X
in short it means their brains grow slow
I believe they are spiritual guides to this world
despite or because of the things they don't know

Like how much money their neighbor makes
or how to climb that corporate ladder
and in their mindful mindless way
I think they know what really matters

But one day their voices will be silenced
Because of our fear and laziness
I mean who would choose a disabled child?
when we can now make princesses

I see Hitler smirking in his grave
"I told you so" he starts to rave
I knew they'd come to my conclusions
and find their own final solutions

Hello my name is Dian Bolling
I'm a constantly trying to recover
Fragile X carrier
In a too surreal and intimate way
I look at myself every day
and feel broken and defective
but I guess I've always suspected
fundamentally
I'm fragile too

When the guilt throws me in hell
I want to find and blame
the ancestral name
that passed to me
this mutant gene
and filled my life with so much pain
...and purpose

I'm glad I didn't know
sometimes I think we know too much

I see the innocence torn from my heart
take root and grow in their eyes
I see them hold a mirror to the world
and give people the chance
to love or despise

When will we cherish our differences
Compliment our compliments
and see what's special
in all of our lives?

Appendix Three

Participant Responses to Selected Survey Items

Stressors

The following list is derived from parent responses to this question: *From your perspective, what aspects of living with a child with a disability are most stressful to you, your spouse, and your marriage?* (Responses listed in order of descending frequency.)

- Stress over behavior and safety issues
- Time demands
- Total or near total responsibility by one parent
- Concern over future of child
- Educational concerns and planning
- Lack of opportunity to spend time with spouse
- Lack of understanding of others
- Financial issues
- Inadequate help from family
- Physical and emotional fatigue
- Denial of child's problems by family and friends
- Stress over child's lack of communication skills
- Stress over lack of child's progress

- Parental isolation
- Limited socialization by child
- Child care issues
- Finding appropriate resources
- Concern over child's physical and emotional health
- Dividing time and attention between child and siblings
- Stress over appropriate decisions
- Parental disagreement
- Envy of normal parenting situations
- Fighting for services
- Concerns about whether to have more children
- Interference by relatives
- Sacrificing careers
- Trying to maintain parental social relationships
- Feeling unappreciated or unsupported
- Being overwhelmed
- Letting go of dreams for self, child, and family
- Stress over child's frustration, suffering, and "differentness"
- Attitudes of employers about parents of children with disabilities
- Spouses at different emotional stages
- Parental health needs
- Alternate lifestyle due to child's needs
- Negative attitudes by professionals and public

Protecting Romance and Passion

The following list is derived from parent responses to the following question: *What have you or your spouse done to protect the romance or passion in your marriage from the daily stresses and pressures?* (Responses listed in order of descending frequency.)

- Spending time together
- Very little
- Intimacy
- Showing affection
- Communication
- Nothing
- Humor

- Prayer
- Time apart
- Family vacations
- Mutual respect
- Remembering love as the reason you married
- Compromise
- Spontaneity
- Honesty
- Be yourself
- Don't take spouse for granted
- Divide roles
- Kindness
- Marriage conferences

Sources of Support

The following list is derived from parent responses to the following question: *Please consider the outside resources and sources of support that have helped sustain your marriage.* (Responses listed in order of descending frequency.)

Outside Resources
- None
- Church
- Therapists
- Wrap around services
- Respite Services
- Therapeutic staff support
- School
- Teacher
- Social workers
- Doctors and specialists
- Paraprofessionals
- Newsletters
- Hospitals
- Workshops
- Family support groups and workshops
- Daycare and respite care
- Family therapy

- Access tickets
- Case managers and advocates

Personal Resources

- None
- Family
- Faith in God
- Time alone with spouse
- Cooperation, communication, and understanding of spouse
- Personal aide for child
- Determination to succeed
- Personal counselor
- Time away from spouse
- Paid babysitter
- Informational resources (articles, Internet)
- Work, travel, exercise

Resources

National Resources for Specific Disabilities

Alexander Graham Bell Association
    for the Deaf
3417 Volta Place, N.W.
Washington, DC 20007
(202) 337-5220 (voice & TTY)
agbell2@aol.com
www.agbell.org

American Council of the Blind
1155 15th Street, N.W., Suite 720
Washington, DC 20005
(202) 467-5081; (800) 424-8666
www.acb.org

American Diabetes Association
1701 N. Beauregard Street
Alexandria, VA 22311
(703) 549-1500; (800) 342-2383
customerservice@diabetes.org
www.diabetes.org

American Foundation for the Blind
11 Penn Plaza, Suite 300
New York, NY 10001
(212) 502-7662 (TTY); (800) 232-5463
afbinfo@afb.org
www.afb.org/afb

American Heart Association National
    Center
7272 Greenville Avenue
Dallas, TX 75231
(214) 373-6300; (800) 242-8721
inquire@amhrt.org
www.americanheart.org

American Speech-Language-Hearing
    Association
10801 Rockville Pike
Rockville, MD 20852
(800) 498-2071
www.asha.org

The ARC
500 E. Border Street, Suite 300
Arlington, TX 76010
(817) 261-6003 (voice)
(817) 277-0553 (TTY)
(800) 433-5255
Info@thearc.org
www.thearc.org

Asthma and Allergy Foundation
    of America
1125 15th Street, N.W., Suite 502
Washington, DC 20005
(202) 466-7643; (800) 727-8462
info@aafa.org
www.aafa.org/

Autism Society of America
7910 Woodmont Avenue, Suite 300
Bethesda, MD 20814-3015
(301) 657-0881; (800) 328-8476
www.autism-society.org

Brain Injury Association
105 North Alfred Street
Alexandria, VA 22314
(703) 236-6000; (800) 444-6443
FamilyHelpline@biausa.org
www.biausa.org

Children and Adults with Attention
    Deficit/Hyperactivity Disorder
8181 Professional Place, Suite 201
Landover, MD 20785
(301) 306-7070; (800) 233-4050
    (to request info. Packet)
national@chadd.org
www.chadd.org

Children's Craniofacial Association
P.O. Box 280297
Dallas, TX 75243-4522
(972) 994-9902; (800) 535-3643
www.childrenscraniofacial.com

DB-LINK
National Information Clearinghouse
    on Children Who Are Deaf-Blind
345 N. Monmouth Ave.
Monmouth, OR 97361
(800) 438-9376 (voice)
(800) 854-7013 (TTY)
dblink@tr.wou.edu
www.tr.wou.edu/dblink

Epilepsy Foundation
4351 Garden City Drive, 5th Floor
Landover, MD 20785-4941
(301) 459-3700; (800) 332-1000
postmaster@efa.org
www.efa.org

Hydrocephalus Association
870 Market Street, #955
San Francisco, CA 94102
(415) 732-7040
hydroassoc@aol.com
www.hydroassoc.org

International Dyslexia Association
Chester Building, #382
8600 LaSalle Road
Baltimore, MD 21286-2044
(410) 296-0232; (800) 222-3123
info@interdys.org
www.interdys.org

International Rett Syndrome
    Association
9121 Piscataway Road, Suite 2B
Clinton, MD 20735-2561
(301) 856-3334; (800) 818-7388
irsa@rettsyndrome.org
www.rettsyndrome.org

Learning Disabilities Association
    of America
4156 Library Road
Pittsburgh, PA 15234
(412) 341-1515; (412) 341-8077
(888) 300-6710
vldanatl@usaor.ne
www.ldanatl.org

Leukemia & Lymphoma Society
600 Third Avenue
New York, NY 10016
(212) 573-8484; (800) 955-4LSA
infocenter@leukemia-lymphoma.org
www.leukemia-lymphoma.org

Muscular Dystrophy Association
3300 E. Sunrise Drive
Tucson, AZ 85718
(520) 529-2000; (800) 572-1717
mda@mdausa.org
www.mdausa.org

National Alliance for the Mentally Ill
    (NAMI)
200 N. Glebe Road, Suite 1015
Arlington, VA 22203-3754
(703) 524-7600; (703) 516-7991 (TTY)
(800) 950-NAMI
namiofc@aol.com
www.nami.org

National Association of the Deaf
814 Thayer Avenue, Suite 250
Silver Spring, MD 20910
(301) 587-1788; (301) 587-1789 (TTY)
nadinfo@nad.org
www.nad.org

National Center for Learning
    Disabilities
381 Park Avenue South, Suite 1401
New York, NY 10016
(212) 545-7510; (888) 575-7373
www.ncld.org

National Down Syndrome Congress
1370 Center Drive, Suite 102
Atlanta, GA 30338
(770) 604-9599; (800) 232-6372
info@ndsccenter.org
www.ndsccenter.org

National Down Syndrome Society
666 Broadway, 8th floor
New York, NY 10012-2317
(212) 460-9330; (800) 221-4602
info@ndss.org
www.ndss.org

National Federation of the Blind
1800 Johnson Street
Baltimore, MD 21230
(410) 659-9314
nfb@access.digex.net
www.nfb.org

National Fragile X Foundation
1441 York Street, Suite 303
Denver, CO 80206
(303) 333-6155; (800) 688-8765
natlfx@sprintmail.com
www.nfxf.org

National Institute on Deafness and
    Other Communication Disorders
    Clearinghouse
1 Communication Avenue
Bethesda, MD 20892-3456
(800) 241-1044 (voice)
(800) 241-1055 (TTY)
nidcdinfo@nidcd.nih.gov
www.nih.gov/nidcd

National Organization for Rare
    Disorders
P.O. Box 8923
New Fairfield, CT 06812-8923
(203) 746-6518 (Voice)
(800) 999-6673
orphan@rarediseases.org
www.rarediseases.org

National Mental Health Association
1021 Prince Street
Alexandria, VA 22314-2971
(703) 684-7722; (800) 969-6642
(800) 433-5959 (TTY)
nmhainfo@aol.com
www.nmha.org

National Multiple Sclerosis Society
733 Third Avenue
New York, NY 10017
(212) 986-3240; (800) 344-4867
info@nmss.org
www.nmss.org

National Organization on Fetal
 Alcohol Syndrome
418 C Street N.E.
Washington, DC 20002
(202) 785-4585; (800) 666-6327
nofas@erols.com
www.nofas.org

National Reye's Syndrome Foundation
P.O. Box 829
Bryan, OH 43506
(419) 636-2679; (800) 233-7393
nrsfc@reyessyndrome.org
www.reyessyndrome.org

National Spinal Cord Injury Association
8300 Colesville Road, Suite 551
Silver Spring, MD 20910
(301) 588-6959; (800) 962-9629
nscia2@aol.com
www.spinalcord.org

National Stuttering Association
5100 E. LaPalma Avenue, Suite 208
Anaheim Hills, CA 92807
(714) 693-7480; (800) 364-1677
nsastutter@aol.com
www.nspstutter.org

Obsessive Compulsive Foundation, Inc.
337 North Hill Road
North Branford, CT 06471
(203) 315-2190
info@ocfoundation.org
www.ocfoundation.org

Spina Bifida Association of America
4590 MacArthur Blvd. N.W., Suite 250
Washington, DC 20007-4226
(202) 944-3285; (800) 621-3141
sbaa@sbaa.org
www.sbaa.org

Tourette Syndrome Association
42-40 Bell Boulevard
Bayside, NY 11361
(718) 224-2999; (800) 237-0717
tsctsa-usa.org
www.tsa-usa.org

United Cerebral Palsy Association, Inc.
1660 L Street, NW, Suite 700
Washington, DC 20036
(202) 776-0406
(202) 973-7197 (TTY)
(800) 872-5827
ucpnatl@ucpa.org
www.ucpa.org

Resources for Disabilities in General

Abilities! (formerly National Center
 for Disability Services)
201 IU Willets Road
Albertson, NY 11507-1599
(516) 465-1601
www.abilitiesonline.org

Clearinghouse on Disability Information
Office of Special Education and
 Rehabilitation Services
Room 3132, Switzer Bldg.
330 C Street S.W.
Washington, DC 20202-2524
(202) 205-8241 (voice & TTY)

Easter Seals, National Office
230 W. Monroe Street, Suite 1800
Chicago, IL 60606
(312) 726-6200 (voice)
(312) 726-4258 (TTY)
(800) 221-6827
info@easter-seals.org
www.easter-seals.org

ERIC Clearinghouse on Disabilities
 and Gifted Education
Council for Exceptional Children
1920 Associated Drive
Reston, VA 20191
(703) 264-9449 (TTY)
(800) 328-0272 (voice & TTY)
ericec@cec.sped.org
www.ericec.org

Family Voices
P.O. Box 769
Algodones, NM 87001
(505) 867-2368; (888) 835-5669
kidshealth@familyvoices.org
www.familyvoices.org

March of Dimes Birth Defects
    Foundation
1275 Mamaroneck Avenue
White Plains, NY 10605
(914) 428-7100
resourcecenter@modimes.org
www.modimes.org

National Father's Network
Kindering Center
16120 N.E. 8th Street
Bellevue, WA 98008
(425) 747-4004, Ext. 218
www.fathersnetwork.org

National Parent Network on
    Disabilities
1130 17th Street N.W., Suite 400
Washington, DC 20036
(202) 463-2299 (voice & TTY)
npnd@cs.com
www.npnd.org

National Parent to Parent Support
    and Information System, Inc.
P.O. Box 907
Blue Ridge, GA 30513
(706) 374-3822; (800) 651-1151
nppsis@ellijay.com
www.nppsis.org

National Rehabilitation Information
    Center
8455 Colesville Road, Suite 935
Silver Spring, MD 20910-3319
(301) 588-9284 (Voice)
(301) 495-5626 (TTY)
(800) 346-2742
www.naric.com

NICHCY
National Dissemination Center for
    Children & Youth with Disabilities
P.O. Box 1492
Washington, DC 20013
(800) 695-0285 (voice & TTY)
(202) 884-8441
nichcy@aed.org
www.nichcy.org

Sibling Support Project
6512 23rd Avenue, #213
Seattle, WA 98117
(206) 297-6368
www.siblingsupport.org

Special Olympics International
1325 G Street N.W., Suite 500
Washington, D.C. 20005
(202) 628-3630
specialolympics@msn.com
www.specialolympics.org

TASH
29 W. Susquehanna Avenue, Suite 210
Baltimore, MD 21204
(410) 828-8274 (voice)
(410) 828-1306 (TTY)
info@tash.org
www.tash.org

References &
Suggested Reading

Introduction

Page, S. (1997). *How One of You Can Bring the Two of You Together: Breakthrough Strategies to Resolve Your Conflicts and Reignite Your Love*. New York: Broadway Books.

Chapter One

Ashner, L. & Meyerson, M. (1997). *When Parents Love Too Much: Freeing Parents and Children to Live Their Own Lives*. Center City, MN: Hazelden.

Gottman, J. M. (1994). *Why Marriages Succeed or Fail: and How You Can Make Yours Last Forever*. New York: Simon & Schuster.

Gottman, J. M. & Silver, N. (1999). *The Seven Principles for Making Marriage Work*. New York: Crown Publishing Group.

Hooks, B. (2000). *All About Love: New Visions*. New York: William Morrow.

Love, P. (2001). *The Truth about Love: The Highs and the Lows and How You Can Make It Last Forever*. New York: Simon & Schuster.

Chapter Four

Ellis, A. & Crawford, T. (2000). *Making Intimate Connections: 7 Guidelines for Great Relationships and Better Communication*. Atascadero, CA: Impact Publisher.

Fanning, P., McKay, M., & Davis, M. (1995). *Messages: The Communication Skills Book*. Oakland, CA: New Harbinger Publications.

Patterson, K. (2002). *Crucial Conversations: Tools for Talking When Stakes Are High*. New York: McGraw Hill.

Paleg, K. & McKay, M. (2001). *When Anger Hurts Your Relationship: 10 Simple Solutions for Couples Who Fight*. Oakland, CA: New Harbinger.

Chapter Five

Knopf, J., Seiler, M., & Meltsner, S. (1991). *Inhibited Sexual Desire*. New York: Warner Books.

Raskin, V. D. (2002). *Great Sex for Moms: Ten Steps to Nurturing Passion While Raising Kids*. New York: Fireside.

Viorst, J. (2002). *Grown-Up Marriage: What We Know, Wish We had Known, and Still Need to Know about Being Married*. New York: Free Press.

Chapter Seven

Brown, J. (1993). "Coping with Stress: The Beneficial Role of Positive Illusions." In Turnbull, A.P., Patterson, J.M., Behr, S.K., Murphy, D.L., Marquis, J.G., & Blue-Banning, M.J., eds. *Cognitive Coping, Families, and Disability*. Baltimore: Paul Brookes Publishing Co.

Cousins, N. (1979). *Anatomy of an Illness*. New York: WW. Norton.

Freebery, N.P. (2002). *Blossom: It's Not What Life Throws at You...It's How You Catch It*. Newark, Delaware: NPF Communications.

Heller, T. (1993). "Self-Efficacy Coping, Active Involvement and Caregiver Well Being Throughout the Life Course Among Families of Persons with Mental Retardation." In Turnbull, A.P., Patterson, J.M., Behr, S.K., Murphy, D.L., Marquis, J.G., & Blue-Banning, M.J., eds. *Cognitive Coping, Families and Disability*. Baltimore: Paul Brookes Publishing Co.

Klein, S.D. & Schive, K. (2001). *You Will Dream New Dreams: Inspiring Personal Stories by Parents of Children with Disabilities*. New York: Kensington Books.

Marsh, J. & Boggis, C., eds. (1994). *From the Heart: Stories by Mothers of Children with Special Needs*. Portland, Maine: Edmund S. Muskie Institute of Public Affairs.

McDonald, K. (1984). *How to Meditate*. Somerville, MA: Wisdom Publications.

Sapolsky, R.M. (1998). *Why Zebras Don't Get Ulcers*. New York: W.H. Freeman and Company.

Thompson, S. (1993). "Individual and Interpersonal Influences on the Use of Cognitive Coping." In Turnbull, A.P., Patterson, J.M., Behr, S.K., Murphy, D.L., Marquis, J.G., & Blue-Banning, M.J. *Cognitive Coping, Families and Disability.* Baltimore, MD: Paul Brookes Publishing Co.

Turnbull, A.P., Patterson, J.M., Behr, S.K., Murphy, D.L. Marquis, J.G., Blue-Banning, M.J., eds. (1993). *Cognitive Coping, Families and Disability.* Baltimore, MD: Paul Brookes Publishing Co.

Chapter Nine
Des Jardins, C. (1993). *How to Get Services by Being Assertive.* Chicago, IL: Family Resource Center on Disabilities.

Santelli, B. & Poyadue, F. (2001). *The Parent to Parent Handbook: Connecting Families of Children with Special Needs.* Baltimore, MD: Paul Brookes Publishing Co.

Thornburgh, G. (1992). *That All May Worship.* Washington, DC: National Organization on Disability.

Chapter Ten
Bilodeau, L. (1992). *The Anger Workbook.* Center City, MN: Hazelden.

Glass, S. & Staeheli, J. C. (2004). *NOT "Just Friends": Rebuilding Trust and Recovering Your Sanity after Infidelity.* New York: Free Press.

Kirshenbaum, M. (1999). *Our Love Is Too Good to Feel So Bad: Ten Prescriptions to Heal Your Relationship.* New York: Avon Books.

Markman, H. J., Stanley, S. M., & Blumberg, L. S. (2001). *Fighting for Your Marriage: Positive Steps for Preventing Divorce and Preserving a Lasting Love,* revised ed. San Francisco: Jossey-Bass.

Potter-Efron, R. (1994). *Angry All the Time: An Emergency Guide to Anger Control.* Oakland, CA: New Harbinger Publications.

Spring, J. A. (1997). *After the Affair: Healing the Pain and Rebuilding the Trust When a Partner Has Been Unfaithful.* New York: HarperCollins.

Weiner-Davis, M. (1993). *Divorce Busting: A Step-by-Step Approach to Making Your Marriage Loving Again.* New York: Fireside.

Weiner-Davis, M. (1999). *Getting Through to the Man You Love: The No-Nagging, No-Nonsense Guide for Women.* New York: Golden Books Publishing.

Chapter Twelve
Hetherington, M. E. & Kelly, J. (2002). *For Better or for Worse: Divorce Reconsidered.* New York: W.W. Norton & Company.

Neuman, M. G. (1999). *Helping Your Kids Cope with Divorce the Sandcastles Way*. New York: Random House.

Wallerstein, J. S. & Blakeslee, S. (2003). *What about the Kids? Raising Your Children Before, During, and After Divorce*. New York: Hyperion.

Wallerstein, J. S., Blakeslee, S., & Lewis, J. M. (2001). *The Unexpected Legacy of Divorce: A 25-Year Landmark Study*. New York: Hyperion.

Chapter Thirteen

Moseley, D., Moseley, N., & Moseley, D. (1998). *Making Your Second Marriage a First-Class Success*. Rocklin, CA: Prima Publishing.

Stepfamily Association of America. (2000). Retrieved, June 30, 2003, from http://saafamilies.org.

Wisdom, S. & Green, J. (2002). *Stepcoupling: Creating and Sustaining a Strong Marriage in Today's Blended Family*. Three Rivers, MI: Three Rivers Press.

Index

About the
Authors

In addition to raising three sons, **Laura E. Marshak, Ph.D.,** is a professor of counseling at Indiana University of Pennsylvania. She is also a founding partner and psychologist at North Hills Psychological Services, where she works with many parents of children with disabilities. She is married and lives in Pittsburgh, Pennsylvania.

Fran Pollock Prezant, M.Ed, CCC-SLP, is currently the Director of Research and Evaluation at Abilities! (formerly National Center for Disability Services) in New York. Trained as a speech and language pathologist, she has been a parent trainer and program director, university instructor, grant writer, researcher, and consultant. Recent work has focused on cultural and arts access for people with disabilities, parent perceptions of professional interactions, and disability representation in children's literature. She has two children and lives with her husband in West Orange, New Jersey.